Unity Android Game Development by Example Beginner's Guide

Learn how to create exciting games using Unity 3D for Android with the help of hands-on examples

Thomas Finnegan

BIRMINGHAM - MUMBAI

Unity Android Game Development by Example Beginner's Guide

First published: December 2013

Production Reference: 1131213

Published by Packt Publishing Ltd.
Livery Place
35 Livery Street
Birmingham B3 2PB, UK.

ISBN 978-1-84969-201-4

www.packtpub.com

Cover Image by Thomas Finnegan (tom@mooingduck.com)

Credits

Author

Thomas Finnegan

Reviewers

Mootez Billeh Chaabani

Valera Kogut

Marc Schaerer

Aris Tsevrenis

Acquisition Editor

Owen Roberts

Commissioning Editor

Llewellyn Rozario

Lead Technical Editor

Ritika Dewani

Technical Editors

Arwa Manasawala

Ankita Thakur

Project Coordinator

Anugya Khurana

Copy Editors

Roshni Banerjee

Deepa Nambiar

Karuna Narayanan

Laxmi Subramanian

Proofreader

Stephen Copestake

Indexer

Rekha Nair

Graphics

Disha Haria

Production Coordinator

Manu Joseph

Cover Work

Manu Joseph

About the Author

Thomas Finnegan completed his graduation from Brown College in 2010. Since then, he has worked on everything from mobile platforms to web development, and even experimental devices. He now works as a freelance game developer. Past clients include Carmichael Lynch, Coleco, and Subaru. His most recent project is Battle Box 3D, a virtual table top. Currently he is teaching game development at the Minneapolis Media Institute in Minnesota.

I would like to thank my fiancée for kicking me into gear whenever I was distracted. Also, I would like to thank my parents for always supporting me. Without my friends and family, life would be dismal.

About the Reviewers

Mootez Billeh Chaabani is a software engineer. Currently he is working as a software engineer (Research and Development) in a French company named SpacEyes. He recently completed his graduation. He studied graphical programming and virtual and augmented reality. He also published two apps: Quizz game in the Windows Marketplace and an Android app in the local appshop, and now he is working on Android/C++ projects based on 3D in SpacEyes. Before this, he was an intern at Microsoft Tunisia in 2011. He also worked as an Android developer in Orange Tunisia in 2012. He also worked on the book *Android NDk Game Development Cookbook*.

> I would like to thank my family, my soulmate, and all of my friends including Bardo Boys (my neighborhood friends).

Valera Kogut is a passionate software developer with different areas of expertise. Before diving into the game industry five years ago, Valera was creating for Web with PHP and Yii frameworks. Having a mathematical background, he finally realized gamedev was his mission. Reusable designs, optimized algorithms, clean code, and elaborated workflows—these things make him happy. He is a co-founder and principal architect at applicat.io, software development agency offering a wide range of services (`http://applicat.io`). However, architectural and management tasks can't stop Valera from digging deeply into code.

Currently, Valera executes one contract as Unity3D C# developer for Kaufcom GmbH, a known games and apps producer from Switzerland http://www.kauf.com (Android games https://play.google.com/store/search?q=kaufcom).

First of all, thanks to the author and team from Packt Publishing for creating this book, and thereby helping the Unity community grow and mature. Special thanks go to my family for the love, education, and freedom they gave me! I would also like to thank my best friends and associates at applicat.io, Paul Kofmann, Alexander Kofmann, and Vitaly Shapovalov; we are the Team! Thanks to the Kaufcom Company! And of course, no progress of mine could be achieved without the support and love of my wife, Irina.

Marc Schaerer is an interactive media software engineer who is creating cutting edge interactive media experiences for training, education, and entertainment purposes on mobile, desktop, and web platforms for customers through his company Gayasoft (http://www.gayasoft.net) located in Switzerland.

His technology of choice is Unity, which he has been using since its early days in 2007.

He has a strong background in 3D graphics, network technology, software engineering, and the interactive media field. Originally, he started programming at the age of 11 and built upon it later while studying Computer Science and Computational Science and Engineering at Swiss Federal Institute of Technology, Zurich, thereby growing into it. This knowledge found, among other projects, usage in Popper (http://www.popper.org), an interactive 3D behavioral research platform by Harvard developed by Gayasoft and powered by Unity, Mathlab, and the ExitGames Photon.

With the rise of serious games, he focused on researching options and technologies for the next generation of interactive and immersive experiences, applying state of the art AR and VR technologies (Vuforia, Metaio, and Oculus Rift) and new innovative input technologies (Razer Hydra, STEM, Leap Motion, and Emotive Insight). He predicts that this will become the base of future experiences in many fields of our daily life.

Aris Tsevrenis is a game developer and director at Terahard Ltd, a game development studio dedicated to creating addictive games that will be remembered for their quality in every aspect. The company's motto, "Terabytes of Quality for Hardcore Gaming", explains a few things about Aris' ambitions. Aris was introduced to games from a very early age in the 90s. Showing great skill, and evolving from chess to modern computer and console games, Aris became famous among the people who knew his numerous feats in the gaming world. He received his BSc in Computer Science with a Computer Vision and Computer Graphics degree in 2009 from Cardiff University in Wales, followed by an MSc in Computer Games and Entertainment degree from Goldsmith's University in London. He entered the games development world and worked in a few different games companies until he set up Terahard Ltd. He currently lives in London, where his games studio is located, and can be contacted at `aris.tsevrenis@terahard.org`.

www.PacktPub.com

Support files, eBooks, discount offers and more

You might want to visit www.PacktPub.com for support files and downloads related to your book.

Did you know that Packt offers eBook versions of every book published, with PDF and ePub files available? You can upgrade to the eBook version at www.PacktPub.com and as a print book customer, you are entitled to a discount on the eBook copy. Get in touch with us at service@packtpub.com for more details.

At www.PacktPub.com, you can also read a collection of free technical articles, sign up for a range of free newsletters and receive exclusive discounts and offers on Packt books and eBooks.

http://PacktLib.PacktPub.com

Do you need instant solutions to your IT questions? PacktLib is Packt's online digital book library. Here, you can access, read and search across Packt's entire library of books.

Why Subscribe?

- ◆ Fully searchable across every book published by Packt
- ◆ Copy and paste, print and bookmark content
- ◆ On demand and accessible via web browser

Free Access for Packt account holders

If you have an account with Packt at www.PacktPub.com, you can use this to access PacktLib today and view nine entirely free books. Simply use your login credentials for immediate access.

Table of Contents

Preface

In this book, we explore the ever-expanding world of mobile game development. Using Unity 3D and the Android SDK, we will learn how to create every aspect of a mobile game. Every chapter explores another piece of the development puzzle. Exploring the special features of development with mobile platforms, every game in the book is designed to increase your understanding of these features. We also finish the book with a total of four complete games and all of the tools we need to create many more.

The first game that we make is Tic-tac-toe. This game functions just as the classic paper version. Two players take turns filling a grid with their symbols; the first to make a line of three wins. It is the perfect game for us to explore the graphical interface options that we have in Unity. By learning how to add buttons, text, and pictures to the screen here, we have all of the understanding and tools needed to add any interface that we might want to any game.

The next game that we create is the Tank Battle game. The player takes control of a tank to drive around a small city and shoot targets and enemies. This game spans three chapters, allowing us to explore many key points of creating games for the Android platform. We start by creating a city and making the player's tank move around, using controls that we learned about when making the Tic-tac-toe game. We also create and animate the targets that the player will shoot at. In the second part of this game, we add some lighting and special camera effects. By the end of the chapter, the environment looks great. In the third part of the game's creation, we create some enemies. Using the power of Unity, these enemies chase the player throughout the city, and attack when they are close.

The third game to be completed is a simple clone of a popular mobile game. Using the power of Unity's physics system, we are able to create structures and throw birds at them. Knock down the structures to gain points, and destroy the target pigs to win the level. We also take the time to explore some of the specific features of a 2D game, such as a parallax scrolling background, and how they can be achieved in Unity. We complete the chapter and the game with the creation of a level selection menu.

Finally, we create the Space Fighter game. This game involves using the special inputs of a mobile device to control the player's ship. As the player's device is tilted, they will be able to steer the ship. When they touch the screen, they can shoot at the enemy ships and asteroids. The second part of this game involves including the special effects that complete the look of every game. We create explosions when ships are destroyed, and engine trails for the ships. We also add the sound effects for shooting and exploding.

The book wraps up with a look at optimization. We explore all of the great features of Unity, and even create a few of our own to make our game run as best as it can. We also take a little bit of time to understand some things that we can do to minimize the file size of our assets while maximizing their look and effect in the game. At this point, our journey ends, but we have four great games that are just about ready to go to market.

What this book covers

Chapter 1, Saying Hello to Unity and Android, explores the feature lists of the Android platform and the Unity 3D game engine, covering why they are great choices for development. We will also cover setting up the development environment, and create a simple Hello World application for your device and emulators.

Chapter 2, Looking Good – Graphical Interface, takes a detailed look at the graphical user interface. By creating a Tic-tac-toe game, we learn about the user interface while making it pleasing to look at.

Chapter 3, The Backbone of Any Game – Meshes, Materials, and Animations, explores meshes, materials, and animations. Through the creation of a Tank Battle game, we cover the core of what players will see when playing.

Chapter 4, Setting the Stage – Camera Effects and Lighting, explains about the camera effects and lighting. With the addition of shadows, lightmaps, distance fog, and a skybox, our Tank Battle environment becomes more dynamic. Utilizing special camera effects, we create extra feedback for the player.

Chapter 5, Getting Around – Pathfinding and AI, shows the creation of mobile enemies in our Tank Battle game. We explore pathfinding and AI to give players a target more meaningful than a stationary dummy.

Chapter 6, Specialties of the Mobile Device – Touch and Tilt, covers the features that make the modern mobile device special. We create a Space Fighter game to understand the touch interface and tilt controls.

Chapter 7, Throwing Your Weight Around – Physics and a 2D Camera, shows the creation of a clone of Angry Birds after taking a short break from the Space Fighter game. Physics and a 2D camera effect are explored here.

Chapter 8, Special Effects – Sound and Particles, returns to the Space Fighter game to add special effects. The inclusion of sound effects and particles allows us to create a more complete game experience.

Chapter 9, Optimization, covers optimization in Unity 3D. We cover the benefits and costs of making our Tank Battle and Space Fighter games as efficient as possible.

What you need for this book

Throughout this book, we will be working with both the Unity 3D game engine and Android. As you can see in the previous section, we will cover both the acquisition and installation of Unity and the Android SDK in *Chapter 1, Saying Hello to Unity and Android*. To get the most of this book, you will need access to an Android-powered device; either a phone or tablet will work well. For simplicity's sake, we will assume that you are working on a Windows-powered computer. Also, the code throughout the book is written in C#, though JavaScript versions of each chapter project are available for reference. To fully utilize the models provided for the chapter projects, you will need Blender, a free modeling program available at http://www.blender.org. To reach all of the challenges, you will need to make use of either Blender or another modeling program that you are comfortable with, for example, a photo-editing program; Photoshop is a common choice, and a source for the creation or acquisition of audio files. All of the audio files provided by this book were found at http://www.freesound.org.

Who this book is for

This book will be optimal for readers who are new to game development and mobile development with Unity. Readers who learn best with real-world examples rather than dry documentation will find every chapter useful. Even if you have little or no programming skills, this book will make a great place to jump in and learn some concepts and standards for programming.

Conventions

In this book, you will find a number of styles of text that distinguish between different kinds of information. Here are some examples of these styles, and an explanation of their meaning.

Code words in text, database table names, folder names, filenames, file extensions, pathnames, dummy URLs, user input, and Twitter handles are shown as follows: "If during the build process, Unity complains about where the Android SDK is, select the `android-sdk` folder inside the location where it was installed."

A block of code is set as follows:

```
public void OnGUI() {
   GUILayout.Label("Hello World");
}
```

Any command-line input or output is written as follows:

```
adb kill-server
adb start-server
adb devices
```

New terms and **important words** are shown in bold. Words that you see on the screen, in menus or dialog boxes for example, appear in the text like this: "Follow that up by clicking on the **Download the SDK Tools for Window**s button".

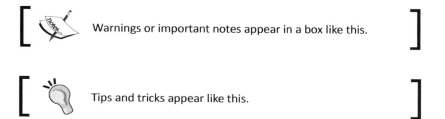

Warnings or important notes appear in a box like this.

Tips and tricks appear like this.

Reader feedback

Feedback from our readers is always welcome. Let us know what you think about this book—what you liked or may have disliked. Reader feedback is important for us to develop titles that you really get the most out of.

To send us general feedback, simply send an e-mail to feedback@packtpub.com, and mention the book title in the subject of your message.

If there is a topic that you have expertise in, and you are interested in either writing or contributing to a book, see our author guide on `www.packtpub.com/authors`.

Customer support

Now that you are the proud owner of a Packt book, we have a number of things to help you to get the most from your purchase.

Downloading the example code

You can download the example code files for all Packt books that you have purchased from your account at `http://www.packtpub.com`. If you purchased this book elsewhere, you can visit `http://www.packtpub.com/support`, and register to have the files e-mailed directly to you.

Downloading the color images of this book

We also provide you with a PDF file that has color images of the screenshots/diagrams used in this book. The color images will help you understand the changes in the output better. You can download this file from: `http://www.packtpub.com/sites/default/files/downloads/2014OT_Images.pdf`.

Errata

Although we have taken every care to ensure the accuracy of our content, mistakes do happen. If you find a mistake in one of our books—maybe a mistake in the text or the code—we would be grateful if you would report this to us. By doing so, you can save other readers from frustration, and help us improve subsequent versions of this book. If you find any errata, please report them by visiting `http://www.packtpub.com/submit-errata`, selecting your book, clicking on the **errata submission form** link, and entering the details of your errata. Once your errata are verified, your submission will be accepted, and the errata will be uploaded on our website or added to any list of existing errata under the Errata section of that title. Any existing errata can be viewed by selecting your title from `http://www.packtpub.com/support`.

Piracy

Piracy of copyright material on the Internet is an ongoing problem across all media. At Packt, we take the protection of our copyright and licenses very seriously. If you come across any illegal copies of our works in any form on the Internet, please provide us with the location address or website name immediately so that we can pursue a remedy.

Please contact us at copyright@packtpub.com with a link to the suspected pirated material.

We appreciate your help in protecting our authors, and our ability to bring you valuable content.

Questions

You can contact us at questions@packtpub.com if you are having a problem with any aspect of the book, and we will do our best to address it.

1
Saying Hello to Unity and Android

*Welcome to the wonderful world of mobile game development. Whether you are still looking for the right development kit or have already chosen one, this chapter will be most important. In this chapter we explore the various features that come with choosing **Unity** as your development environment and **Android** as the target platform. Through comparison with major competitors, it is discovered why Unity and Android stand on the top of the pile. Following that, we examine how Unity and Android work together. Finally, the development environment is set up and we create a simple Hello World application to test that everything is set up correctly. For the purposes of this book, it is assumed you are working in a Windows-based environment.*

In this chapter, we will cover the following topics:

- Major Unity features
- Major Android features
- Unity licensing options
- Installing the JDK
- Installing the Android SDK
- Installing Unity 3D
- Installing Unity Remote

Understanding what makes Unity great

Perhaps the greatest feature of Unity is how open-ended it is. Nearly all game engines currently on the market are limited in what one can build. It makes perfect sense but it can limit the capabilities of a team. The average game engine has been highly optimized for creating a specific game type. This is great if all you plan on making is the same game again and again. When one is struck with inspiration for the next great hit, only to find that the game engine can't handle it and everyone has to retrain in a new engine or double the development time to make it capable, it can be quite frustrating. Unity does not suffer this problem. The developers of Unity have worked very hard to optimize every aspect of the engine, without limiting what types of games can be made. Everything ranging from simple 2D platformers to massive online role-playing games is possible in Unity. A development team that just finished an ultra-realistic first-person shooter can turn right around and make 2D fighting games without having to learn an entirely new system.

Being so open ended does, however, bring a drawback. There are no default tools optimized for building that perfect game. To combat this, Unity grants the ability to create any tool one can imagine, using the same scripting that creates the game. On top of that, there is a strong community of users that have supplied a wide selection of tools and pieces, both free and paid, to be quickly plugged in and used. This results in a large selection of available content, ready to jump-start you on your way to the next great game.

When many prospective users look at Unity, they think that because it is so cheap, it is not as good as an expensive AAA game engine. This is simply not true. Throwing more money at the game engine is not going to make a game any better. Unity supports all of the fancy shaders, normal maps, and particle effects you could want. The best part is, nearly all of the fancy features you could want are included in the free version of Unity and 90 percent of the time beyond that, one does not need to even use the Pro only features.

One of the greatest concerns when selecting a game engine, especially for the mobile market, is how much girth it will add to the final build size. Most are quite hefty. With Unity's code stripping, it becomes quite small. Code stripping is the process by which Unity removes every extra little bit of code from the compiled libraries. A blank project, compiled for Android, that utilizes full code stripping ends up being around 7 megabytes.

Perhaps one of the coolest features of Unity is the multi-platform compatibility. With a single project one can build for several different platforms. This includes the ability to simultaneously target mobile, PC, and consoles. This allows one to focus on real issues, such as handling inputs, resolution, and performance.

In the past, if a company desired to deploy their product on more than one platform, they had to nearly double the development costs in order to essentially reprogram the game. Every platform did, and still does, run by its own logic and language. Thanks to Unity, game development has never been simpler. We can develop games using simple and fast scripting, letting Unity handle the complex translation to each platform.

There are of course several other options for game engines. Two major ones that come to mind are **cocos2d** and **Unreal Engine**. While both are excellent choices, we can always find them to be a little lacking in certain respects.

The engine of Angry Birds, cocos2d, could be a great choice for your next mobile hit. However, as the name suggests, it is pretty much limited to 2D games. A game can look great in it, but if you ever want that third dimension, it can be tricky to add. A second major problem with cocos2d is how bare bones it is. Any tool for building or importing assets needs to be created from scratch, or they need to be found. Unless you have the time and experience, this can seriously slow down development.

Then there is the staple of major game development, Unreal Engine. This game engine has been used successfully by developers for many years, bringing great games to the world; Unreal Tournament and Gears of War not the least among them. These are both, however, console and computer games, which is the fundamental problem with the engine. Unreal is a very large and powerful engine. Only so much optimization can be done for mobile platforms. It has always had the same problem; it adds a lot of girth to a project and its final build. The other major issue with Unreal is its rigidity in being a first-person shooter engine. While it is technically possible to create other types of games in it, such tasks are long and complex. A strong working knowledge of the underlying system is a must before achieving such a feat.

All in all, Unity definitely stands strong among the rest. Perhaps you have already discovered this, and that is why you are reading this book. But these are still great reasons for choosing Unity for game development. Projects can look just as great as AAA titles. Overhead and girth in the final build is small and very important when working on mobile platforms. The system's potential is open enough to allow you to create any type of game you might want, where other engines tend to be limited to a single type of game. And should your needs change at any point in the project's life cycle, it is very easy to add, remove, or change your choice of target platforms.

Understanding what makes Android great

With over 30-million devices in the hands of users, why would you not choose the Android platform for your next mobile hit? Apple may have been the first one out of the gate with their iPhone sensation, but Android is definitely a step ahead when it comes to smartphone technology. One of its best features is its blatant ability to be opened up so you can take a look at how the phone works, both physically and technically. One can swap out the battery and upgrade the micro SD card, should the need arise. Plugging the phone into a computer does not have to be a huge ordeal; it can simply function as removable storage media.

From the point of view of cost of development, the Android market is superior as well. Other mobile app stores require an annual registration fee of about 100 dollars. Some also have a limit on the number of devices that can be registered for development at one time. The Google Play market has a one-time registration fee, and there is no concern about how many or what type of Android devices you are using for development.

One of the drawbacks about some of the other mobile development kits is that you have to pay an annual registration fee before you have access to the SDK. With some, registration and payment are required before you can view their documentation. Android is much more open and accessible. Anybody can download the Android SDK for free. The documentation and forums are completely viewable without having to pay any fee. This means development for Android can start earlier, with device testing being a part of it from the very beginning.

Understanding how Unity and Android work together

Because Unity handles projects and assets in a generic way, there is no need to create multiple projects for multiple target platforms. This means that you could easily start development with the free version of Unity and target personal computers. Then, at a later date, you can switch targets to the Android platform with the click of a button. Perhaps, shortly after your game is launched, it takes the market by storm and there is a great call to bring it to other mobile platforms. With just another click of the button, you can easily target iOS without changing anything in your project.

Most systems require a long and complex set of steps to get your project running on a device. For the first application in this book, we will be going through that process because it is important to know about it. However, once your device is set up and recognized by the Android SDK, a single-button click will allow Unity to build your application, push it to a device, and start running it. There is nothing that has caused more headaches for some developers than trying to get an application on a device. Unity makes it simple.

With the addition of a free Android application, Unity Remote, it is simple and easy to test mobile inputs without going through the whole build process. While developing, there is nothing more annoying than waiting for 5 minutes for a build every time you need to test a minor tweak, especially in the controls and interface. After the first dozen little tweaks the build time starts to add up. Unity Remote makes it simple and easy to test it all without ever having to hit the Build button.

These are the big three: generic projects, a one-click build process, and Unity Remote. We could, of course, come up with several more great ways in which Unity and Android can work together. But these three are the major time and money savers. You could have the greatest game in the world but, if it takes 10 times as long to build and test, what is the point?

Differences between Pro and Basic

Unity comes with two licensing options, Pro and Basic, which can be found at `https://store.unity3d.com`. In order to follow the bulk of this book, Unity Basic is all that is required. However, real-time shadows in *Chapter 4, Setting the Stage – Camera Effects and Lighting*, the whole of *Chapter 5, Getting Around – Pathfinding and AI*, and some of the optimization features discussed in *Chapter 9, Optimization*, will require Unity Pro. If you are not quite ready to spend the $3,000 required to purchase a full Unity Pro license with the Android add-on, there are other options. Unity Basic is free and comes with a 30-day free trial of Unity Pro. This trial is full and complete, just as if one has purchased Unity Pro. It is also possible to upgrade your license at a later date. Where Unity Basic comes with mobile options for free, Unity Pro requires the purchase of Pro add-ons for each of the mobile platforms.

License comparison overview

License comparisons can be found at `http://unity3d.com/unity/licenses`. This section will cover the specific differences between Unity Android Pro and Unity Android Basic. We will explore what the feature is and how useful it is.

- **NavMeshes, Pathfinding, and crowd Simulation**: This feature is Unity's built-in pathfinding system. It allows characters to find their way from point to point around your game. Just bake your navigation data in the editor and let Unity take over at runtime. This feature is great if you don't have the ability or inclination to program a pathfinding system yourself. There is a whole slew of tutorials online about how to program pathfinding and do crowd simulation. It is completely possible to do all of this in Unity Basic; you just need to provide the tools yourself.

◆ **LOD Support: LOD (Level-of-detail)** lets you control how complex a mesh is, based on its distance from the camera. When the camera is close to an object, render a complex mesh with a bunch of detail in it. When the camera is far from that object, render a simple mesh, because all that detail is not going to be seen anyway. Unity Pro provides a built-in system to manage this. However, this is another system that could be created in Unity Basic. Whether using Pro or not, this is an important feature for game efficiency. By rendering less complex meshes at a distance, everything can be rendered faster, leaving more room for awesome gameplay.

◆ **Audio Filter:** Audio filters allow you to add effects to audio clips at runtime. Perhaps you created gravel footstep sounds for your character. Your character is running, and we can hear the footsteps just fine, when suddenly they enter a tunnel and a solar flare hits, causing a time warp and slowing everything down. Audio filters would allow us to warp the gravel footstep sounds to sound like they are coming from within a tunnel and are slowed by a time warp. Of course, you could also just have the audio guy create a new set of tunnel gravel footsteps in the time warp sounds. But this might double the amount of audio in your game and limits how dynamic we can be with it at runtime. We either are or are not playing the time warp footsteps. Audio filters would allow us to control how much time warp is affecting our sounds.

◆ **Video Playback and Streaming**: When dealing with complex or high-definition cut scenes, being able to play a video becomes very important. Including them in a build especially with a mobile target can require a lot of space. This is where the streaming part of this feature comes in. This feature not only lets us play video, it also lets us stream that video from the internet. There is, however, a drawback to this feature. On mobile platforms, the video has to go through the device's built-in, video-playing system. This means the video can only be played full-screen and cannot be used as a texture. Theoretically, though, you could break your video into individual pictures for each frame and flip through them at runtime, but this is not recommended for build size and video quality reasons.

◆ **Fully Fledged Streaming with Asset Bundles**: Asset bundles are a great feature provided by Unity Pro. They allow you to create extra content and stream it to the users, without ever requiring an update to the game. You could add new characters, levels, or just about any other content you can think of. Their only drawback is that you cannot add more code. The functionality cannot change, but the content can. This is one of the best features of Unity Pro.

◆ **100,000 Dollar Turnover**: This one isn't so much a feature as it is a guideline. According to Unity's End User License Agreement, the basic version of Unity cannot be licensed by any group or individual that made $100,000 in the previous fiscal year. This basically means, if you make a bunch of money, you have to buy Unity Pro. Of course, if you are making that much money, you can probably afford it without issue. That is the view of Unity at least, and the reason why it is there.

- **Mecanim: IK Rigs**: Unity's new animation system, Mecanim, supports many exciting new features, one of which is IK. If you are unfamiliar with the term, IK allows one to define the target point of an animation and let the system figure out how to get there. Imagine you have a cup sitting on a table and a character that wants to pick it up. You could animate the character to bend over and pick it up, but what if the character is slightly to the side? Or any number of other slight offsets that a player could cause, completely throwing off your animation. It is simply impractical to animate for every possibility. With IK, it hardly matters that the character is slightly off. We just define the goal point for the hand and leave the arm to the IK system. It calculates for us how the arm needs to move in order to get the hand to the cup. Another fun use is making characters look at interesting things as they walk around a room. A guard could track the nearest person, the player character could look at things that they can interact with, or a tentacle monster could lash out at the player without all the complex animation. This will be an exciting one to play with.

- **Mecanim: Sync Layers & Additional Curves**

  - Sync layers, inside Mecanim, allow us to keep multiple sets of animation states in time with each other. Say you have a soldier that you want to animate differently based on how much health he has. When at full health, he walks around briskly. After a little damage, it becomes more of a trudge. If health is below half, a limp is introduced to his walk. And when almost dead, he crawls along the ground. With sync layers, we can create one animation state machine and duplicate it to multiple layers. By changing the animations and syncing the layers, we can easily transition between the different animations while maintaining the state machine.

  - Additional curves are simply the ability to add curves to your animations. This means we can control various values with the animation. For example, in the game world, when a character picks up their feet for a jump, gravity will pull them down almost immediately. By adding an extra curve to that animation, in Unity, we can control how much gravity is affecting the character, allowing them to actually get in the air when jumping. This is a useful feature for controlling such values right alongside the animations, but one could just as easily create a script that holds and controls the curves.

- **Custom Splash Screen**: Though pretty self-explanatory, it is perhaps not immediately evident why this feature is specified, unless you have worked with Unity before. When an application built in Unity initializes on any platform, it displays a splash screen. In Unity Basic this will always be the Unity logo. By purchasing Unity Pro, you can substitute the Unity logo with any image you want.

◆ **Build Size Stripping**: This is an important feature for mobile platforms. Build size stripping removes all of the excess from your final build. Unity does a very good job at only including the assets that you have created that are used in the final build. With the stripping, it also only includes the parts of the engine itself that are used in the game. This is of great use when you absolutely have to get under that limit for downloading from the cell towers. On the other hand, you could create something similar to the asset bundles. Just let the users buy the framework, and download the assets later.

◆ **Realtime Directional Shadows**: Lights and shadows add a lot to the mood of a scene. This feature allows us to go beyond blob shadows and use realistic looking shadows. This is all well and good if you have the processing space for it. Most mobile devices do not. This feature should also never be used for static scenery. Instead, use static lightmaps, which is what they are for. But if you can find a good balance between simple needs and quality, this could be the feature that creates the difference between an alright and an awesome game.

◆ **HDR, tone mapping**: HDR (**High Dynamic Range**) and tone mapping allow us to create more realistic lighting effects. Standard rendering uses values from zero to one to represent how much of each color in a pixel is on. This does not allow for a full spectrum of lighting options to be explored. HDR lets the system use values beyond this range and process them using tone mapping to create better effects, such as a bright morning room or the bloom from a car window reflecting the sun. The downside of this feature is in the processor. The device can still only handle values between zero and one, so converting them takes time. Additionally, the more complex the effect, the more time it takes to render it. It would be surprising to see this used well on handheld devices, even in a simple game. Maybe the modern tablets could handle it.

◆ **Light Probes**: Light probes are an interesting little feature. When placed in the world, light probes figure out how an object should be lit. Then, as a character walks around, they tell it how to be shaded. The character is, of course, lit by the lights in the scene but there are limits on how many lights can shade an object at once. Light probes do all the complex calculations beforehand, allowing for better shading at runtime. Again, however, there are concerns about the processing power. Too little and you won't get a good effect; too much and there will be no processing left for playing the game.

◆ **Lightmapping with Global Illumination and area lights**: All versions of Unity support lightmaps, allowing for the baking of complex static shadows and lighting effects. With the addition of global illumination and area lights, you can add another touch of realism to your scenes. However, every version of Unity also lets you import your own lightmaps. This means, you could use some other program to render the lightmaps and import them separately.

- **Static Batching**: This feature speeds up the rendering process. Instead of spending time on each frame grouping objects for faster rendering, this allows the system to save the groups generated beforehand. Reducing the number of draw calls is a powerful step towards making a game run faster. That is exactly what this feature does.

- **Render-to-Texture Effects**: This is a fun feature, but of limited use. It simply allows you to redirect the rendering of the camera from going to the screen and instead go to a texture. This texture could then, in its most simple form, be put onto a mesh and act like a surveillance camera. You could also do some custom post processing, such as removing the color from the world as the player loses their health. However, that option could become very processor-intensive.

- **Full-Screen Post-Processing Effects**: This is another processor-intensive feature that probably will not make it into your mobile game. But you can add some very cool effects to your scene. Such as, adding motion blur when the player is moving really fast, or a vortex effect to warp the scene as the ship passes through a warped section of space. One of the best is using the bloom effect to give things a neon-like glow.

- **Occlusion Culling**: This is another great optimization feature. The standard camera system renders everything that is within the camera's view frustum, the view space. Occlusion culling lets us set up volumes in the space our camera can enter. These volumes are used to calculate what the camera can actually see from those locations. If there is a wall in the way, what is the point of rendering everything behind it? Occlusion culling calculates this and stops the camera from rendering anything behind that wall.

- **Navmesh: Dynamic Obstacles and Priority**: This feature works in conjunction with the pathfinding system. In scripts, we can dynamically set obstacles, and characters will find their way around them. Being able to set priorities means different types of characters can take different types of objects into consideration when finding their way around. A soldier must go around the barricades to reach his target. The tank, however, could just crash through, should it desire to.

- **.Net Socket Support**: This feature is only useful if you plan on doing fancy things over a user's network. Multiplayer networking is already supported in every version of Unity. The multiplayer that is available, though, does require a master server. With the use of sockets, one could create connections to other devices locally.

- **Profiler and GPU profiling**: This is a very useful feature. The profiler provides tons of information about how much load your game puts on the processor. With this information we can get right down into the nitty-gritties and determine exactly how long a script takes to process. Towards the end of the book, though, we will also create a tool for determining how long specific parts of your code take to process.

◆ **Script Access to Asset Pipeline**: This is an alright feature. With full access to the pipeline, there is a lot of custom processing that can be done on assets and builds. The full range of possibilities are beyond the scope of this book. But think of it as being able to tint all of the imported textures slightly blue.

◆ **Dark Skin**: This is entirely a cosmetic feature. Its point and purpose are questionable. But if a smooth, dark-skinned look is what you desire, this is the feature you want. There is an option in the editor to change it to the color scheme used in Unity Basic. For this feature, whatever floats your boat goes.

Setting up the development environment

Before we can create the next great game for Android, we need to install a few programs. In order to make the Android SDK work, we will first install the JDK. Then, we will be installing the Android SDK. After that is the installation of Unity. We then have to install an optional code editor. To make sure everything is set up correctly, we will connect to our devices and take a look at some special strategies if the device is a tricky one. Finally, we will install Unity Remote, a program that will become invaluable in your mobile development.

Time for action – installing the JDK

Android's development language of choice is Java, so to develop for it we need a copy of the Java SE Development Kit, JDK, on our computers. The process of installing the JDK is given in the following steps:

1. The latest version of the JDK can be downloaded from `http://www.oracle.com/technetwork/java/javase/downloads/index.html`. So, open the site in a web browser.

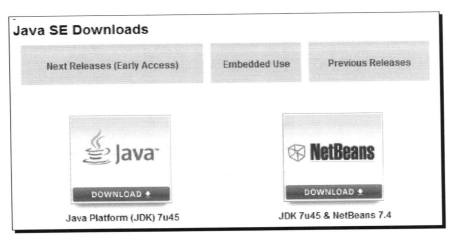

2. Select **Java Platform (JDK)** from the available versions and you will be brought to a combination of license agreement and type selection page.

3. Accept the license agreement, and select your appropriate Windows version from the bottom of the list. If you are unsure which to choose, then **Windows x86** is usually a safe choice.

4. Once the download is completed, run the new installer.

5. A scan, two **Next** button-clicks, an initialization, and one more **Next** button will install the JDK to the default location. It is as good there as anywhere else, so once it is done installing, hit **Close**.

What just happened?

We installed the **JDK (Java Development Kit)**. We need this so that our Android development kit will work. Luckily, the installation process for this keystone is short and sweet.

Time for action – installing the Android SDK

In order to actually develop and connect to our devices, we need to have the Android SDK installed. Having it fulfills two primary requirements. First, it makes sure we have the bulk of the latest drivers for recognizing devices. Second, we are able to use the **ADB (Android Debug Bridge)**. ADB is the system used for actually connecting to and interacting with the device. The process of installing the Android SDK is given in the following steps:

1. The latest version of the Android SDK can be found at `http://developer.android.com/sdk/index.html`, so open a web browser and go to the given site.

2. Once there, scroll to the bottom and select **USE AN EXISTING IDE**.

3. Follow that up by clicking on the **Download the SDK Tools for Windows** button.

> **Download the SDK**
> ADT Bundle for Windows
>
> If you prefer to use an existing version of Eclipse or another IDE, you can instead take a more customized approach to installing the Android SDK. See the following instructions.
>
> ˄ USE AN EXISTING IDE
>
> If you already have an IDE you want to use for Android app development, setting up a new SDK requires that you download the SDK Tools, then select additional Android SDK packages to install (such as the Android platform and system image). If you'll be using an existing version of Eclipse, then you can add the ADT plugin to it.
>
> Download the SDK Tools for Windows
>
> ˅ SYSTEM REQUIREMENTS
> ˅ DOWNLOAD FOR OTHER PLATFORMS

4. You will then be sent to a Terms and Conditions agreement. Read it if you prefer, but agree to it to continue and hit the download button to start downloading the installer.

5. Once it has finished downloading, start it up.

6. Hit the first **Next** button and the installer will try to find an appropriate version of the JDK. You will come to a page complaining about it, if you do not have it installed.

7. If you skipped ahead and do not have the JDK installed, hit the **Visit java.oracle.com** button in the middle of the page and go back to the previous section for guidance on installing it. If you do have it, continue with the process.

8. Hitting **Next** again will bring us to a page about selecting who to install the SDK for.

9. Select **Install for anyone using this computer**, because the default install location is easier to get to for later purposes.

10. Hit **Next** twice, followed by **Install** to install to the default location.

11. Once it is done, hit **Next** and **Finish** to complete the installation of the Android SDK Manager.

12. If the Android SDK Manager does not start right away, start it up. Either way, give it a moment to initialize. The SDK Manager makes sure that we have the latest drivers, systems, and tools for developing with the Android platform. But first, we have to actually install them.

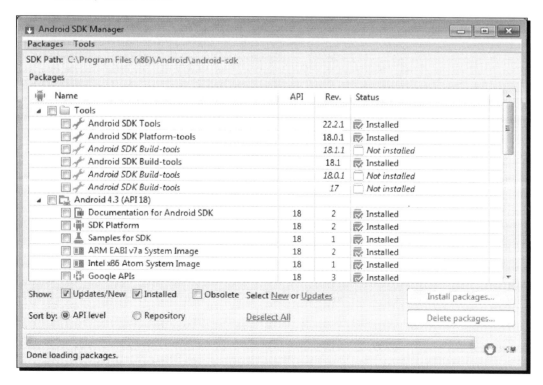

13. By default it should select a number of options to install. If not, select the latest Android API, 4.3 (API 18) as of the time of writing this, **Android Support Library** and **Google USB Driver** found in **Extras**. Be absolutely sure that **Android SDK Platform-tools** is selected. This one will be very important later. It actually includes the tools we need to connect to our device.

14. Once everything is selected, hit **Install packages** in the bottom-right corner.

15. The next screen is another set of license agreements. Every time a component is installed or updated through the SDK Manager, you have to agree to the license terms before it gets installed. Accept all of the licenses and hit **Install** to start the process.

16. You can now sit back and relax. It takes a while for the components to be downloaded and installed. Once it is all done, you can close it out. We have completed the process, but you should occasionally come back to it. Periodically checking the SDK Manager for updates will make sure you are using the latest tools and API's.

What just happened?

We installed the Android SDK. Without it, we would be completely unable to do anything with the Android platform. Besides the long wait to download and install components, this was a pretty easy installation.

Time for action – installing Unity 3D

Perhaps the most important part of this whole book, without which none of the rest has meaning, is installing Unity.

1. The latest version of Unity can be found at `http://www.unity3d.com/unity/download`. As of the time of writing this, the current version is 4.2.2.

2. Once downloaded, launch the installer and click **Next** until you reach the **Choose Components** page.

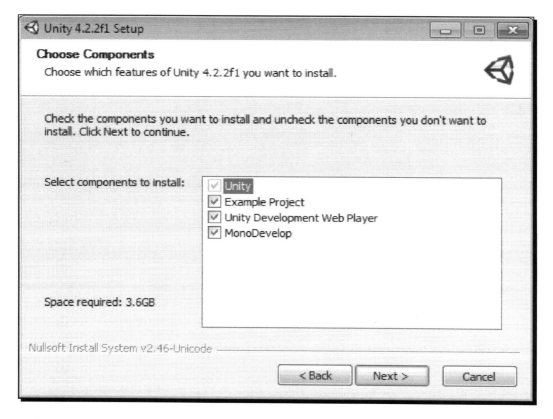

3. Here, we are able to select the features of Unity installation. None of these options are actually necessary for following the rest of this book, but they warrant having a look at since Unity will ask every time you update or reinstall it.

    ❏   The **Example Project** is the current project built by Unity to show off some of its latest features. If you want to jump in early and take a look at what a complete Unity game looks like, leave this checked.

     ❑   The **Unity Development Web Player** is required if you plan on developing browser applications with Unity. As this book is focused on Android development, it is entirely optional. It is, however, a good one to check. You never know when you may need a web demo and since it is entirely free to develop for the web using Unity, there is no harm in having it.

     ❑   The last option is **MonoDevelop**. It is a wise choice to leave this option unchecked. There is more detail in the next section, but it will suffice for now to say that it just adds an extra program for script editing that is not nearly as useful as it should be.

4. Once you have selected or deselected your desired options, hit **Next**. If you wish to follow the book exactly, we will be unchecking **MonoDevelop** and leaving the rest checked.

5. Next is the install location. The default location works well, so hit **Install** and wait. This will take a couple of minutes, so sit back, relax, and enjoy your favorite beverage.

6. Once the installation is complete, the option to run Unity will be displayed. Leave it checked and hit **Finish**. If you have never installed Unity before, you will be presented with a license activation page.

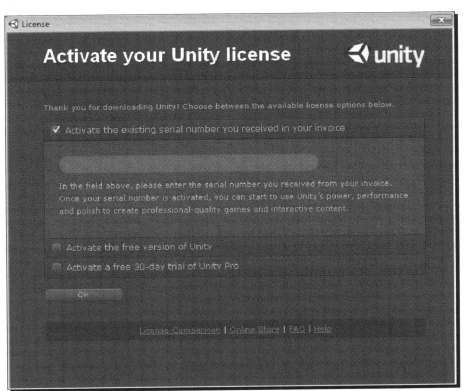

7. While Unity does provide a feature–rich, free version, in order to follow the entirety of this book, one requires to make use of some of the Unity Pro features. At `https://store.unity3d.com` you have the ability to buy a variety of licenses. To follow the whole book, you will at least need to purchase Unity Pro and Android Pro licenses. Once purchased, you will receive an e-mail containing your new license key. Enter that in the provided text field.

8. If you are not ready to make a purchase, you have two alternatives. We will go over how to reset your license in the *Building a simple application* section later in the chapter.

   ❑ The first alternative is that you can check the **Activate the free version of Unity** checkbox. This will allow you to use the free version of Unity. As discussed earlier, there are many reasons to choose this option. The most notable at the moment is cost.

   ❑ Alternatively, you can select the **Activate a free 30-day trial of Unity Pro** option. Unity offers a fully functioning, one-time installation, and free 30-day trial of Unity Pro. This trial also includes the Android Pro add-on. Anything produced during those 30 days is completely yours, just as if you had purchased a full Unity Pro license. They want you to see how great it is, so you will come back and make a purchase. The downside is the Trial Version watermark that will be constantly displayed in the corner of the game. After the 30 days, Unity will revert to the free version. This is a great option, should you choose to wait before making a purchase.

9. Whatever your choice is, hit **OK** once you have made it.

10. The next page simply asks you to log in with your Unity account. This will be the same account you used to make your purchase. Just fill out the fields and hit **OK**.

11. If you have not yet made a purchase, you can hit **Create Account** and have it ready to go when you do make a purchase.

12. The next page is a short survey on your development interests. Fill it out and hit **OK** or scroll straight to the bottom and hit **Not right now**.

13. Finally there is a thank you page. Hit **Start using Unity**.

14. After a short initialization, the project wizard will open and we can start creating the next great game. However, there is still a bunch of work to do: in connecting the development device. So, for now, hit the **X** button in the top-right corner to close the project wizard. We will cover how to create a new project in the *Building a simple application* section later on.

What just happened?

We just installed Unity 3D. The whole book relies on this step. We also had to make a choice about licenses. If you chose to purchase the Pro version, you will be able to follow everything in this book without issues. The alternatives, though, will have a few shortcomings. You will either not have full access to all of the features or be limited to the length of the trial.

Optional code editor

Now a choice has to be made about code editors. Unity comes with a system called **MonoDevelop**. It is similar in many respects to Visual Studio. And, like Visual Studio, it adds many extra files and much girth to a project, all of which it needs to operate. All this extra girth makes it take an annoying amount of time while it starts up, before one can actually get to the code.

Technically, you can get away with a plain text editor as Unity doesn't really care. This book recommends using Notepad++, found at `http://notepad-plus-plus.org/download`. Free to use, it is essentially Notepad with code highlighting. There are several fancy widgets and add-ons for Notepad++ that add even greater functionality, but they are not necessary for following this book. If you choose this alternative, installing Notepad++ to the default location will work just fine.

Connecting to a device

Perhaps the most annoying step in working with Android devices is setting up the connection to your computer. Because there are so many different kinds of devices, it can get a little tricky at times just to have the device recognized by your computer.

Time for action – simple device connection

The simple device-connection method involves changing a few settings and a little work in the command prompt. It might seem a little scary but if all goes well, you will be connected to your device shortly.

1. The first thing we need to do is turn on some developer settings on the phone. At the top of the settings page, there should be a **Development** option; select it. If you do not have that option, look for an **Applications** option.

2. Find the **Unknown sources** check box and check it. This lets us install our development applications on the device.

3. The next checkbox to be checked is **USB debugging**. This allows us to actually detect our device from the development environment.

4. If you are using Kindle, be sure to go into **Security** and turn on **Enable ADB** as well.

 There are several warning pop ups that are associated with turning these various options on. They essentially amount to the same malicious software warnings associated with your computer. Applications with immoral intentions can mess with your system and get to your private information. All these settings need to be turned on if your device is only going to be used for development. But, as the warnings suggest, if malicious applications are a concern, turn them off when not developing.

5. Next, start a command prompt. This can be done most easily by hitting your Windows key, typing `cmd.exe`, and hitting *Enter*.

6. We now need to navigate to the ADB commands. If you did not install to the default location, replace the path in the following commands with the path you installed to.

    ❏ If you are running a 32-bit version of Windows and installed to the default location, type the following in the command prompt:

    ```
    cd c:\program files\android\android-sdk\platform-tools
    ```

    ❏ If you are running a 64-bit version, type the following in the command prompt:

    ```
    cd c:\program files (x86)\android\android-sdk\platform-tools
    ```

7. Now connect your device to your computer, preferably using the USB cable that came with it.

8. Wait for your computer to finish recognizing the device. There should be a "Device drivers installed" type of message pop-up when it is done.

9. The following command lets us see which devices are currently connected and recognized by the ADB system. Emulated devices will show up as well. Type into the command prompt:

    ```
    adb devices
    ```

10. After a short pause for processing, the command prompt will display a list of devices attached along with the unique IDs of all attached devices. If this list now contains your device, congratulations, you have a developer-friendly device. If not, things get a little trickier.

What just happened?

We made our first attempt at connecting to our Android devices. For most, this should be all that you need to connect to your device. For some, this process is not quite enough. The next little section covers solutions to resolve the issue.

Time for action – connecting trickier devices

For trickier devices, there are a few general things we can try. If these steps fail to connect your device, you may need to do some special research.

1. Start by typing the following commands. These will restart the connection system and display the list of devices again.

```
adb kill-server
adb start-server
adb devices
```

2. If you are still not having any luck, try the following commands. These commands force an update and restart the connection system.

```
cd ../tools
android update adb
cd ../platform-tools
adb kill-server
adb start-server
adb devices
```

3. If your device is still not showing up, you have one of the most annoying and tricky devices. Check the manufacturer's website for data syncing and management programs. If you have had your device for quite some time, you have probably been prompted to install this more than once. If you have not already done so, install the latest version, even if you never plan on using it. The point is to obtain the latest drivers for your device, and this is the easiest way.

4. Restart the connection system again using the first set of commands, and cross your fingers.

5. If you are still unable to connect, the best, professional recommendation that can be made is to Google it. Conducting a search for your device brand with adb at the end should turn up a step-by-step tutorial specific to your device in the first couple of results. http://www.xda-developers.com/ is also an excellent resource for finding out all about the nitty-gritties of Android devices.

What just happened?

Some of the devices that you will encounter while developing will not connect easily. We just covered some quick steps and managed to connect these devices. If we could have covered the processes for every device, we would have. However, the variety of devices is just too large, and they keep making more.

Unity Remote

Unity Remote is a great application created by the Unity team. It allows developers to connect their Android powered devices to the Unity Editor and provide mobile inputs for testing. This is a definite must for any aspiring Unity and Android developer. If you are using a non-Amazon device, acquiring Unity Remote is quite easy. At the time of writing this book, it could be found on Google Play at `https://play.google.com/store/apps/details?id=com.unity3d.androidremote`. It is free and does nothing but connect to the Unity Editor, so the permissions are negligible.

If, however, you are like the ever-growing Amazon market or seek to target Amazon's line of Android devices, adding Unity Remote becomes a little trickier. First, you need to download the APK. It can be found at: `http://files.unity3d.com/ricardo/AndroidRemote.apk`. Be sure to download the file to a location that you can easily get the whole file path for. In the next section, we build a simple application and put it on our device. Follow along from the **Start Console** step, replacing the simple application with the downloaded APK.

Building a simple application

We are now going to create a simple Hello World application. This will familiarize you with the Unity interface and how to actually put an application on your device.

Time for action – Hello World

To make sure everything is set up properly, we need a simple application to test with, and what better to do that with than a Hello World application?

1. The first step is pretty straightforward and simple; start Unity.
2. If you have been following along so far, once it is done you should see a screen resembling the next screenshot. As the tab might suggest, this is the screen through which we open our various projects. Right now, though, we are interested in creating one, so select **Create New Project** from the second tab on top, and we will do just that.

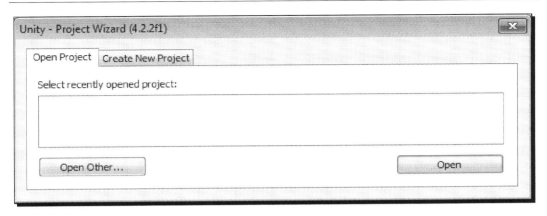

3. Use the **Browse** button to select an empty folder to keep your project in. Be sure that the folder is empty, because Unity will delete everything in it before creating the new project. Ch1_HelloWorld_CS works well for a project name.

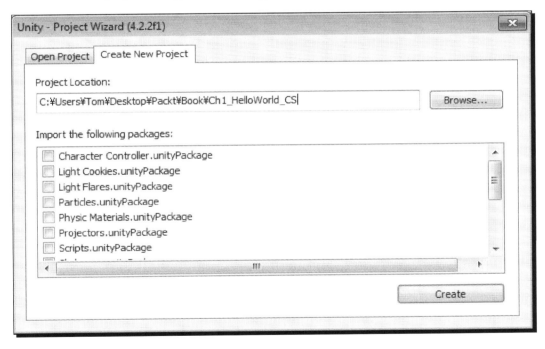

4. For now we can ignore the packages. These are bits of assets and functionality provided by Unity. They are free for you to use in your projects.

5. Hit the **Create** button, and Unity will create a brand new project for us.

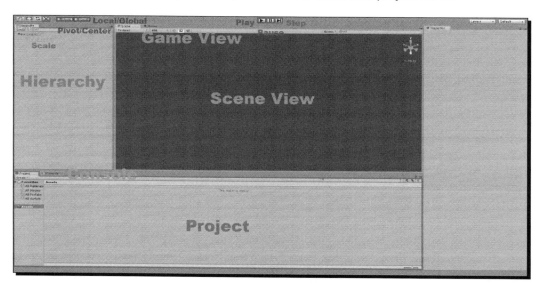

6. The default layout of Unity contains a decent spread of windows needed to create a game.

    ❑ Starting from the left-hand side, **Hierarchy** contains a list of all the objects that currently exist in our scene. They are organized alphabetically and are grouped under parent objects, if any.

    ❑ Next to that is the **Scene** view. This window allows us to edit and arrange objects in the 3D space. In the top-left hand side, there are two groups of buttons. These affect how you can interact with the **Scene** view.

    ❑ The button on the far left that looks like a hand lets you pan around when clicking and dragging with the left-mouse button.

    ❑ The next button over, the crossed arrows, lets you move objects around. Its behavior and the gizmo it provides will be familiar if you have made use of any modeling programs.

    ❑ The third button changes the gizmo to rotation. It allows you to rotate objects.

    ❑ The fourth button is for scale. It changes the gizmo as well.

    ❑ The second to last button toggles between **Pivot** and **Center**. This will change the position of the gizmo used by the last three buttons to be either at the pivot point of the selected object, or at the average position point of all the selected objects.

- The last button toggles between **Local** and **Center**. This changes whether the gizmo is orientated parallel with the world origin or rotated with the selected object.

- Underneath the **Scene** view is the **Game** view. This is what is currently being rendered by any cameras in the scene. It is what the player will see when playing the game and is used for testing your game. There are three buttons that control the playback of the **Game** view in the upper-middle section of the window.

- The first is the **Play** button. It toggles the playing of the game. If you want to test your game, press this button.

- The second is the **Pause** button. While playing, pressing this button will pause the whole game, allowing you to take a look at the game's current state.

- The third is the **Step** button. When paused, this button will let you progress through your game one frame at a time.

- On the right-hand side is the **Inspector** window. This displays information about any object that is currently selected.

- In the bottom left-hand side is the **Project** window. This displays all of the assets that are currently stored in the project.

- Behind it is the **Console**. It will display debug messages and compile errors, warnings, and runtime errors.

7. At the top, underneath **Help** is an option called **Manage License....** By selecting this, we are given options to control the license. The button descriptions cover what they do pretty well, so we will not cover them in more detail at this point.

8. The next thing we need to do is connect our optional code editor. At the top, go to **Edit** followed by **Preferences...**, which opens the following window:

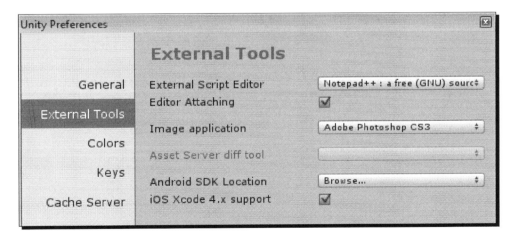

9. By selecting **External Tools** on the left, we can select other software to be used for managing asset editing.

10. If you do not desire to use MonoDevelop, select the drop-down list to the right of **External Script Editor** and navigate to the executable of **Notepad++**, or the other code editor of your choice.

11. Your **Image application** can also be changed here to **Adobe Photoshop CS3** or any other image-editing program you prefer, in the same way as the script editor.

12. If you installed the Android SDK to the default location, do not worry about it. Otherwise, click on **Browse...** and find the `android-sdk` folder.

13. Now, for the actual creation of this application, right-click inside of your **Project** window.

14. From the new window that pops up, select **Create** and **C# Script** from the menu.

15. Type in a name for the new script, `HelloWorld` will work well, and hit *Enter* twice: once to confirm the name and once to open it.

>
> Because this is the first chapter, it will be a simple Hello World application. Unity supports C#, JavaScript, and Boo as scripting languages. For consistency, this book will be using C#. If you, instead, wish to use JavaScript for your scripts, copies of all of the projects can be found with the other resources for this book and an _JS suffix for JavaScript.

16. Every script that is going to attach to an object inherits from MonoBehaviour. JavaScript does this automatically, but C# scripts must define it explicitly. However, as you can see from the default code in the script, we do not have to worry about setting this up initially; it is done automatically. Inheriting from MonoBehaviour lets our scripts access various values of the game object, such as the position, and lets the system automatically call certain functions during specific events in the game, such as the Update cycle and the GUI rendering.

17. For now we will delete the `Start` and `Update` functions that Unity insists on including in every new script. Replace them with a bit of code that simply renders the words **Hello World** in the top-left corner of the screen. You can now close the script and return to Unity.

```
public void OnGUI() {
  GUILayout.Label("Hello World");
}
```

18. Drag the `HelloWorld` script from the **Project** window and drop it on the **Main Camera** object in the **Hierarchy** window. Congratulations, you have just added your first bit of functionality to an object in Unity.

19. If you select the **Main Camera** in **Hierarchy**, then **Inspector** will display all of the components attached to it. At the bottom of the list is your brand new `HelloWorld` script.

20. Before we can test it, we need to save the scene. To do this, go to **File** at the top, and select **Save Scene**. Give it a name of `HelloWorld` and hit **Save**.

21. You are now free to hit the **Play** button in the upper-middle section of the editor and witness the magic of Hello World.

22. We now get to build the application. At the top, select **File** followed by **Build Settings...**.

23. By default the target platform is **PC**. Under **Platform**, select **Android** and hit **Switch Platform** in the bottom-left corner of the **Build Settings** window.

24. Underneath the **Scenes In Build** box, there is a button labeled **Add Current**. Click on it to add our currently opened scene to the build. Only scenes that are in this list and checked will be added to the final build of your game. The scene with the number zero next to it will be the first scene loaded when the game starts.

25. There is one last thing to change before we can hit the **Build** button. Select **Player Settings...** at the bottom of the **Build Settings** window.

26. The **Inspector** window will open **Player Settings** for the application. From here we can change the splash screen, icon, screen orientation, and a handful of other technical options.

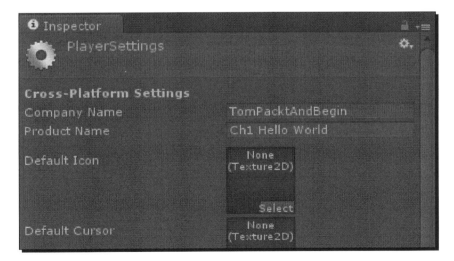

27. At the moment, there are only a few options that we care about. At the top, **Company Name** is the name that will appear under the information about the application. **Product Name** is the name that will appear underneath the icon on your Android device. You can largely set these to anything you want, but they do need to be set immediately.

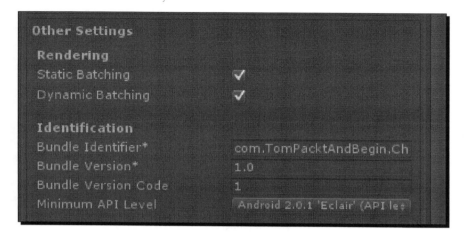

28. The important setting is **Bundle Identifier** underneath **Other Settings**. This is the unique identifier that singles out your application from all other applications on the device. The format is `com.CompanyName.ProductName`, and it is good practice to use the same company name across all of your products. For this book, we will be using `com.TomPacktAndBegin.Ch1.HelloWorld` for **Bundle Identifier**, opting to use an extra dot for organization.

29. Go up to **File** and click on **Save** again.

30. Now you can hit the **Build** button in the **Build Settings** window.

31. Pick a save location and a file name; `Ch1_HelloWorld.apk` works well. Be sure to remember where it is, and hit **Save**.

32. If, during the build process, Unity complains about where the Android SDK is, select the `android-sdk` folder inside the location where it was installed. The default would be `C:\Program Files\Android\android-sdk` for 32-bit Windows and `C:\Program Files (x86)\Android\android-sdk` for 64-bit Windows.

33. Once the loading bar finishes, which should not be very long, your `apk` has been made and we are ready to continue.

34. We are finished with Unity for this chapter. You can close it down and start a command prompt.

35. Just as we did when we were connecting our devices, we need to navigate to the `platform tools` folder in order to connect to our device. If you installed it to the default location, use:

1. For 32-bit Windows:

```
cd c:\program files\android\android-sdk\platform-tools
```

2. For 64-bit Windows:

```
cd c:\program files (x86)\android\android-sdk\platform-tools
```

36. Double-check to make sure that the device is connected and recognized using:

```
adb devices
```

37. Now we install the application. This command tells the system to install an application on the connected device. The `-r` indicates that it should override if an application is found with the same Bundle Identifier as the application we are trying to install. That way you can just update your game as you develop, rather than uninstalling before installing the new version each time you need to make an update. The path to the `.apk` file that you wish to install is shown in quotes as follows:

```
adb install -r "c:\users\tom\desktop\packt\book\ch1_helloworld.apk"
```

38. Replace it with the path to your apk file; capital letters do not matter, but be sure to have all the correct spacing and punctuations.

39. If all goes well, the console will display an upload speed when it has finished pushing your application to the device and a success message when it is finished installing. The most common causes for errors at this stage are not being in the `platform-tools` folder when issuing commands and not having the correct path to your `.apk` file surrounded by quotes.

40. Once you have received your success message, find the application on your phone and start it up.

41. Now, gaze in wonder at your ability to create Android applications with the power of Unity.

What just happened?

We created our very first Unity and Android application. Admittedly, it was just a simple Hello World application, but that is how it always starts. Also, it served very well for double-checking the device connection and for learning about the build process without all of the clutter from a game.

Have a go hero – working ahead

Try changing the icon for the application. It is a fairly simple procedure that you will undoubtedly want to perform as your game develops. How to do this was mentioned earlier in this section. But, as a reminder, take a look at **Player Settings**. Also, you will need to import an image. Take a look under **Assets**, in the menu bar, to know how to do this.

Summary

There were a lot of technical things in this chapter. First, we discussed the benefits and possibilities when using Unity and Android. That was followed by a whole lot of installation; the JDK, the Android SDK, Unity 3D, and Unity Remote. We then figured out how to connect to our devices through the command prompt. Our first application was quick and simple to make. Finally, we built it and put it on a device.

The next chapter will see us creating a game that is significantly more interactive, Tic-tac-toe. We will be exploring the wonderful world of graphical user interfaces. So, not only will we make the game, but we will make it look good too.

Looking Good – Graphical Interface

2

In the previous chapter, we covered the features of Unity and Android. We also discussed the benefits of using them together. After we finished installing a bunch of software and setting up our devices, we created a simple Hello World application to confirm that everything was connected correctly.

*This chapter is all about **Graphical User Interface (GUI)**. We will start by creating a simple Tic-tac-toe game, using the basic pieces of GUI that Unity provides. Following that we will discuss Unity's GUI Styles and GUI Skins. Using what we learned, we will improve the look of our game. Also, we will explore some tips and tricks for handling many different screen sizes of Android devices. Finally, we will learn about a much quicker way to put our games on the device, which was covered in the previous chapter. With all that said, let's jump in.*

In this chapter, we will cover the following topics:

- User preferences
- Buttons and labels
- GUI Skins and GUI Styles
- Dynamic GUI positioning
- Build and run

In this chapter, we will be creating a new project in Unity. The first section here will walk you through its creation and setup.

Creating a Tic-tac-toe game

The project for this chapter is a simple Tic-tac-toe-style game, similar to what any of us might play on paper. As with anything else, there are several ways you could make this game. We are going to use Unity's GUI system, in order to better understand how to create a GUI for any of our other games.

Time for action – creating Tic-tac-toe

The basic Tic-tac-toe game involves two players and a 3 x 3 grid. The players take turns filling X's and O's. The player who first fills a line of three squares with his/her letter wins the game. If all squares are filled without a player achieving a line of three, the game is a tie. Let's perform the following steps to create our game:

1. The first thing to do is to create a project for this chapter. So, start up Unity and we will do just that.

2. If you have been following along so far, Unity should boot up into the last project that was open. This isn't a bad feature, but it can become extremely annoying. Think of it like this: you have been working on a project for a while and it has grown large. Now you need to quickly open something else, but Unity defaults to your huge project. If you wait for it to open before you can work on anything else, it can consume a lot of time. To change this feature, go to the top of the Unity window and click on **Edit** followed by **Preferences**. This is the same place where we changed our script editor's preferences. This time, though, we are going to change settings in the **General** tab. The following screenshot shows the options present under the **General** tab:

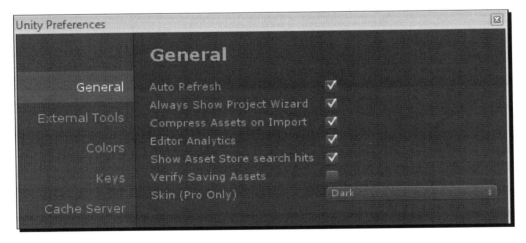

3. At this moment, the primary concern is the **Always Show Project Wizard** option; however, we will still cover all of the options in turn. All the options under the **General** tab are explained in detail as follows:

    ❑ **Auto Refresh**: This is one of the best features of Unity. As assets are changed outside of Unity, this option lets Unity automatically detect the change and refresh the asset inside your project.

    ❑ **Always Show Project Wizard**: This is a great first option to go check whenever installing Unity. Instead of opening the last project, Unity opens **Project Wizard**. From there, you can open any project of your choice or create a new one. This is always a good one to turn on.

    ❑ **Compress Assets on Import**: This is the checkbox for automatically compressing your game assets when they are first imported to Unity.

    ❑ **Editor Analytics**: This is the checkbox for Unity's anonymous usage statistics. Leave it checked and the Unity Editor sends info occasionally to the Unity source. It doesn't hurt anything to leave it on, and helps the Unity team make the Unity Editor better. But it comes down to personal preference.

    ❑ **Show Asset Store search hits**: This setting is only relevant if you are planning to use the Asset Store. The Asset Store can be a great source of assets and tools for any game; however, since we are not going to use it, the relevance to this book is rather limited. It does what the name suggests. When you search the Asset Store for something from within the Unity Editor, the number of results is displayed based on this checkbox.

    ❑ **Verify Saving Assets**: This is a good one to be left off. If this is on, every time you click on **Save** in Unity. A dialog box will pop up so that you can make sure you save any and all of the assets that have changed since your last save. It is not so much about your models and textures, but concerned with Unity's internal files, the materials, and prefabs. Best to leave it off for now.

    ❑ **Skin (Pro Only)**: This option only applies to Unity's pro users. It gives the option to switch between the light and dark versions of the Unity Editor. It is purely cosmetic, so go with your gut for this one.

4. With your preferences set, now go up to **File** and follow it with selecting **Open Project**.

5. Select the **Create New Project** tab, followed by the **Browse...** button to pick a location and name for the new project.

6. We will not be using any of the included packages, so click on **Create** and we can get on with it.

7. Once Unity finishes initializing the new project, create two new scripts in the **Project** panel, just as we did for the *Hello World* project in the previous chapter. Name the new scripts as `TicTacToeControl` and `SquareState`. Open them and clear out the default functions; again, just as we did in *Chapter 1, Saying Hello to Unity and Android*.

8. The `SquareState` script will hold the possible states of each square of our game board. To do that, clear everything out of the script and replace it with a simple enumeration. An enumeration is just a list of potential values. This one is concerned with the player who controls the square. Do X's control it, O's control it, or is it clear because the game board is traditionally clear by default. `Clear` becomes the first and therefore the default state.

```
public enum SquareState {
  Clear,
  XControl,
  OControl
}
```

9. In our other script, `TicTacToeControl`, we start with two variables that will largely control the flow of the game. The first defines our game board. Traditionally the game is played on a 3 x 3 grid, therefore nine squares. The second line dictates whose turn it is. How it is going to change will be made clear in a little bit, but for now suffice it to say that if it is X's turn, the value will be true. If it is not X's turn, the value will be false.

```
public SquareState[] board = new SquareState[9];
public bool xTurn = true;
```

In Unity, every script by default inherits from the `MonoBehaviour` class. This gives our scripts two primary benefits.

First, it allows us to add our scripts to objects as components. The filename of the script also needs to be the exact same as the class name within the script, if you plan on adding the script to an object.

The second benefit of the `MonoBehaviour` class is the variety of variables and functions that come with it. The variables give us access to all the parts that make up objects in Unity. The functions provide a number of automatic features and access to the game initialization and loop. This is what we are most interested in at this particular moment.

10. In order to draw anything in each GUI frame, one needs to utilize the `OnGUI` function provided by the `MonoBehaviour` class. That is where we will draw our game board. The `OnGUI` function lets us draw our interface every frame. Inside it, we will first define the width and height of our board squares.

```
public void OnGUI() {
   float width = 75;
   float height = 75;
```

11. Following that is a pair of for-loops. Because our board is a 3 x 3 grid, we need the loops to count three rows of three squares.

```
for(int y=0;y<3;y++) {
    for(int x=0;x<3;x++) {
```

12. Inside the loops we must first figure out which square we are currently drawing. It becomes hard to play a game, if you don't know which square was touched.

```
int boardIndex = (y * 3) + x;
```

13. The next line of code defines whether the square is going to be drawn as a `Rect` class. A `Rect` class is defined in GUI space as x position, y position, width, and height. In Unity, GUI space is defined as the top-left corner being (0,0) and the bottom-right is `Screen.width, Screen.height`. The width and height of the screen are the number of pixels.

```
Rect square = new Rect(x * width, y * height, width, height);
```

14. We then figure out who controls the square. The following line of code is a little complicated, but it is really just a compressed `if` statement. Basically, it works like this: first check a condition and if it is true return the first value, whatever is between the question mark and the colon. If the condition is false, return the value after the colon. Two of these compressed `if` statements were combined here; if the square is owned by X, set our owner to X. Otherwise, if it is owned by O, set the owner to O. If neither of the conditions is true, nobody owns the square and we set our owner to an empty string.

```
string owner = board[boardIndex] == SquareState.XControl ? "X" :
board[boardIndex] == SquareState.OControl ? "O" : "";
```

15. Now that all the hard work of figuring out where we are is done, we actually draw our game board square. This is done through the use of a wonderful little function provided by Unity, `GUI.Button`. To use this function in its basic form, we must tell the function where the button should be drawn and what text to display, hence rect and string. We give it our square and owner variables, it does all the hard work of actually drawing on screen, and we are given back a Boolean result, whether or not the button was pressed. Therefore, we check it with an `if` statement and if true, we send to a new function which square was pressed, letting it handle setting the owner. Also, don't forget the extra curly braces to close up the loops and the function.

```
if(GUI.Button(square, owner))
   SetControl(boardIndex);
```

```
          }
       }
   }
```

16. The `SetControl` function is pretty short; it simply sets the owner for whichever square is passed to it. It first makes sure that the index given is actually within the range for our board. If it is not, we'll exit the function early. The next line of code sets control of the board square based on whose turn it is. If it is X's turn, set the square to `XControl`; otherwise set control to `OControl`. Finally we change whose turn it is. This is done by simply setting our `xTurn` Boolean to the opposite of itself, indicating that it is the other person's turn.

```
public void SetControl(int boardIndex) {
    if(boardIndex < 0 || boardIndex >= board.Length) return;

    board[boardIndex] = xTurn ? SquareState.XControl : SquareState.
OControl;
    xTurn = !xTurn;
}
```

17. We are just about ready to play our game. We just need to set up the scene. To do this, start by dragging our `TicTacToeControl` script from the **Project** pane of the Unity Editor to the **Main Camera** object in the **Hierarchy** pane of the Unity Editor.

18. Now save the scene, just as we did in *Chapter 1, Saying Hello to Unity and Android*, as `TicTacToe`.

19. It is possible to play the game at this point. It is also possible to do so on a device; just follow the same steps as in *Chapter 1, Saying Hello to Unity and Android*, but for now just perform testing in the Unity Editor. Later in this chapter we will cover a much easier way to build to our devices.

Downloading the example code

You can download the example code files for all Packt books you have purchased from your account at http://www.packtpub.com. If you purchased this book elsewhere, you can visit http://www.packtpub. com/support and register to have the files e-mailed directly to you.

What just happened?

We created the very base of what we need to play Tic-tac-toe. We did this with two short and simple scripts. However, while playing the game now, you probably noticed a few things about it. For starters, it doesn't look particularly fantastic. That is extremely odd, considering it is the point of this chapter, but we will address that soon enough. Second, there are no checks to determine whether or not somebody already controls a square.

Also, there are no checks to see if anybody won the game. Finally, if you decided to build to device, you might have noticed one of the great things about Unity's GUI functions. There is no special programming needed to make any of the GUI functions work with touch inputs rather than the mouse. A lot of time is saved when you don't have to worry about special inputs, especially if you plan on multiplatform targeting.

Finishing the game

If you didn't want to go through the process of building the application and putting it on your device, it is still possible for you to try out interacting with the buttons, and touching them with your fingers. In *Chapter 1, Saying Hello to Unity and Android*, we installed the application, Unity Remote. Plug the device into your computer and start it up; when you click on **Play** in the Unity Editor, you should see the game running on your device. If you can see the game playing in the Unity Editor but not on the device, just restart Unity. Make sure to save it; it would be awful to lose all of your hard work.

Undoubtedly the first thing you will notice when using Unity Remote is that the game doesn't look good. It is almost certainly stretched and pixelated. If it doesn't concern you now, don't worry, it gets worse when the project becomes more complicated. Now, before you start freaking out, grumbling about why you had to install such a useless program, you must understand the point of Unity Remote. We went over it sometime back, but we will dig a little deeper. Unity Remote is for testing device inputs: touch screen, tilt, and so on. What it looks like is a result of freeing up bandwidth so that the frame rate is the same as it is in the Unity Editor.

There is something you can and should do about the stretching. At the top-left corner of the **Game** window of the Unity Editor is a drop-down list. By default it is set to **Free Aspect**, which means the window will fill all the space available. If you click on it, a variety of aspect ratio options will be presented. Clicking through these options, you will see black bars in the **Game** window. This is Unity resizing the **Game** window and blacking out the unused space. The options change based on what the build target is. In the **Build Settings** window, change your platform to Android. In the **Game** window's drop-down menu, find an aspect ratio that matches your device. With that selected, your game will no longer appear stretched when using Unity Remote.

Time for action – finish creating the game

Let us finish the creation of our game by creating an opening screen. We will then add some checks to stop players from selecting squares more than once. Follow that with a check to see if anyone won and finally display a game over screen. With that, the game will be ready for us to make it look great.

Let's perform the following steps for finishing our game:

1. We will do all this by first creating another script like our `SquareState` script. Create the new `GameState` script and clear out the default contents. Add the following code snippet and we will have the values needed to track the current state of our game:

```
public enum GameState {
  Opening,
  MultiPlayer,
  GameOver
}
```

2. We now need to update our `TicTacToeControl` script. For starters, because we want to be able to play multiple games, add the `NewGame` function to the script. This function initializes our control variables so that we can start a fresh game with a clear board. It will not do very well for players to start a new game and have the board already filled in. This function will be used by our main menu, which we will be writing shortly.

```
public void NewGame() {
  xTurn = true;
  board = new SquareState[9];
}
```

3. But first, we need to update our `OnGUI` function. To do that, start by moving all of the current contents of `OnGUI` to a new function called `DrawGameBoard`.

4. Now, we need to change our cleared `OnGUI` function to the following code snippet in order to allow it to check and draw the proper screen based on the current game state. A `switch` statement works the same as a bunch of `if` and `else if` statements. In our case, we check the game state and call a different function based on what it is. For example, if the game state is equal to `GameState.MultiPlayer`, we will call the `DrawGameBoard` function, which should now contain what used to be in the `OnGUI` function.

```
public void OnGUI() {
  switch(gameState) {
    case GameState.Opening:
      DrawOpening();
      break;
    case GameState.MultiPlayer:
      DrawGameBoard();
      break;
    case GameState.GameOver:
      DrawGameOver();
      break;
  }
}
```

5. By this point you are probably wondering where that game state variable is coming from. If you guessed that it was automatically provided by Unity, you are wrong. We have to track our own game state. That is why we created the GameState script earlier. Add the following line of code to the top of our TicTacToeControl class, right above where we defined our game board:

```
public GameState gameState = GameState.Opening;
```

6. Next, we need to create the other two game state screens. Let us start with the opening screen. When we draw our opening screen, we start by defining the Rect class used by our title. We follow that with a quick call to GUI.Label. By passing it a Rect class to position itself by and some text, the text is simply drawn on screen. This function is the best way to draw a section of text on the screen.

```
public void DrawOpening() {
  Rect titleRect = new Rect(0, 0, 300, 75);
  GUI.Label(titleRect, "Tic-Tac-Toe");
```

7. The following line of code defines the Rect class used by our New Game button. We want to be sure that it was right under the title, so it starts with the title's x position. We then combine the title's y position with its height to find the position right underneath it. Next, we used the width from the title so that our button will cover the entire position under it. Finally, the height is set to 75 because it is a good size for fingers and we don't want it to change based on the title. We could have just as easily used all the values from the title or just put in the numbers but our title will change later when we start styling everything.

```
  Rect multiRect = new Rect(titleRect.x, titleRect.y + titleRect.
height, titleRect.width, 75);
```

8. Finally, we make a call that will draw our button. You may remember our use of the GUI.Button function from when we drew the game board. If the button is pressed, the game state is set to MultiPlayer that will start our game. The NewGame function is also called, which will reset our game board. And of course, there is an extra curly brace to finish off the function.

```
  if(GUI.Button(multiRect, "New Game")) {
    NewGame();
    gameState = GameState.MultiPlayer;
  }
}
```

9. We have one screen left to draw, the game over screen. To do this, we will create the function referenced by our `OnGUI` function. However, in order for a game to end, there must be a winner, so add the following line of code right under our game state variable. We are making extended use of the `SquareState` enumeration. If the winner variable is equal to `Clear`, nobody won the game. If it is equal to `XControl` or `OControl`, the relevant player has won. Don't worry, it will make more sense when we create the game over screen next and the winner check system in a little bit.

    ```
    public SquareState winner = SquareState.Clear;
    ```

10. There is nothing particularly new in the `DrawGameOver` function. First, we'll define where we are going to write who won the game. We'll then figure out who won, using our winner variable. After drawing the winner title, the `Rect` class used is shifted down by its height so it can be reused. Finally, we'll draw a button that changes our game state back to `Opening`, which is of course our main menu.

    ```
    public void DrawGameOver() {
      Rect winnerRect = new Rect(0, 0, 300, 75);
      string winnerTitle = winner == SquareState.XControl ? "X Wins!"
    : winner == SquareState.OControl ? "O Wins!" : "It's A Tie!";
      GUI.Label(winnerRect, winnerTitle);

      winnerRect.y += winnerRect.height;
      if(GUI.Button(winnerRect, "Main Menu"))
        gameState = GameState.Opening;
    }
    ```

11. To make sure we are not overwriting squares that somebody already controls, we need to make a few changes to our `DrawGameBoard` function. First, it would be helpful if the players could easily tell whose turn it is. To do this, we'll add the following code snippet to the end of the function. This should start to become familiar. We'll first define where we want to draw. Then, we'll use our xTurn Boolean to determine what to write about whose turn it is. Finally, it is the `GUI.Label` function to draw it on screen.

    ```
    Rect turnRect = new Rect(300, 0, 100, 100);
    string turnTitle = xTurn ? "X's Turn!" : "O's Turn!";
    GUI.Label(turnRect, turnTitle);
    ```

12. We now need to change the bit where we draw the board square, the `GUI.Button` function. We need to only draw that button if the square is clear. The following code snippet will do just that by moving the button inside of a new `if` statement. It checks whether the board square is clear. If it is, we draw the button. Otherwise, we use a label to write the owner to the button's location.

    ```
    if(board[boardIndex] == SquareState.Clear) {
      if(GUI.Button(square, owner))
    ```

```
        SetControl(boardIndex);
    }
    else GUI.Label(square, owner);
```

13. The last thing we need to do is make a system that checks for a winner. We will do this in another function provided by the `MonoBehaviour` class. `LateUpdate` is called at the end of every frame, just before things are drawn on the screen. You might be wondering to yourself, why don't we just create a function that is called at the end of `OnGUI`, which is already called every frame? The reason is that the `OnGUI` function gets a little weird when drawing some of the GUI elements. It will sometimes be called more than once so that it can draw everything. So, for the most part, the functionality should never be controlled by `OnGUI`. That is what `Update` and `LateUpdate` are for. `Update` is the normal game loop where most of a game's functionality is called from. `LateUpdate` is for things that need to happen after the objects' update, such as our check for a game over.

14. Add the following `LateUpdate` function to our `TicTacToeControl` class. We'll start with a check to make sure we should even be checking for a winner. If the game isn't in a state where we are playing, in this case `MultiPlayer`, exit here and go no further.

```
public void LateUpdate() {
    if(gameState != GameState.MultiPlayer) return;
```

15. Follow that with a short `for` loop. A victory in this game is a run of three matching squares. We start by checking the column that is marked by our loop. If the first square is not `Clear`, compare it to the square below; if they match, check it against the square below that. Our board is stored as a list but drawn as a grid, so we have to add three to go down a square. The `else if` statement follows checks of each row. By multiplying our loop value by three, we will skip down a row of each loop. We'll again compare the square to `SquareState.Clear`, then to the square one to its right, and finally two to the right. If either set of conditions is correct, we'll send the first square in the set out to another function to change our game state.

```
    for(int i=0;i<3;i++) {
        if(board[i] != SquareState.Clear && board[i] == board[i + 3]
&& board[i] == board[i + 6]) {
            SetWinner(board[i]);
            return;
        }
        else if(board[i * 3] != SquareState.Clear && board[i * 3] ==
board[(i * 3) + 1] && board[i * 3] == board[(i * 3) + 2]) {
            SetWinner(board[i * 3]);
            return;
        }
    }
```

16. The following code snippet is largely the same as the `if` statements we just wrote previously. However, these lines of code check the diagonals. If the conditions are true, again send out to the other function to change game states. You have probably also noticed the returns after the function calls. If we have found a winner at any point, there is no need to check any more of the board. So, we'll exit the `LateUpdate` function early.

```
if(board[0] != SquareState.Clear && board[0] == board[4] &&
board[0] == board[8]) {
    SetWinner(board[0]);
    return;
}
else if(board[2] != SquareState.Clear && board[2] == board[4] &&
board[2] == board[6]) {
    SetWinner(board[2]);
    return;
}
```

17. This is the last little bit for our `LateUpdate` function. If no one has won the game, as determined by the previous parts of this function, we have to check for a tie. This is done by checking all of the squares of the game board. If any one of them is `Clear`, the game has yet to finish and we exit the function. But, if we make it through the entire loop without finding a `Clear` square, we go set the winner but declare a tie.

```
for(int i=0;i<board.Length;i++) {
    if(board[i] == SquareState.Clear)
        return;
}
SetWinner(SquareState.Clear);
}
```

 Do remember to close the last curly brace. It is needed to close off the `LateUpdate` function. If you forget it, some annoying errors will come your way.

18. Finally, we'll create the `SetWinner` function that is called repeatedly in our `LateUpdate` function. Short and sweet, we'll pass to this function that is going to win. It sets our winner variable and changes our game state to `GameOver`.

```
public void SetWinner(SquareState toWin) {
    winner = toWin;
    gameState = GameState.GameOver;
}
```

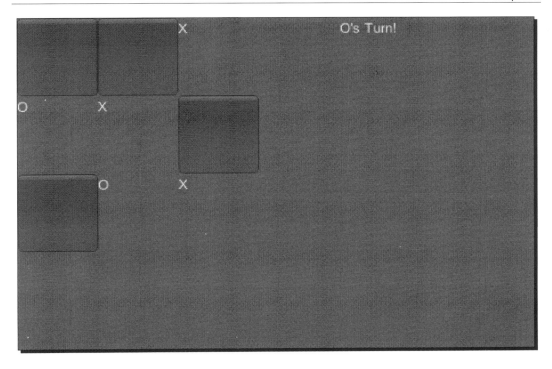

What just happened?

That is it. Congratulations! We now have a fully functioning Tic-tac-toe game and you survived the process. In the next sections, we will finally get to make it all look pretty. That is a good thing because, as the screenshot shows, the game does not look great right now.

GUI Skins and GUI Styles

GUI Styles are how we change the look and feel of GUI elements, buttons, and labels in Unity. A GUI Skin contains several GUI Styles and allows us to change the look of the entire GUI without explicitly defining GUI Styles for each element. To create a GUI Skin, right-click in the **Project** window of the Unity Editor, just as with creating a new script. Go to **Create** but, instead of selecting **Script**, go to the bottom and select **GUI skin**. Selecting this option will create the new GUI Skin and let us name it to GameSkin. By looking at our GameSkin in the **Inspector** window, you can see what we have to work with.

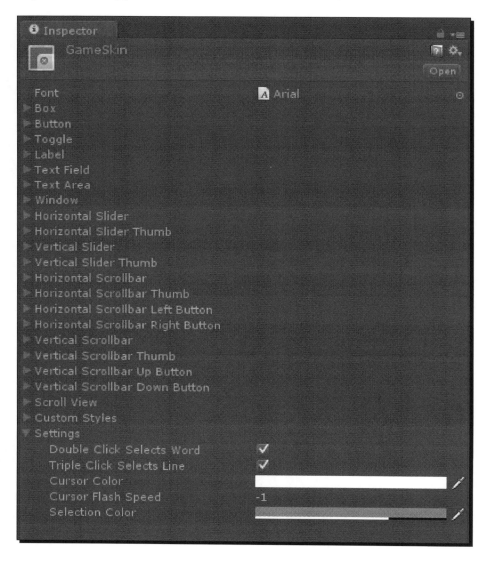

♦ At the top is a **Font** attribute. By importing font files to your project and placing one here, you can change the default font used by text in the whole game.

♦ Under that is a long list of GUI elements, including our good friends **Button** and **Label**. These are all GUI Styles and coincide with the GUI functions that we use to draw things on screen. For example, unless otherwise specified, when we use the `Button` function, it will draw using the **Button** GUI Style.

♦ Following the list of GUI elements is a **Custom Styles** attribute. This is where we can put any extra styles that we want to use. Of our dozen buttons, perhaps we want one to have red text. That GUI Style would go here.

♦ At the bottom is a **Settings** attribute. By expanding it, we can see it is fairly short. It includes options for whether or not multiclicks can be used for selection, what color of cursor and how fast it should flash when in a text field, and what color the highlight on selected words should be. The defaults here are just fine. Unless there is a very specific look or need, these values can be ignored.

Now, let us go over what it takes to be a GUI Style. Expand the **Button** GUI Style from our `GameSkin` example. No matter what the GUI Style is used for, they all are made up the same. It may look like there are many attributes that make up a GUI Style, but most of them are nearly identical, making it much simpler.

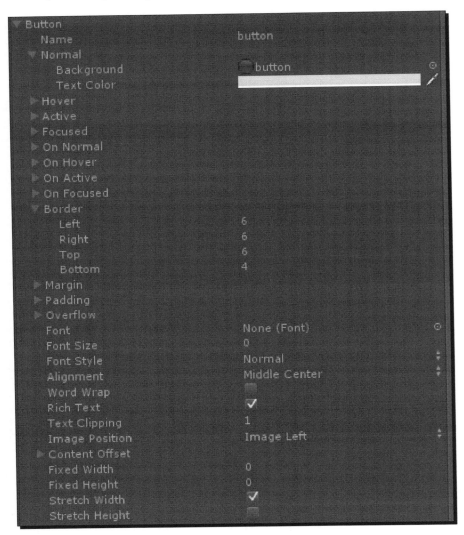

◆ The first attribute is fairly straightforward, but perhaps the most important. **Name** is what Unity uses to find GUI Styles and apply them to GUI elements. It lets us know what the style is supposed to be; however, if there is a typo between it and the code, you will never see your style in the game.

- The next several groups of values describe how the GUI element should look when in a particular state. This is where the bulk of your styling will go. The primary states of any element are **Normal, Hover, Active**, and **Focused**. Secondary to these are **On Normal, On Hover, On Active**, and **On Focused**. These secondary states only occur as the GUI element transfers into the corresponding primary state. Not every GUI element makes use of every state, and you have the ability to control which states an element can go into, but we will discuss that a little later. Let's see in detail how these states work:

  - **Normal**: This is the default state of any GUI element. It is always used and occurs any time the element is not being interacted with.

  - **Hover**: This state is used primarily by buttons and other clickable elements. When your mouse is on top of a GUI element, it will enter this state, if it can. However, since the focus of this book is touch screens, we do not have a mouse to really concern ourselves with. So, we will not be using this state.

  - **Active**: This has to be the second most important state. An element enters this state when it is activated. For example, when one presses a button, it is active. By clicking on or touching a button, it enters the **Active** state. All of the GUI elements that can be interacted with use this state.

  - **Focused**: This is a rarely used state. In terms of Unity's GUI, focused means having keyboard control. The only element that uses it by default is the **Text Field**.

- If you were to expand any of the states, you would see that it has two attributes, **Background** and **Text Color**. The **Background** attribute is a texture. It can be any texture in your game. The **Text Color** attribute is simply the color of any text that appears in the GUI element. Except for the **Normal** state, if a state does not have a background texture, it will not be used. This can be both good and annoying. If we do not want our buttons to show that they have been hovered over, simply remove the texture from the Hover state's **Background** attribute. It becomes annoying when we want a GUI element that does not have a background image of its own, but we do want the text to change color between states. How do we make use of the active state, but not use a texture for the background? The answer is that we create a blank image, but it is not quite as simple as saving off a 100 percent transparent PNG and using that. The GUI Style is too smart for that. It detects that the image is completely blank, making it no different than if there was no image. And so, the state still is not used. To get around this, create a small, blank PNG image, but take a single pixel and make it 90 percent transparent white. This might seem like a hack solution, but it is, unfortunately, the only way. At such a low transparency, we can't detect the pixel; though it is not actually clear. However, Unity sees that there is a slightly white pixel that must be drawn and does so.

◆ Now, you might be thinking, that's stupid. I'm just going to create images of all of my buttons and not worry about the text. It is indeed stupid but the response to that is, what if you need to slightly change the text of a button? Or perhaps the text on the button is dynamic based on the player's name. In nearly every project I have been a part of there has been a need to create the not quite blank image.

◆ Below the GUI element's states are **Border**, **Margin**, **Padding**, and **Overflow**. These attributes control how an element interacts with its background images and contained text. Inside each you will find **Left**, **Right**, **Top**, and **Bottom** values. Since every element is drawn as a rectangle, these correspond to each side of the said rectangle. They are defined in pixels, just like our GUI space. Let's see all these attributes in detail as follows:

  ❑ **Border**: This lets us define how many pixels from each side should not be stretched. When defining a GUI element, the background is normally stretched evenly across the space occupied. If you were to create a blue box with red edging and rounded corners, these values would keep your edges and corners regular while still stretching the blue on the inside.

  ❑ **Margin**: This is only used by Unity's automatic GUI layout system named GUILayout. It is how much extra space should be around the outside of the element.

  ❑ **Padding**: This is the space between the borders of an element and the text that it contains. If you want the text of a button left-justified but in slightly, you should use **Padding**.

  ❑ **Overflow**: This defines an extra space for your background image. When creating our buttons, we defined a `Rect` class for how much space the button takes up. If we are to use `Overflow`, the button itself would be where the `Rect` class is, but the background would extend beyond each edge as dictated by the values. This would be useful for buttons with a shadow or glow around them.

◆ The next several values have to do with the text in an element. The **Font** attribute is a font that is used specifically by this style. If this value is left empty, the font from the GUI Skin is used. **Font Size** is how big the letters of the text should be. This works just like your favorite word processor, except that a value of zero means to use the default font size defined in the font object. **Font Style** also works like your word processor. It lets you choose between **Normal**, **Bold**, and **Italic** text. This only makes a difference if it is supported by your chosen font.

◆ **Alignment** defines where to justify the text in the GUI element. Imagine splitting your element into a 3 x 3 grid. **Alignment** is the same as the position of the grid.

- **Word Wrap** defines whether or not text should split into multiple lines if it is too long. It again works on the same principle as your word processor. If checked and the line of text would extend beyond the sides of the GUI element, the text is split into as many lines as necessary to keep it within the bounds.

- **Rich Text** is a fairly new and interesting feature of GUI Styles. It allows us to use HTML style markup to control text. You could put the tags `<b>` and `</b>` around a word in your Label's text, and instead of writing those tags, Unity will make the words in between bold. We can make use of the bold, italics, size, and color tags. This allows for selectively making parts of our text bold or italics. We can make certain words larger or smaller. And, the color of any part of the text can be altered using hexadecimal values.

- **Text Clipping** became weird in the recent updates. It used to be a nice drop-down list of values, but now it is an integer field. Either way, it still serves its function. If the text extends beyond the edges of the GUI element, this attribute dictates what to do. A value of zero means don't clip the text, let it extend beyond the edges. Any value that is not zero will cause the text to be clipped. Any text that extends beyond the borders will simply not be drawn.

- **Image Position** is used in conjunction with GUIContent. GUIContent is a way of passing GUI elements the text, an icon image, and a tool tip. **Image Position** describes how the image and text interact. The image can either go to the left of the text or above. Or, we can choose to only use either the image or the text. Since tool tips aren't really useful in a touch environment, GUIContent is of limited use to us. For that reason, we will not be using it extensively, if at all.

- **Content Offset** adjusts anything contained inside the GUI element by the values provided. If all of your text is normally centered in your button, this will allow you to move it slightly to the right and up. It is an aesthetic thing, for when you need a very specific look.

- **Fixed Width** and **Fixed Height** provides approximately the same function. If any value other than zero is provided for these attributes, they will override the corresponding values in the `Rect` class used for the GUI element. So, if you wanted buttons to always be one hundred pixels wide, no matter where they are in the game, you could set **Fixed Width** to one hundred and they will do just that.

- **Stretch Width** and **Stretch Height** also serves about the same function. They are used by GUILayout for automatic placement of GUI elements. It pretty much gives the system permission to make elements wider/skinnier and taller/shorter, respectively, in order to satisfy its conditions for a better layout. The way GUILayout arranges elements is not always the best. It is good, if you need something up quick. But it gets complicated if you want any sort of deeper control.

A prettier form of Tic-tac-toe

Finally, we get to put what we learned about GUI Skins and GUI Styles into action and make our game look better. Or, at least make the game look like it isn't using default assets. Whatever your artistic talents, you will need to find or create a few images to continue following along.

Time for action – styling the game

If you do not want to look far, the assets used for this chapter are found along with the resources for the book. All of the needed images are available, and they will work just well, until you have an opportunity to create some of your own.

1. First, we need five small textures: `ButtonActive`, `ButtonNormal`, `ONormal`, `XNormal`, and `Title`. To create these, you will have to use a separate photo-editing program or use the ones supplied with the included projects.

2. The easiest way to get the images into your Unity project is to simply save them into the `Assets` folder that is created when you create a new project. Alternatively, you can go up to the top and click on **Assets** followed by **Import New Asset**. This will open a file browser and let you navigate to the asset you want. When you have found the asset you desire to import and have clicked on the **Import** button, a copy of the asset is put in your project. Unity will not move or remove files that exist outside of the current project.

❑ And now a note about import settings for textures. By default, Unity assumes any image files imported to your project are going to be used as game model textures. Because of that, Unity compresses them and adjusts them to fit a power of two.

 In case you didn't know, in computer graphics it is much faster to render images that can be divided in half evenly, down to a single unit. There are deeper reasons, but suffice it to say that it is because of the binary switches that actually make up a computer.

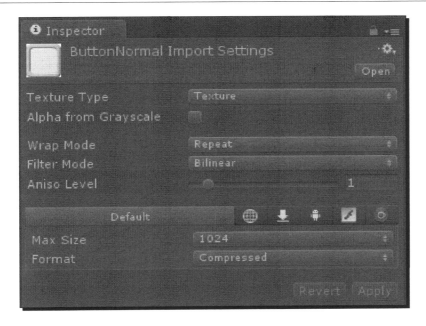

    ❑   Making our images recognized as being for the GUI is quite simple. To the right of **Texture Type**, click on **Texture** and select **GUI** from the drop-down menu.

    ❑   You will notice that we were given a new **Filter Mode** drop-down menu. This is essentially how much effort Unity will put into making the image look nice as it is resized for the various GUI elements. **Trilinear** is the best, **Point** is the fastest, and **Bilinear** is in the middle.

    ❑   Once the import settings have been changed, be sure to click on **Apply**, or Unity will complain when you try to do anything else. If you do not want to commit the changes, clicking on **Revert** will discard any changes just made and set back the **Import Settings** window to the last configuration that was used.

3. So, set all of **Texture Types** for your images to GUI and we will get on with it.

4. Let us start with the beginning of the game. Open your `TicTacToeControl` script and add the following lines of code at the beginning. These allow us to attach references to other assets inside of the Unity Editor. The first will hold our `GameSkin`, so we can style all of our GUI elements. The second, as you can see in the following lines of code, will hold our fancy title image:

```
public GUISkin guiSkin;
public Texture2D titleImage;
```

5. Now go to the Unity Editor and select **Main Camera** from the **Hierarchy** window.

- ❑ Every object that you see listed in the **Hierarchy** window is a GameObject. A GameObject is given a purpose and a meaning by the various components that are attached to it, for example, our TicTacToeControl script.

- ❑ An empty GameObject is just a point in space, as defined by the Transform component that is always the first component on any GameObject.

- ❑ You can see in the **Inspector** window, the **Main Camera** object has a **Camera** component. It gives a purpose to the GameObject and controls how the **Camera** component functions, just as our TicTacToeControl component at the bottom lets it control our Tic-tac-toe game.

- ❑ The **Inspector** window also lets us see all of the public variables that can be changed in the Unity Editor. If they are changed, those values are saved and used when the game is played. So, by creating a variable in our script, we can add the reference to our GameSkin and it will be used in the game. To add the reference, simply click-and-drag the object to the desired variable on the component in the **Inspector** window.

6. Drag GameSkin to the **GUI Skin** slot and our title image to the **Title Image** slot.

> Be sure to save. Saving regularly is the only thing that stands between you and premature baldness, the next time your computer decides to die.

7. Inside of our TicTacToeControl script, add the following line of code at the beginning of the OnGUI function. It first checks to make sure there is a GUI Skin available. If it is, it is set into the GUI.skin variable. This variable controls the GUI Skin that is used in the game. Once set, any GUI elements drawn after that will use the new GUI Skin. This could allow you to set one GUI Skin and draw half of the GUI, then set a different GUI Skin and draw the other half in a completely different style.

```
if(guiSkin != null) GUI.skin = guiSkin;
```

8. If you play your game now, it won't look like much. The defaults of a new GUI Skin are the exact same as the default GUI Skin that Unity uses. Let us change that by selecting our GameSkin and expanding **Button** and **Label** in the **Inspector** window.

9. For **Button** we created a **ButtonNormal** and **ButtonActive** image. By dragging those to the **Background** properties of the respective states, the look of the buttons will change.

10. The supplied button images have a yellow background, which will make the white text hard to read. So, by clicking on the color next to the **Text Color** property, the **Color Picker** window will open and we can select a new color. A navy blue for the **Normal** state and a faded blue for the **Active** state works well.

11. Also, to keep it from looking weird in the Unity Editor, remove the **Hover** state. With a touch interface, there is no cursor to hover over buttons; therefore, there is no need for a hover state. To remove it, first click on the little circle to the right of the **Background** image.

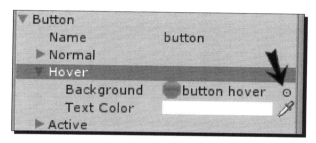

12. The new window that pops up allows us to select any image that is currently in our project. However, since we want nothing to be in there select **None**, the first option in the list.

13. The borders on the button images are much larger than those of the default buttons. So, we need to adjust the **Border** attribute to accommodate them. Values of 15 for each side works well.

14. The text is also too small, so for the **Font Size** attribute choose a value of 40. This will give us a large and easily readable text.

15. For the **Label** element, we are only going to make two changes. First, the text is too small. So, it will also get a value of 40 for its font size. Second, we want the text to be centered in the GUI elements. That requires setting the alignment to middle center.

16. Play the game now. It is already looking better or at least different. However, it is a little difficult to tell at a glance who controls which square. To fix this we are going to create two custom GUI Styles. To do this, expand the **Custom Styles** attribute of our GameSkin in the **Inspector** window. By default, one blank style is already in there. We are going to need two, but don't change the quantity just yet.

17. Expand the custom GUI Style, by default called Element 0.

18. On clicking to the right of the **Name** attribute, more or less in the middle of the **Inspector** window, will allow us to rename the style. The name is very important. Whatever we call it here we need to call it exactly the same in code or it won't be used. Give it the name XSquare because it will be used to mark which squares are controlled by the X player.

19. Inside of the **Normal** state, add the **XNormal** image to the **Background** attribute. The **Text Color** attribute can be left as black. We also need to adjust the font size and alignment properties to the same as we did for the **Label** element. So, set them to **40** and **MiddleCenter** respectively.

20. Now that we have created the first style, creating the second becomes fast and easy. Collapse the **XSquare** style.

21. Set the size of the **Custom Styles** attribute to **2**. When increasing the size of arrays in the Unity Editor, Unity duplicates whatever was the last item in the array to each of the new slots. So, we should now have two XSquare GUI Styles.

22. Expand the second GUI Style and change its name to `Osquare`.

23. Also, replace the `XNormal` **Background** image with the `ONormal` image.

> If you are having trouble in dragging-and-dropping in the **Inspector** window, the `GameSkin` keeps losing focus perhaps; there is a lock at the top of the **Inspector** window. Clicking on that will stop the window from changing to anything else when a new object is selected. Clicking it again will toggle off this feature.

24. Just because we have our spiffy new custom GUI Styles, doesn't mean they will work automatically. But, just a little bit of coding will make them work. Inside our `DrawGameBoard` function of the `TicTacToeControl` script, we need to change the line that draws our label by adding a little bit to the end of it. The addition of a second string will tell the GUI system to look for a specific GUI Style. A little bit earlier in the function, we figure out who owns the square, is it X or O. By adding this to `Square` we create the names of our two custom GUI Styles, `XSquare` and `OSquare`.

```
else GUI.Label(square, owner, owner + "Square");
```

25. If you play the game now, you will see that when a player claims control of a square, our custom styles appear.

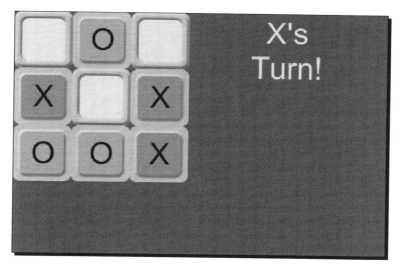

26. There is one more thing to do to change the look of our Tic-tac-toe game. Do you remember the title image that was created and for which we added a variable? Now is the time to place that. Inside of `TicTacToeControl` go to the `DrawOpening` function. To draw our image, we need to replace the call to `GUI.Label` with a call to `GUI.DrawTexture`. Instead of using GUI Styles, this function simply draws an image to the screen. It uses a `Rect` class, just as with all of our **Buttons** and **Labels**, to define a size and position. The image is, by default, stretched to fill the whole `Rect` class. For now, this suits us just fine.

```
GUI.DrawTexture(titleRect, titleImage);
```

27. We can fix the stretching by updating the previous line of code, where we defined the `Rect` class for our title to accommodate. As you can see by the following code snippet, we use the width and height of `titleImage` to determine the width and height of `titleRect`. The `Rect` class now automatically determines how large it should be based on the size of our title image. If the `Rect` class is of the same size and shape as the image, it won't be stretched. In addition to that, because of the way we defined the `Rect` class for our **New Game** button, it will still be directly under and just as wide as our title image.

```
Rect titleRect = new Rect(0, 0, titleImage.width, titleImage.
height);
```

28. That is all there for styling our Tic-tac-toe game. Click on the **Play** button and take a look at all your hard work.

What just happened?

We made our Tic-tac-toe game look great, or at least not like the defaults. We achieved this through the use of a handful of images and some custom GUI Skins and GUI Styles. With the addition of a special function for drawing textures on screen, we also add a unique title image to our opening screen.

Have a go hero – backgrounds

Your challenge here is to make a background image and draw it behind the game. It also has to cover the whole of the screen. The default blue is great, but we could do so much better. As a note, whichever GUI element was drawn last is drawn on top, so think carefully about where to call the function to have the image drawn in the background. Also, since stretching is only good for exercising and rubber bands, take a look at also passing the function a `ScaleMode`, which is a special value type that Unity uses to determine how images should stretch. Look in the scripting reference or search online to find more information about it.

Dynamic positioning

You are probably thinking that it is all well and good that the game is all styled now, but everything is still sitting in the top-left corner of the screen. Well then, you are in luck. That is exactly the topic of this section. It is not enough to simply adjust the numbers in our `Rects` until our GUI is centered. While working with the Android platform and other mobile devices, we have to be prepared for a large variety of possibilities. Not every device that our games will be played on will have the same screen size. So, you may position your GUI to be centered on your tablet, but it will be far off screen on a phone.

Time for action – the dynamic GUI

We will be covering two excellent ways of dynamically adjusting our GUI to meet any screen requirements. The opening screen and the game over screen will both be centered. We will stretch the game board to fill the available space. The turn indicator text will also be set up to automatically change position based on the screen orientation.

1. Again, let's start with our main menu. Open up the `TicTacToeControl` script and go to the `DrawOpening` function.

2. To center the menu, we will wrap up the contents as a GUI group by adding the following line of code at the beginning of the `DrawOpening` function. Think of GUI's grouping as **picture-in-picture** (**PIP**) that some televisions can do. Pick a rectangle section on screen and draw some other channel in it. So, first we are deciding where to draw our group. We do this by finding the center of the screen, `Screen.width` and `Screen.height` is divided by two. But, because GUI content is positioned at the top-left corner, we must subtract half our content's size to find that corner. For the width, that is simply the width of our title image. But the height is a combination of the image and the button below.

   ```
   Rect groupRect = new Rect((Screen.width / 2) - (titleImage.
   width / 2), (Screen.height / 2) - ((titleImage.height + 75) / 2),
   titleImage.width, titleImage.height + 75);
   ```

3. The `BeginGroup` function of the GUI is what gives us the PIP effect. Any GUI elements that are drawn after a call to this function are confined to the `Rect` class that was passed to the function. Instead of positions starting from the top-left corner of the screen, elements within the group will start at the top-left corner of the group `Rect`. Anything that extends beyond the edges of the group is also not drawn, just as if it extended beyond the edges of the screen.

```
GUI.BeginGroup(groupRect);
```

4. Before we can see the group in action, we must add a line to the end of our `DrawOpening` function. `EndGroup` is the direct counterpart to `BeginGroup`. If ever you use `BeginGroup`, there must be a corresponding call to `EndGroup`. Should you fail to pair up the function calls, Unity will make no end of complaints until the problem is fixed. It is really quite annoying.

```
GUI.EndGroup();
```

5. With that line added, play the game. The main menu will now center itself. It will do this no matter the screen size. Also, it will do this whether the screen is in landscape or in portrait mode. In this case, the trick to keeping everything on screen is to plan for the smallest screen size and make images and GUI elements that fit accordingly.

6. Skipping ahead a little, we can use a similar method for centering the game over screen. Add the following line of code to the beginning of the `DrawGameOver` function. You can see that we are doing the same thing we did a moment ago. Figure out where the center of the screen is and subtract half of the total size of our content. In this case we supplied solid numbers instead of keying off the size of an image. Also, because the math is easy, we already did the divisions to come up with `150` and `75`.

```
Rect groupRect = new Rect((Screen.width / 2) - 150, (Screen.height
/ 2) - 75, 300, 150);
GUI.BeginGroup(groupRect);
```

7. Be sure to add your `EndGroup` function call to the end of the `DrawGameOver` function.

```
GUI.EndGroup();
```

8. After that, find the line where we define the `winnerRect` variable class. We need to change it so it is easier to adjust the size and fit the contents, should we want to. Because of the way we set up the **winner** label and **main menu** button, this will cause each to take up the whole width of the group. They will also split the available height evenly; hence the division is by two.

```
Rect winnerRect = new Rect(0, 0, groupRect.width, groupRect.height
/ 2);
```

9. Now we have the tricky part to do. For the game board, we want it to expand evenly so that it fills whichever direction is shortest. The turn indicator should be centered in the remaining space. Because the board needs to dynamically expand and the turn indicator needs to be either in the right or bottom of the screen, based on orientation, we can't get away with using our GUI group functions. Instead, we first need to figure out which side of our screen is smaller, the width or the height. This is fairly simple with the following lines of code added to the beginning of the `DrawGameBoard` function. Recognize the conditional statement, our good old friend? First, we create a variable to hold the result of comparing the width and height of the screen; we will be using it again later. If the width is smaller, obviously the small side is the width; otherwise it is the height.

```
bool widthSmaller = Screen.width < Screen.height;
float smallSide = widthSmaller ? Screen.width : Screen.height;
```

10. Next we change our width and height definitions. Because the game board is a 3 x 3 grid, once we have the small side it is a simple matter to figure out how big the squares should be to fill the space. The change to the height is to keep the board squares actually square. Perhaps you remember from your first geometry lessons? The width and height of the sides of a square are equal.

```
float width = smallSide / 3;
float height = width;
```

11. Playing the game at this point, we will be able to experience a game board that scales with our game screen. Try it out!

12. Remember when we were connecting Unity Remote? Use the drop-down menu in the top-left corner of the **Game** window to select different screen sizes and orientations. This does, however, reveal another small error. The turn indicator text sometimes appears over the top of our game board. Other times it may be beyond the edges of the screen. Or, perhaps you already noticed that one? Either way, to make it better we need to find the `Rect` class that will cover the remaining negative space.

13. After the initial definition of our `turnRect`, add the following code snippet. Using our conditional friends, we figured out all we need to place the `Rect` class in the negative space. If the width is smaller in portrait mode, the negative space starts at the left side of the screen, zero. The y position of the space begins where the board ends, the equivalent of the width; it is a square board, after all. The total width of the negative space is also equivalent to the width of the screen. The height becomes whatever is left over from the difference between the height and the width. If we are in landscape mode instead, the height being smaller than the width, the positioning is largely determined in the same way.

```
turnRect.x = widthSmaller ? 0 : smallSide;
turnRect.y = widthSmaller ? smallSide : 0;
turnRect.width = widthSmaller ? Screen.width : Screen.width -
Screen.height;
turnRect.height = widthSmaller ? Screen.height - Screen.width :
Screen.height;
```

14. This is all well and good. Looks pretty good with the turn text actually positioned where it can easily be seen and read. But, in some of those screen sizes there is an awful lot of empty space. If only there was some way we could scale the text to better fit the space. It just so happens that there is a good way to do just that. After we are done messing with the turn indicator's `Rect`, we can add the following line of code. This touch of code gets the label GUI Style from the current GUI Skin and creates a duplicate. In code, if we ever create a new GUI Style and pass another one as the argument, all of the values are copied into the new GUI Style. This allows us to cause temporary and dynamic changes without ruining the whole GUI Skin being used.

```
GUIStyle turnStyle = new GUIStyle(GUI.skin.GetStyle("label"));
```

15. In the next line of code we'll adjust the font size. To do this we have to figure out how much space is left on the long side of the screen after the game board is scaled up. Adding the width and height of the screen results in the total amount of screen distance available. By subtracting the smaller of the two sides, the distance that the game board covers multiplied by two, we are left with the excess negative space. Dividing all of that by one hundred, the amount of space that we had previously used for our turn indicator, will scale the font size to proportionately fit the change in space. It is finally wrapped in an explicit conversion to the integer type because the font size value must be defined as an integer.

```
turnStyle.fontSize *= (int)((Screen.width + Screen.height -
(smallSide * 2)) / 100);
```

16. To actually see this dynamic font size in action, we need to make a change to the line that draws the turn indicator. We change the call to the `Label` function to use the temporary style. Instead of providing the name of the GUI Style to GUI functions, we can provide a specific GUI Style. The function will then use this style to draw the GUI element.

```
GUI.Label(turnRect, turnTitle, turnStyle);
```

17. Try it out. By clicking on the **Game window** tab and dragging it into the **Game** window, you can undock the window and make it free floating. Changing the aspect ratio, that drop-down menu in the top-right corner of the **Game** window, to **Free Aspect** allows us to freely re-size the window and witness our great work in action.

What just happened?

We made our game change dynamically based on the screen of our devices. Both of the menu screens will center themselves. We also caused our game board to grow and shrink until it fills as much of the screen as it can. We then used a carefully applied bit of code magic to make the turn indicator automatically position itself and change font size to fill the remaining space.

Have a go hero – scaling menus

The second challenge is a little tougher. Continue to use the GUI groups, but make the opening screen and the game over screen scale with the screen size. If you want a subchallenge with this one, see what you can do about scaling the text with it as well. And, don't forget about the text used to indicate control of the game board squares.

If you want to prepare for even more devices, change the Rects that we use throughout the section. Wherever we used specific numbers for position or size on screen, change them to percent. You will have to calculate the pixel size using percent and the size of the screen. That calculated amount can then be passed to and used in our Rects.

A better way to build to device

Now for the part of the build process that everyone itches to learn. There is a quicker and easier way to have your game built and playing on your Android device. The long and complicated way is still very good to know. Should this shorter method fail, and it will at some point, it is helpful to know the long method so you can debug any errors. Also, the short path is only good for building to a single device. If you have multiple devices and a large project, it will take significantly more time to load them all with the short path.

Time for action – build and run

With this alternate build method, we can quickly and easily test games on our devices as follows:

1. Start by opening the **Build Settings** window. Remember, it can be found under **File** at the top of the Unity Editor.

2. Click on the **Add Current** button to add our current scene, also the only scene, to the list of **Scenes In Build**. If this list is empty, there is no game.

3. Be sure to change your **Platform** to **Android**, if you haven't already done so. It is after all still the point of this book.

4. Do not forget to set the **Player Settings**. Click on the **Player Settings** button to open them up in the **Inspector** window. Do you remember this from *Chapter 1, Saying Hello to Unity and Android.*

5. At the top, set the **Company Name** and **Product Name** fields. Values of `TomPacktAndBegin` and `Ch2 TicTacToe` respectively will match the included completed project. Remember, these are seen by the people playing your game.

6. The **Bundle Identifier** field under **Other Settings** needs to be set as well. The format is still `com.CompanyName.ProductName`, so `com.TomPactAndBegin.Ch2.TicTacToe` will work well.

7. So that we can see our cool dynamic GUI in action on a device, there is one other setting that should be changed. Click on **Resolution** and **Presentation** to expand the options.

8. We are interested in **Default Orientation**. The default is **Portrait**, but this option means the game will be fixed in the portrait display mode. Click on the drop-down menu and select **Auto Rotation**. This option tells Unity to automatically adjust the game to be upright in whichever orientation the device is being held.

   ❑ The new set of options that popped up when **Auto Rotation** was selected allow for the limiting of the orientations that are supported. Perhaps you are making a game that needs to be wider and held in landscape orientation. By unchecking **Portrait** and **Portrait Upside Down**, Unity will still adjust (but only for the remaining orientations). On your Android device, along one of the shorter sides, are the controls of some sort usually a home, menu, back, and search set of buttons. This side is generally recognized as the bottom of the device and it is the position of these buttons that dictates what each orientation is. **Portrait** is when those buttons are down relative to the screen. **Landscape Right** is when they are to the right. The pattern begins to come clear, does it not?

9. For now, leave all of the orientation options checked and we will go back to **Build Settings**.

10. The next step (and this is very important) is to connect your device to your computer and give it a moment to be recognized. If your device is not first connected to your computer, this shorter build path will fail.

11. In the bottom-right corner of the **Build Settings** window, click on the **Build And Run** button. You will be asked to give the application file, the APK, a relevant name and save it to an appropriate location. A name `Ch2_TicTacToe.apk` will be fine and it is suitable enough to save the file to the desktop.

12. Click on **Save** and sit back to watch the wonderful loading bar that is provided. If you paid attention to the loading bar when we built the *Hello World* project in *Chapter 1, Saying Hello to Unity and Android*, you will notice that there is an extra step taken this time around. After the application is built, there is a pushing to device step. This means the build was successful and Unity is now putting the application on your device and installing it. Once done, the game will be started on the device and the loading bar will be finished.

What just happened?

We just learned about the **Build And Run** button provided by the **Build Settings** window. Quick, easy, and free from command prompt pain; isn't the short build path wonderful? But if the build process fails for any reason including being unable to find the device, the application file will not be saved. You will have to sit through the entire build process again, if you want to try installing again. This isn't so bad for our simple Tic-tac-toe game, but might consume a lot of time for a larger project. Also, you can only have one Android device connected to your computer while building. Any more and the build process is a guaranteed failure. Unity also doesn't check for multiple devices until after it has gone through the rest of the potentially long build process.

Other than those words of caution, the **Build And Run** option is really quite nice. Let Unity handle the hard part of getting the game to your device. This gives us much more time to focus on testing and making a great game.

Have a go hero – single player mode

This is a tough one. Create a single player mode. You will have to start by adding an extra game state. Is the choice of MultiPlayer for a game state starting to make sense? The opening screen is going to need an extra button for selecting the second game mode. Also, any logic for the computer player should go in the Update function that is provided by the MonoBehaviour class. The computer needs to take its turn before we check for victory in LateUpdate. The Update function is just the place to do it. Also, take a look at Random. Range for randomly selecting a square to take control of. Or, you could do a little more work and make the computer search for a square where it can win or create a line of two matches.

Summary

At this point, you should be familiar with Unity's GUI system including GUI Skins, GUI Styles, and a variety of GUI functions.

In this chapter, we learned all about the GUI by creating a Tic-tac-toe game. We first became familiar with drawing buttons and the like to the GUI. After delving into the depths and gaining understanding of GUI Styles and GUI Skins, we applied the knowledge to make our game look even better. The game continued to improve when we added some dynamic positioning to our GUI elements. The opening and closing screens became centered, while the game board dynamically scaled to fill the screen. Finally, we explored an alternative build method for putting our game onto devices.

In the next chapter, we will be starting a new and more complex game. The Tank Battle game that we will be creating will be used to gain understanding with the basic building blocks of any game: meshes, materials, and animations. When all is done, we will be able to drive a tank around a colorful city and shoot animated targets.

3
The Backbone of Any Game – Meshes, Materials, and Animations

In the previous chapter we learned about the GUI. We started by creating a simple Tic-tac-toe game to learn about the basic pieces. This was followed by styling the GUI to change the look of the game. Finally, we adjusted the game so it would expand automatically to fit a screen of any size.

This chapter is about the core of any game: meshes, materials, and animations. Without these blocks there is generally nothing to show players. You could, of course, just use flat images in the GUI. But, where is the fun in that? If you are going to choose a 3D game engine, you might as well make full use of its capabilities.

To understand meshes, materials, and animations, we will be creating a Tank Battle game. This project will be used in a few other chapters. By the end of the book, it will be one of the two robust games we will create. For this chapter, the player will get to drive a tank around a small city, he/she will be able to shoot at animated targets, and we will add a counter to track the scores.

This chapter covers the following topics:

- Importing the meshes
- Creating the materials
- Animations
- Creating the prefabs
- Ray tracing

We will be starting a new project for this chapter, so follow along in the first section to get it started.

Setting up

Though this project will eventually grow to become much larger than the previous ones, the actual setup is similar and not overly complex. You will also need a number of starting assets for this project; they will be described during the setup process. Due to the complexity and specific nature of these assets, it is recommended to use the ones provided for now.

Time for action – the setup

As we have done in the previous two chapters, we will need to create a new project so that we can create our next game. Obviously, the first thing to do is to start a new Unity project. For organizational purposes, name it `Ch3_TankBattle_CS`.

1. This project will also grow to become much larger than our previous projects, so we should create some folders to keep things organized. For starters, create six folders. The top level folders will be the `Models`, `Scripts`, and `Prefabs` folders. Inside `Models`, create `Environment`, `Tanks`, and `Targets`. Having these folders makes the project significantly more manageable. Any complete model can consist of a mesh file, one or more textures, a material for every texture, and potentially dozens of animation files.

2. Before we go too far, it is a good idea to change your target platform to Android, if you haven't already done so. Every time the target platform is changed, all of the assets in the project need to be re-imported. This is an automatic step carried out by Unity, but will take an increasing amount of time as your project grows. By setting our target platform before there is anything in the project, we save loads of time later.

3. We will also make use of a very powerful part of Unity. Prefabs are special objects that make the process of creating a game significantly easier. The name means prefabricated—created beforehand and replicated. What this means for us is, we can completely set up a target for our tank to shoot at and turn it into a prefab. Then, we can place instances of that prefab throughout the game world. If we ever need to make a change to the targets, all we need to do is modify the original prefab. Any change made to a prefab is also made on any instance of that prefab. Don't worry; it makes more sense when used.

4. We will also need to create some meshes and textures for this project. To start with, we will need a tank. It is kind of hard to have a battle of tanks without any tanks. The tank that is provided has a turret and cannon, which are separate pieces. We will also use a trick to make the tank's treads look like they are moving, so that each of them are separate pieces and also use a separate texture.

5. For the location of our battle, a portion of a city was created. Instead of applying a specific texture to the city, some tile-able textures will be used. Also, there is a wall around the city to keep the player from falling out of the world.

6. Finally, we will need an animated target. The one that is provided is rigged up like the human arm, with a bull's eye for the hand. It has four animations. The first starts in a curled position and goes to an extended position. The second is the reverse of the first one, going from the extended position to the curled position. The third starts in the extended position and is flung back, as if hit in the front, and returns to the curled position. The last is just like the third one, but it goes forward as if hit from behind. These are fairly simple animations, but they will serve us well in learning about Unity's animation system.

What just happened?

Very little happened here, we simply created the project and added some folders. There was also a little discussion about the assets we would be using for this chapter's project.

Importing the meshes

There are several ways to import assets to Unity. We will be going over perhaps the simplest and certainly the best ways for groups of assets.

Time for action – importing the tank

Let's get started.

1. Inside the Unity Editor, start by right-clicking on your `Tanks` folder and selecting **Show in Explorer** from the menu.

2. This opens the folder that contains the asset that was selected. In this case, the `Models` folder is opened in the Windows folder browser. We just need to put our tank and its textures into the `Tanks` folder.

The files provided for this chapter are `Tank.blend`, `Tanks_Type01.png`, and `TankTread.png` files. Also, utilizing `.blend` files in Unity requires Blender to be installed on your system. Blender is a free modeling program available at `http://www.blender.org`. Unity makes use of it in order to convert the previously mentioned files into ones that it can fully utilize.

3. When we return to Unity, the fact that we added files will be detected and they will be automatically imported. This is one of the best things about Unity. There is no need to explicitly tell Unity to import. If there are changes within the project's assets, it just does so.

4. You might also notice that an extra folder and some files were created when Unity imported our tank. Whenever a new mesh is imported, by default Unity will try to pair it with the materials. We will go into more detail about what a material is in Unity in the next section. For now, it is an object that keeps track of how to display a texture on a mesh. Based on the information in the mesh, Unity looks in the project for a material with the correct name. If one cannot be found, a `Materials` folder is created next to the mesh and the missing materials are created inside it. When creating these materials, Unity also searches for the right textures. This is why it is important to add textures to the folder at the same time as the mesh, so that they all can be imported together. If you did not add the textures at the same time as the tank, the section about creating materials will describe how to add textures to materials.

What just happened?

We just imported our tank into Unity. It is really quite simple. Changes made to any of the assets or folders of the project are automatically detected by Unity, and anything that needs to be is suitably imported.

Tank import settings

When importing any asset into Unity, it is done by using a default group of settings. Any of these settings can be changed from the **Inspector** window. With your new tank selected, we will go over the import settings for a model here.

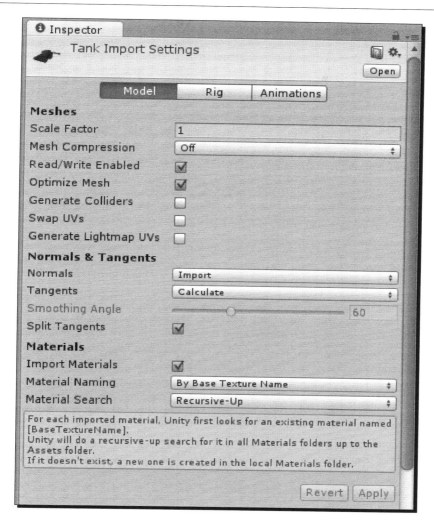

- The top of the Unity Editor has three tabs: **Model**, **Rig**, and **Animations**. The **Model** page handles the mesh itself, while **Rig** and **Animations** are for importing animations. For now, we only care about the **Model** page, so select it if it is not already selected.

- The **Meshes** section of the **Import Settings** window starts with the **Scale Factor** attribute. This is a value that tells Unity how big the mesh is by default. One generic unit or one meter from your modeling program translates to one unit in Unity. This tank was made in generic units, so the tank's scale factor is one. If you were working in centimeters when making the tank, the scale factor would be 0.01, because a centimeter is a hundredth of a meter.

- The next option, **Mesh Compression**, will become important in the final chapter when we go over the optimization of our games. The higher the compression is set, the smaller the file is in the game. However, this will start to introduce weirdness to your mesh as Unity works to make it smaller. For now, leave it **Off**.

- **Read/Write Enabled** is useful if you want to make changes to the mesh while the game is playing. This could allow you to do some really cool things such as destructible environments where your scripts break the meshes into pieces based on where they are being shot at. However, it also means that Unity has to keep a copy of the mesh in memory, which could really start to lag a system if it is complex. This is outside the scope of this book, so unchecking the option is a good idea.

- **Optimize Mesh** is a good one to leave on, unless you are doing something specific and fancy with the mesh. With it on, Unity does some special magic behind the scenes. In computer graphics and especially Unity, every mesh is ultimately a series of triangles being drawn on screen. This option allows Unity to reorder the triangles in the file so that the whole mesh will be drawn faster and more easily.

- The next option, **Generate Colliders**, is a useful one if doing complex things with **Physics**. Unity has a set of simple collider shapes that should be used whenever possible, because they are easier to process. However, there are situations where they won't quite get the job done, for example, rubble or a half-pipe where the collision shape is too complex to be made with a series of simple shapes. That is why Unity has a **Mesh Collider** component. With this option checked, a **Mesh Collider** component is added to every mesh in our model. We will be sticking with simple colliders in this chapter, so leave the **Generate Colliders** option off.

- **Swap UVs** and **Generate Lightmap UVs** are primarily used when working with lighting, especially lightmaps. Unity can handle two sets of UV coordinates on a model. Normally, the first is used for the texture and the second for the lightmap or shadow texture. If they are in the wrong order, **Swap UVs** will change them, so that the second set now comes first. If you need an unwrap for a lightmap, but did not create one, **Generate Lightmap UVs** will create one for you. We are not working with lightmaps in this project, so both of these can remain off.

- The next section of options, **Normals & Tangents**, begins with the **Normals** option. This defines how Unity will get a hold of the normals of your mesh. By default, they are imported from the file; but there is also the option to make Unity calculate them based on the way the mesh is defined. Or, if we set this option to **None**, Unity will not import the normals. **Normals** are needed if we want our mesh to be affected by real-time lighting or make use of normal maps. We will be making use of real-time lighting in this project, so leave it set to **Import**.

◆ **Tangents**, **Smoothing Angle**, and **Split Tangents** are used if your mesh has a normal map. Tangents are needed to determine how lighting interacts with a normal-mapped surface. By default, Unity will calculate these for you. Importing tangents is only possible from a few file types. The smoothing angle dictates whether shading across an edge would be smooth or sharp, based on the angle between the two faces. The **Split Tangents** option is there to handle a few specific lighting quirks. If lighting is broken by seams, enabling this option will fix it. Normal maps are great for making a low-resolution game look like a high-resolution one. However, because of all the extra files and information needed to use them, they are not ideal for a mobile game. Therefore, we will not be using them in this book and all of these options can be turned off to save memory.

◆ The last section, **Materials**, defines how Unity should look for materials. The first option, **Import Materials**, is to decide whether or not a material should be imported. If it is turned off, a default white material will be applied. This material will not show up anywhere in your project; it is a hidden default. For models that will not have any textures, such as collision meshes, this could be turned off. For our tank and nearly every other case, this should be left on.

◆ The last two options, **Material Naming** and **Material Search**, work together to name and find the materials for the mesh. Directly below them, there is a text box that describes how Unity will go about searching for the material. The name of the material being searched for can be the name of the texture used in the modeling program, the name of the material created in the modeling program, or the name of the model plus the material. If a texture name cannot be found, the material name will be used instead. By default, Unity does a **Recursive-Up** search. This means that we start by looking in the `Materials` folder, followed by any materials that are in the same folder. We then check the parent folder for matching materials, followed by the folder above that. This continues until we either find the material that has the correct name or we reach the root assets folder. Alternatively we have the options of checking the entire project by only looking in the `Materials` folder that is next to our model. The defaults for these options are just fine. In general, they do not need to be changed. They are most easily changed with the Unity Editor scripting, which will not be covered in this book.

◆ Next, we have a pair of buttons: **Revert** and **Apply**. Whenever changes are made to the import settings, one of these two buttons must be chosen. The **Revert** button cancels the changes and switches the import settings back to what they were before changes were made. **Apply** confirms the changes and re-imports the model with the new settings. If these buttons are not selected, Unity will complain with a pop up and force a choice before letting you mess with anything else.

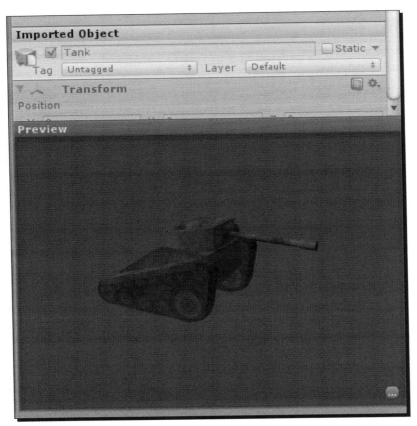

◆ Finally, we have two types of previews. The **Imported Object** section is a preview of what the object will look like in the **Inspector** window, if added to the **Scene** view and selected. The **Preview** window is what the model will look like in the **Scene** view. You can click-and-drag in this window to rotate the object and look at it from different angles. Also, there is a little blue button in this window. By clicking on this button, you will be able to add labels to the object. Then, these labels are also searchable in the **Project** window.

Setting up the tank

Now that we have the tank imported, we need to set it up. We will be adjusting the arrangement of the tank as well as creating a few scripts.

Time for action – creating the tank

At this point, the creation of our tank will primarily consist of the creation and arrangement of the tank's components.

1. Start by dragging the tank from the **Project** window to the **Hierarchy** window. You will notice that the name of the tank appears in blue color in the **Hierarchy** window. This is because it is a prefab instance. Any model in your project largely acts like a prefab. But, we want our tank to do more than just sit there. So, being a prefab of a static mesh is not helpful. Therefore, select your tank in the **Hierarchy** window and we will start making it useful by removing the Animator component. To do this, select the gear to the right of the Animator component in the **Inspector** window. From the new drop-down list, select **Remove Component** and it will be removed.

2. If you are using the tank provided by default, selecting the different parts of it will reveal that all the pivot points are at the base. This will not be useful for making our turret and cannon pivot properly. The easiest way to solve this is by adding new empty GameObject to act as pivot points.

 Any object in the scene is a GameObject. Any empty GameObject is one that only has a **Transform** component.

3. At the top of the Unity Editor, **Create Empty** is the first option under the **GameObject** button. It creates the objects we need. Create two empty GameObjects, and position one at the base of the turret and the other at the base of the cannon. Also, rename them to TurretPivot and CannonPivot respectively. This can be done with the textbox at the very top of the **Inspector** window, if the object is selected.

4. In the **Hierarchy** window, drag `TurretPivot` onto `Tank`. This changes the parent of `TurretPivot` to `Tank`. Then, drag the object, that is, the turret mesh, onto `TurretPivot`. In code, we will be rotating the pivot point, not the mesh directly. When a parent object moves or rotates, all of the children objects move with it. When you make this change, Unity will complain about the change to the original hierarchy of the object; just checking to make sure it is a change you want to do and not an accident.

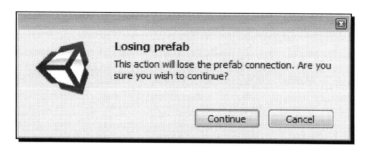

5. Because losing that connection to the prefab can potentially break a game, Unity just wants to be sure that we actually want it to happen. So, click on **Continue** and we can finish working with the tank without other complaints from Unity. We also need to make `CannonPivot` a child of `TurretPivot`, and the cannon a child of `CannonPivot`.

6. To finish off our hierarchy changes, we need to place the camera. Because we want it to appear as if the player is actually in the tank, the camera should be placed behind and above the tank with a tilt slightly downward to focus on a spot a few tank lengths ahead. Once positioned, make it a child of `TurretPivot` as well.

What just happened?

We set up the basic structure that our tank will use. By making use of multiple objects in this way, we can control their movements and actions independently from each other. At this point, instead of having a rigid tank that only points forward, we can tilt, rotate, and aim each piece independently.

 Also, the tank should be centered above the point that you want the whole thing to pivot around. If yours is not, you can select everything that is under the base tank object in the **Hierarchy** window and move it around.

Time for action – keeping score

A short script for keeping track of the player's score will constitute the focus of this short section.

1. To make this tank work, we are going to need three scripts. The first is fairly simple. Create a new script and name it `ScoreCounter`. It will, as the name implies, track the score. Create it in the `Scripts` folder and clear out the default functions, just like every other script we have made so far.

2. Add the following line of code to the new script:

```
public static int score = 0;
```

   - For the most part, this should look familiar from the previous chapter. First we define an integer counter. Because it is static, other scripts (such as the ones we will create for the targets) will be able to modify this number and give us the score.

3. We follow with an `OnGUI` function that defines a `Rect` class and displays the score using the `GUI.Box` function. A Box is just like a Label, but it has a black background by default. This will make it easier to see as we move around.

```
public void OnGUI() {
  Rect scoreRect = new Rect(0, 0, 100, 30);
  GUI.Box(scoreRect, "" + score);
}
```

What just happened?

We just created a very simple script. It will track our score throughout the game. Also, instead of doing any of the score incrementation itself, other scripts will update the counter to give points to the player.

Time for action – controlling the chassis

A normal tank rotates in place, and it can easily move forward and back. We will make our tank do this with the creation of a single script.

1. The second script is called `ChassisControls`. It will make our tank move around. Create it in the `Scripts` folder as well.

2. The first three lines of the script define the variables the tank will need to move around. We will also be able to change them in the **Inspector** window, in case our tank is too fast or too slow. The first line defines a variable that holds a connection to a `CharacterController` component. This component will easily move the tank around, but will allow it to be stopped by walls and other colliders. The next two lines of code define how fast we move and rotate:

```
public CharacterController characterControl;
public float moveSpeed = 10f;
public float rotateSpeed = 45f;
```

3. Now let's add our good friend `OnGUI` to the mix. This should look mostly familiar. We are creating four buttons that will sit in the bottom-left corner of the screen. When the first two buttons are pressed, we make a call to a function that will move our tank and give it a value for how fast it can move. A positive value is going to move us forward and a negative value will move us backward. The last two buttons do the same thing, except with rotation instead of movement. A positive value will rotate to the right and a negative value will rotate the tank to the left. These buttons are also `RepeatButtons`. A normal button will only activate once for each time it is pressed. A repeat button is active as long as it is held down. The good side of this is that it will allow our tank to move every frame the button is held down. The down side is a quirk in how the `RepeatButton` and `OnGUI` functions work. If one of these buttons is active, nothing will be drawn after that button in the `OnGUI` function. It is a bit annoying, but suits our needs for now.

```
public void OnGUI() {
  Rect fore = new Rect(50, Screen.height - 150, 50, 50);
  if(GUI.RepeatButton(fore, "f")) {
    MoveTank(moveSpeed);
  }

  Rect back = new Rect(50, Screen.height - 50, 50, 50);
  if(GUI.RepeatButton(back, "b")) {
    MoveTank(-moveSpeed);
  }

  Rect left = new Rect(0, Screen.height - 100, 50, 50);
  if(GUI.RepeatButton(left, "l")) {
    RotateTank(-rotateSpeed);
  }

  Rect right = new Rect(100, Screen.height - 100, 50, 50);
  if(GUI.RepeatButton(right, "r")) {
    RotateTank(rotateSpeed);
  }
}
```

4. Only two functions left to go. We start the following line of code by defining our MoveTank function. It needs to be passed with a speed value to dictate how far and in which direction to go. It was mentioned a moment ago; a positive value will go forward and a negative value will go backwards.

```
public void MoveTank(float speed) {
```

5. In order to move in three-dimensional spaces, we need a vector—a value with both direction and magnitude. Therefore, we define a movement vector and set it to the tank's forward direction, multiplied by the tank's speed, and again multiplied by the amount of time since the last frame. If you remember from the geometry class, 3D space has three directions: x, y, and z. In Unity, the following convention applies: x is to the right, y is up, and z is forward. The **Transform** component holds an object's position, rotation, and scale. We can access the **Transform** component of any object in Unity by calling upon the .transform value that Unity provides. The **Transform** component also provides a forward value that will give us a vector that points forward relative to the object. Also, we want to move at a regular pace, for example, a certain number of meters per second, hence we make use of Time.deltaTime. This is a value provided by Unity that holds how many seconds it has been since the last frame of the game was drawn on screen. Think of it like a flip book. In order to make it look like a guy is walking across the page, he needs to move slightly on each page. In the case of a game, the pages are not flipped regularly. So, we have to modify our movement by how long it has taken to flip to the new page. This helps us to maintain an even pace.

```
Vector3 move = characterControl.transform.forward * speed *
Time.deltaTime;
```

6. Next, we want to stay on the ground. In general, any character you want to control in a game does not automatically receive all of the physics that a boulder would, such as gravity. For example, when jumping, you temporarily remove gravity so the character can go up. That is why the next line of code does a simple implementation of gravity by subtracting the normal speed of gravity and again keeps it in pace with our frame rate:

```
move.y -= 9.8f * Time.deltaTime;
```

7. Finally, for the MoveTank function, we actually do the moving. The CharacterController component has a special Move function that will move the character but constrain it by collisions. We just need to tell it how far and in which direction we want to move this frame by passing the Move vector to it. That final curly brace, of course, closes off the function.

```
characterControl.Move(move);
}
```

8. The `RotateTank` function is the last one. This function also needs a speed value to dictate how fast and in which direction to rotate. We start by defining another vector; but, instead of defining which direction to move, this one will dictate which direction to rotate around. In this case, we will be rotating around our up direction. We then multiply that by our speed and `Time.deltaTime` to move fast enough and keep pace with our frame rate.

```
public void RotateTank(float speed) {
    Vector3 rotate = Vector3.up * speed * Time.deltaTime;
```

9. The last bit of the function actually does the rotation. The **Transform** component provides a `Rotate` function. Rotation, especially in 3D space, can become weird and difficult very quickly. The `Rotate` function handles all of that for us; we just need to supply it with the values to be applied for rotation. Also, don't forget the curly brace to close off the function.

```
    characterControl.transform.Rotate(rotate);
}
```

What just happened?

We created a script to control the movement of our tank. It will draw a group of buttons on the screen, so that our tank can move forward and back. This is done using a special `Move` function from the `CharacterController` component. We also used a special `Rotate` function provided by the **Transform** component to rotate our tank using another set of buttons.

Time for action – controlling the turret

This script will allow the player to rotate their turret and aim the cannon.

1. The last script we need to create for our tank is `TurretControls`. This script will allow players to rotate the turret left and right and tilt the cannon up and down. As with all of the others, create it in the `Scripts` folder.

2. The first two variables we define will hold pointers to the turret and cannon pivots, the empty `GameObjects` that we created for our tank. The second set is the speed that our turret and cannon will rotate at. Finally we have some limit values. If we didn't limit how much our cannon could rotate, it would just spin around and around, passing through our tank. This isn't the most realistic behavior for a tank, so we must put some limits on it. The limits are in the range of 300 because straight ahead is zero degree and down is 90 degree. We want it to be the upwards angle, so it is in the range of 300. We also use 359.9 because Unity will change 360 to zero so it can continue to rotate.

```
public Transform turretPivot;
public Transform cannonPivot;
```

```
public float turretSpeed = 45f;
public float cannonSpeed = 20f;

public float lowCannonLimit = 315f;
public float highCannonLimit = 359.9f;
```

3. The next step is to create the OnGUI function to draw buttons and give the player control of the turret. This function is almost identical to the OnGUI function we made for the ChassisControls script. The differences are in the fact that the Rects class will move to the bottom-right corner of the screen, and that we are calling the RotateCannon and RotateTurret functions. When we send a speed to RotateCannon, we need a positive value to go up and a negative value to go down. RotateTurret will largely function like the RotateTank function; a positive speed will rotate to the right and a negative speed will rotate to the left.

```
public void OnGUI() {
  Rect up = new Rect(Screen.width - 100, Screen.height - 150, 50,
50);
  if(GUI.RepeatButton(up, "u")) {
    RotateCannon(cannonSpeed);
  }

  Rect down = new Rect(Screen.width - 100, Screen.height - 50, 50,
50);
  if(GUI.RepeatButton(down, "d")) {
    RotateCannon(-cannonSpeed);
  }

  Rect left = new Rect(Screen.width - 150, Screen.height - 100,
50, 50);
  if(GUI.RepeatButton(left, "l")) {
    RotateTurret(-turretSpeed);
  }

  Rect right = new Rect(Screen.width - 50, Screen.height - 100,
50, 50);
  if(GUI.RepeatButton(right, "r")) {
    RotateTurret(turretSpeed);
  }
}
```

4. Next is the `RotateTurret` function. It works exactly in the same way as the `RotateTank` function. However, instead of looking at a `CharacterController` component 's `Transform` variable, we act upon the `turretPivot` variable that was defined at the beginning of the function.

```
public void RotateTurret(float speed) {
    Vector3 rotate = Vector3.up * speed * Time.deltaTime;
    turretPivot.Rotate(rotate);
}
```

5. The last function, `RotateCannon`, gets a little more down-and-dirty with rotations. The fault completely lies with the need to put limits on the rotation of the cannon. After opening the function, the first step is to figure out how much we are going to be rotating this frame. We are using a float value instead of a vector because we have to set the rotation ourselves.

```
public void RotateCannon(float speed) {
    float rotate = speed * Time.deltaTime;
```

6. Next, we define a variable that holds our current rotation. We do this because Unity will not let us act on the rotation directly. Unity actually keeps track of rotation as a quaternion. This is a complex method of defining rotations that is beyond the scope of this book. Luckily, Unity gives us access to an x, y, z method of defining rotations called `EulerAngles`. It is a rotation around each of the three axes in 3D space. The `localEulerAngles` value of a **Transform** component is the rotation relative to the parent `GameObject`.

```
Vector3 euler = cannonPivot.localEulerAngles;
```

 It is called `EulerAngles` because of *Leonhard Euler*, a Swiss mathematician who defined this method of defining rotations.

7. Next, we adjust the rotation and apply the limits in one go through the use of the `Mathf.Clamp` function. `Mathf` is a group of useful math functions. The `Clamp` function takes a value and makes it no lower and no higher than the other two values passed to the function. So, we first send it our x axis rotation, which is the result of subtracting `rotate` from the current x rotation of `euler`. Because the positive rotation is clockwise around an axis, we have to subtract our rotation to go up instead of down with a positive value. Next, we pass our lower limit to the `Clamp` function, followed by our higher limit: the `lowCannonLimit` and `highCannonLimit` variables that we defined at the top of the script.

```
euler.x = Mathf.Clamp(euler.x - rotate, lowCannonLimit,
highCannonLimit);
```

8. Finally, we have to actually apply the new rotation to our cannon's pivot point. This is simply setting the `localEulerAngles` value of the **Transform** component to the new value. And again, be sure to use the curly brace to close off the function.

```
cannonPivot.localEulerAngles = euler;
}
```

What just happened?

We created a script that will control the turret of the tank. Through the use of buttons on the screen, the player is able to tilt the cannon and rotate the turret. This script functioned in a very similar manner to the `ChassisControls` script we created earlier. The difference came in limiting the amount the cannon can tilt.

Time for action – putting the pieces together

That was the last of the scripts, for the moment. We have our tank and our scripts; the next step is to put them together.

1. Now, we need to add them to our tank. Remember how we added our `Tic-tac-toe` script to the camera in the last chapter? Start by selecting your tank in the **Hierarchy** window. Before they work, we will first need to add the `CharacterController` component to our tank. So, go to the top of the Unity Editor and select **Component**, then select **Physics**, and finally click on the **Character Controller** option.

- You will notice that a green capsule also appears on the tank in the Scene view; at the same time the new component is added. This capsule represents the space that will collide and interact with other colliders. The values on the CharacterController component let us control how it interacts with other colliders. For most cases, the defaults for the first four are just fine.

Slope Limit: This attribute shows us how steep an incline the controller can move up.

Step Offset: This attribute shows us how high a step can be before it starts to block movement.

Skin Width: This defines how far another collider can penetrate this controller's collider before it is completely stopped. This is mostly used for squeezing between objects.

Min Move Distance: This attribute is for limiting jitter. It is the minimum amount of movement that has to be applied in a frame before it will actually move.

Center, **Radius**, and **Height**: These attributes define the size of the capsule that you see in the Scene view. They are used for the collision.

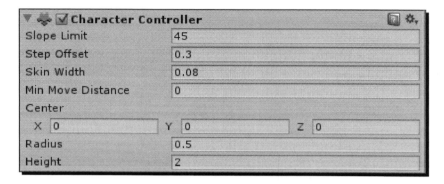

2. The last three values are what we care about right now. We need to adjust these values to match our tank's values as closely as possible. Admittedly the capsule is round and our tank is square, but a CharacterController component is the easiest way to move a character with collision and will be used most often. Use values of 2.3 for the **Radius** attribute and the **Y** portion of the **Center** attribute; everything else can be left at the default values.

3. It is now time to add the scripts to our tank. Do this by selecting the tank in the **Hierarchy** window and dragging the ChassisControls, TurretControls, and ScoreCounter scripts onto the **Inspector** window. This is just as we did it in the previous chapters.

4. Before the tank will work, we need to finish creating the connections that we started in our scripts. Start by clicking the CharacterController component's name and dragging it to the **Character Control** value that is on our new ChassisControls script component. Unity lets us connect object variables in the Unity Editor, so that they do not have to be hard coded.

5. We also need to connect our turret and cannon pivot points. So, click-and-drag the points from the **Hierarchy** window to the corresponding variable on the TurretControls script component.

6. Save the scene as TankBattle and try it out.

What just happened?

We just finished putting our tank together. Unless you look at the **Scene** view while using the movement controls, it is hard to tell that the tank is moving. The turret controls can be seen in the **Game** view, though. Other than not having a point of reference for whether or not our tank is moving, it runs pretty well. The next step and the next section will give us that reference point as we add our city.

Have a go hero – cannon alignment

You might notice a quick jump when you first try to tilt the cannon. Such behavior is annoying and makes the game look broken. Try adjusting the cannon to fix it. If you are having trouble with it, take a look at the cannon's starting rotation.

Creating the materials

In Unity, the materials are the defining factor for how models are drawn on the screen. They can be as simple as coloring it all blue, or as complex as reflective water with waves. In this section, we will cover the details of the controls for a material. We will also create our city and some simple materials to texture it with.

Time for action – creating the city

Creating a city gives our tanks and our players a good place to play.

1. For the purposes of this section, no part of the provided city was given a specific texture. It was just unwrapped and some tile-able textures were created. So, we need to start by importing the city and the textures to the `Environment` folder. Do it the same way that we imported the tank.

     The files are `TankBattleCity.blend`, `brick_001.png`, `brick_002.png`, `brick_003.png`, `dirt_001.png`, `dirt_003.png`, `pebbles_001.png`, `rocks_001.png`, `rubble_001.png`, and `water_002.png`.

2. Because the city was unwrapped, Unity still created a single material for it. However, textures were never applied in any modeling program. So, the material is plain white. We have several extra textures, so we are going to need more than that one material for the whole city. Creating a new material is simple; it is done just as with creating a new script. Right-click on the `Materials` folder inside the `Environment` folder, and select **Create** followed by **Material**, which is about halfway down the menu.

3. This will create a new material in the folder and immediately allow us to name it. Name the material, `Pebbles`.

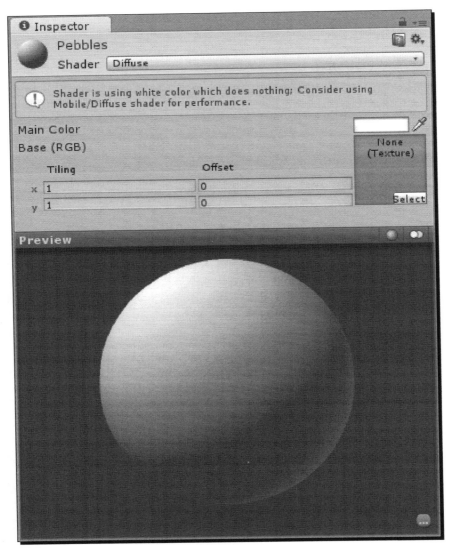

4. With your new material selected, take a look at the **Inspector** window. When we have a material selected, we get the options needed to change its look.

❑ At the very top of the **Inspector** window, we have the material's name, followed by a **Shader** drop-down list. A shader is essentially a short script that tells the graphics card how to draw something on screen. You will use the **Diffuse** shader most often, so it is always selected by default. This is where you would select from your Bump-mapped shaders, specular, transparent, and a plethora of other options. If you were to create some custom shaders, they would also be found here.

❑ The next little block will only be visible if Unity has something to warn you about. In this case, it is advising us to use a different shader for performance reasons. However, that is a discussion for *Chapter 9, Optimization*, so we will ignore it for now.

❑ Then, we have the **Main Color** value with a colored square next to it. By clicking on that square, the **Color Picker** window will open and let us select any color we want. This color value changes the tinting on the texture being drawn by the material. Because we don't have a texture yet, you will notice that it just changes the color of the ball in the **Preview** window.

❑ The **Base (RGB)** value is under the **Main Color** value. This is the texture. The box on the right, with **None (Texture)** and a **Select** button in it, is a preview box for the texture being used by this material. To add a texture to the material, either drag one to this box from the **Project** window, or click on the **Select** button. The button opens a new window that holds the thumbnails of every texture that is currently in the project. You can scroll through or use the search bar to find the texture that you need and double-click to select it.

❑ To the left of the box, we have our **Tiling** and **Offset** controls. The **Tiling** values dictate how many times the texture will repeat across the normalized UV space in the x and y directions. The **Offset** is how far off zero the texture starts in the normalized UV space. You can select the number fields and input values to modify them. Doing so, and paying attention to the **Preview** window below, you will see how they change the texture. Tiling textures are most commonly used for large surfaces where the texture is similar enough across the surface that it just repeats.

❑ Our **Preview** window is at the bottom of the **Inspector** window. It functions just as the one we saw for our tank mesh. What makes this one special, though, is the two buttons in the top-right corner of this window. The one to the left scrolls through a set of preview shapes. By clicking on it you'll be able to see how the texture looks on a sphere, cube, cylinder, or torus. The other button toggles between the two types of lighting.

5. Add the `pebbles_001` texture to this material by dragging it from the **Project** window and dropping it on the **Base (RGB)** preview box.

6. Use values of 30 for the material's **Tiling** and a light tan color for the **Main Color** option, so that the texture can be sized right and more pleasing to look at.

7. To see our new material in action, first drag your city to the **Hierarchy** window, so that it is added to the **Scene** view. By right-clicking-and-dragging, you can look around in your **Scene** view. Look over at the streets of the city.

8. Now, drag your new material from the **Project** window into your **Scene** view. While dragging the material around, you should see the meshes change to appear as if they are using the material. Once you are over the streets, let go of your left mouse button. The material is now applied to the mesh.

9. However, we currently have a whole quarter of a city to texture. So, create more materials and use the remaining textures on the rest of the city. Create a new material for each extra texture, plus four extra of `brick_002`, so, we can have different colors for each building height.

10. Apply your new materials to the city, either by comparison with the following figure or through your own artistic whim:

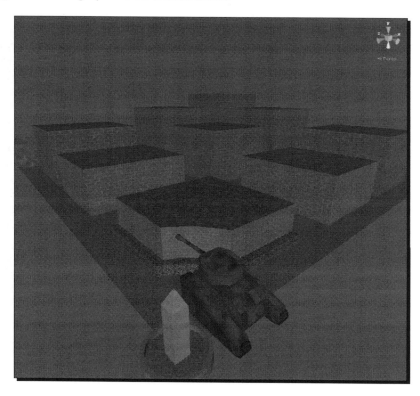

When trying to get to the center fountain, if your tank is in the way, select your tank in the **Hierarchy** window and use the **Gizmo** option in the **Scene** view to drag it out of the way.

❑ If you were to try to play the game now, you might notice that we have a couple of problems. For starters, we only have a quarter of a city; perhaps you have more if you made your own city. There is still no collision on the city, so we fall right through it when moving. Also, the tank is a little large for this city, and it is too dark to see where we are going. Turning on the lights is the quickest solution to fix this problem.

11. At the top of the Unity Editor, select **GameObject**, followed by **Create Other**, and finally **Directional Light**. This creates an object that emits light in a single direction. The next chapter explains lights and how to control them, so the details will be left for later.

12. Changing the size of our tank is also pretty simple. Select it in the **Hierarchy** window and look for the **Scale** label in our **Transform** component. Changing the **X**, **Y**, and **Z** values under **Scale** will change the size of our tank. Be sure to change them evenly or some weirdness will occur when we start rotating the tank. Values of 0.5 make the tank small enough to fit through the small streets.

13. Next up is collision for the city. For the most part, we will be able to get away with simple collision shapes that are faster to process. However, the circular center of the city will require something special. Start by double-clicking on the walls of one of the square buildings in the **Scene** view.

When dealing with prefabs, which the city still is, clicking on any object that makes up the prefab will select the root prefab object. Once a prefab is selected, clicking on any part of it will select that individual piece. Because this behavior is different from non-prefab objects, you need to be mindful of it when selecting objects in the **Scene** view.

14. With a set of walls selected, go to the top of the Unity Editor and select **Component**, followed by **Physics**, and finally **Box Collider**.

15. Because we are adding the collider to a specific mesh, Unity does its best to automatically fit the collider to the shape. For us, this means that the new `BoxCollider` component is already sized to fit the building. Continue by adding `BoxColliders` to the rest of the square buildings and the outer wall. Our streets are essentially just a plain, so a `BoxCollider` component will work just fine for them as well. Though pointed at the top, the obelisk in the center of the fountain is essentially just a box; so, another `BoxCollider` will suit it fine.

16. We have one last building and the fountain ring to deal with. These are not boxes, spheres, or capsules. So, our simple colliders will not work. Select the walls of the last building, the one next to the center fountain. A few options down from where you were selecting **Box Collider**, there is a **Mesh Collider** option. This will add a `MeshCollider` component to our object. This component does what its name suggests; it takes a mesh and turns it into a collider. By adding it to a specific mesh, the `MeshCollider` component automatically selects that mesh to be collideable. You should also add `MeshColliders` to the short ledge around the center building and the ring wall around the fountain.

17. The last problem to solve is the duplication of our city quarter. Start by selecting the root `city` object in your hierarchy, `TankBattleCity`, and remove the `Animator` component from it. The city is not going to animate, so it does not need this component.

18. Now, right-click on the city in the **Hierarchy** window and select **Duplicate**. This creates a copy of the object that was selected.

19. Duplicate the city quarter twice more and we will have the four parts of our city. The only problem is that they are all in the exact same position.

20. We need to rotate three of the pieces to make a full city. Select one and set the **Y Rotation** value in the **Transform** component to `90`. This will rotate it 90 degrees around the vertical axis and give us half of a city.

21. We will complete the city by setting one of the remaining pieces to `180` and another to `270`.

22. That leaves one last thing to do. We have four center fountains. In three of the four city pieces, select the three meshes that make up the center fountain (the `Obelisk`, `Wall`, and `Water`) and click on the *Delete* key on your keyboard. Confirm that you want to break the prefab connection each time, and our city will be complete.

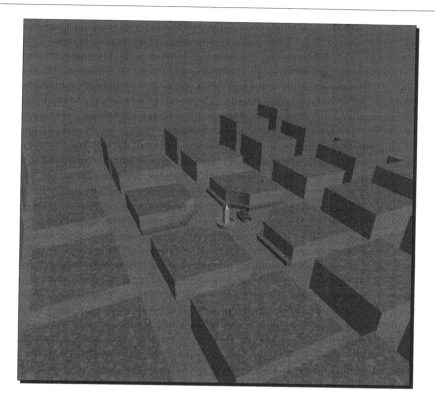

What just happened?

Try out the game now. We can drive around the city and rotate our turret. It is so much fun. We created materials and textured the city. After making it possible to collide with the buildings and road, we duplicated the section so that we could have a whole city.

Have a go hero – decorating the city

Now that you have all the skills needed to import meshes and create materials, the challenge is to decorate the city. Create some rubble and tank traps and practice importing them to Unity and setting them up in the scene. If you really want to go above and beyond, try your hand at creating your own city. Choose something from the world, or choose something from your imagination. Once it is created, we can release the tanks in it.

Time for action – moving treads

1. There is just one thing left to do, and then we will be done with materials and can go on to make the game even more fun. Remember the **Offset** value of the materials? It turns out that we can actually control that with a script. Start by opening up the `ChassisControls` script.

2. First, we need to add a few variables to the beginning of the script. The first two will hold references to our tank tread renderers, the part of the mesh object that keeps track of the material that is applied to the mesh and actually does the drawing. This is just like how the `characterControl` variable holds a reference to our `CharacterController` component.

```
public Renderer rightTread;
public Renderer leftTread;
```

3. The second two variables will keep track of the amount of offset applied to each tread. We store it here because it is a faster reference than trying to look it up from the thread's material each frame.

```
private float rightOffset = 0;
private float leftOffset = 0;
```

4. To make use of the new values, these lines need to be added to the end of the `MoveTank` function. The first line here adjusts the offset for the right tread as per our speed and keeps in time with our frame rate. The second line utilizes the material value of a `Renderer` component to find our tank tread material. The `mainTextureOffset` value of the material is the offset of the primary texture in the material. In the case of our diffuse materials, it is the only texture. Then, we have to set the offset to a new `Vector2` value that will contain our new offset value. `Vector2` is just like `Vector3` we used for moving, but works in 2D space instead of 3D space. A texture is flat, hence 2D space. The last two lines of the code do the same thing as the other two, but for the left tank tread.

```
rightOffset += speed * Time.deltaTime;
rightTread.material.mainTextureOffset = new Vector2(rightOffset, 0);
leftOffset += speed * Time.deltaTime;
leftTread.material.mainTextureOffset = new Vector2(leftOffset, 0);
```

5. To make the connections to the `Renderer` components of our treads, do the same thing that we did for the pivot points: drag the tread meshes from the **Hierarchy** window to the corresponding value in the **Inspector** window. Once done, be sure to save it and try it out.

What just happened?

We updated our `ChassisControls` script to make the tank treads move. As the tank is driven around, the textures pan in the appropriate direction. This is the same type of functionality that is used to make waves in water and other textures that move.

Have a go hero – turning with the treads

The movement of the material doesn't quite match the speed of the tank. Figure out how to add a speed value for the tank's treads. Also, it would be cool if they moved in opposite directions when the tank is rotating. Real tanks turn by making one tread go forward and the other back.

Animations

The next topic we will be covering is animation. As we explore animations in Unity, we will be creating some targets for our tank to shoot at. Much of the power of Unity's animation system, Mecanim, lies in working with humanoid characters. But, setting up and animating human type characters is a book unto itself, so it will not be covered here. However, there is still much we can learn and do with Mecanim.

◆ Before we continue with the explanation of the animation import settings, we need an animated model to work with. We have one last set of assets to import to our project. Import the `Target.blend` and `Target.png` files into the `Targets` folder of our project. Once imported, adjust the **Import Settings** window on the **Model** page for the target, just as we did for the tank. Now switch to the **Rig** tab.

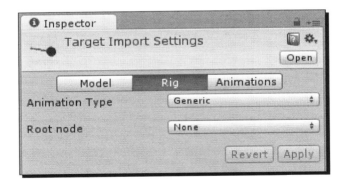

- ◆ The **Animation Type** attribute tells Unity what type of skeleton the current model is going to use when animating.

  - ❑ The **Humanoid** option adds many more buttons and switches to this page for working with human type characters. But again, it is too complex to cover here.

  - ❑ A **Generic** rig still uses Mecanim and many of its features. Really, this is just any animation skeleton that does not resemble a human in structure.

  - ❑ The third option, **Legacy**, utilizes Unity's old animation system. But, this system will be phased out over the next few versions of Unity, so it will not be covered either.

  - ❑ The last option, **None**, indicates that the object will not be animating. You could select this option for both the tank and the city, because it also keeps Unity from adding that `Animator` component and saves space in the final project size.

  - ❑ The **Root Node** value is a list of every object that is in the model file. Its purpose is to select the base object of your animation rig. For this target, select **Bone_Arm_Upper**, which is underneath the second **Armature** option.

♦ The last page of the import settings, **Animations**, contains everything that we need to get the animations from our files into Unity. At the top of the **Target Import Settings** window, we have the **Import Animation** checkbox. If an object is not going to animate, it is a good idea to turn this option off. Doing so will also save space in your project.

♦ The option below that, **Bake Animations**, is only used when your animations contain Kinematics and are from 3Ds Max or Maya. This target is from Blender, so the option is grayed out.

♦ The next four options, **Anim. Compression**, **Rotation Error**, **Position Error**, and **Scale Error**, are primarily for smoothing jittery animations. Nearly all of the time, the defaults will suit just fine.

♦ The **Clips** section is what we are really concerned about. This will be a list of every animation clip that is currently being imported from the model. On the left-hand side of the list, we have the name of the clip. On the right-hand side, we can see the start and end frames of the clip.

   ❑ Unity will add the **Default Take** animation clip to every new model. This is a clip generated from the default preview range of your modelling program, when the file was saved.

   ❑ In Blender, it is also possible to create a series of actions for each rig. By default, they are imported by Unity as animation clips. In this case, the **ArmatureAction** clip is created.

❑ Below and to the right-hand side of the clips, there is a little tab with + and - buttons. These two buttons add a clip to the end and remove the selected clip respectively.

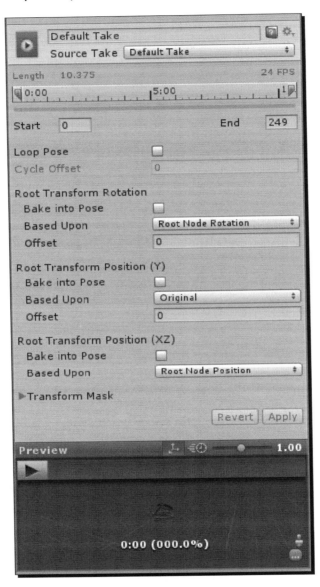

◆ When a clip is selected, the next section appears. It starts with a text field for changing the name of the clip.

- Below the text field, there is a **Source Take** drop-down list. This list is the same as the default animations. Most of the time, you will just use **Default Take**; but if your animation is ever appearing wrong or is missing, try changing the **Source Take** drop-down list first.

- Then, we have a small timeline, followed by input fields for the start and end frames of the animation clip. Clicking-and-dragging on the two blue flags in the timeline will change the numbers in the input fields.

- Next we have **Loop Pose** and **Cycle Offset**. If we want our animation to repeat, check the box next to **Loop Pose**. When an animation is looping, **Cycle Offset** will become available. This value lets us adjust the frame that the looping animation starts on.

- The next three small sections, **Root Transform Rotation**, **Root Transform Position (Y)**, and **Root Transform Position (XZ)**, allow us to control the movement of a character through the animation.

  - All three of these sections have a **Bake into Pose** option. If these are left unchecked, the movement of the root node (we selected it under the **Rig** page) within the animation is translated into movement of the whole object. Think of it like this: say you were to animate a character running to the right and inside of the animation program, you actually move them, rather than animating in place as normal. With Unity's old animation system, for the physical part of a character to move the collider, the GameObject had to be moved with code. So, if you were to use that animation, the character would appear as if it had moved, but it would have no collision. With this new system, the whole character will move when that animation is played. However, this requires a different and more complex setup to work completely. So, it was not chosen to be used on the tank, though we could have used it.

  - Each of the three sections also has a **Based Upon** drop-down option. The choice of this option dictates the object's center for each of the sections. There are more choices if you are working with humanoid characters, but for now we only have two.

    A choice of **Root Node** means the pivot point of the root node object is the center.

    A choice of **Original** means the origin as defined by the animation program is the center of the object.

  - There is also an **Offset** option for the first two of these sections that works to correct errors in the motion. When animating a walk cycle for a character, if the character is pulling to the side slightly, adjusting the **Offset** option under **Root Transform Rotation** will correct it.

◆ The last option for our animation clip is a **Transform Mask** option. By clicking on the arrow to the left, you can expand a list of all objects in the model. Each object has a checkbox next to it. The objects that are not checked will not be animated when this clip is played. This is useful in the case of a hand-waving animation. Such an animation would only need to move the arm and hand, so we would uncheck all of the objects that might make up the body of the character. We could then layer animations, making our character capable of waving while standing, walking, or running, without the need to create three extra animations.

◆ Finally, we have our **Revert** button, **Apply** button, and the **Preview** window at the bottom. Just as with all of our other import settings, we have to hit one of these buttons when changes are made. This **Preview** window is made special by the speed slider in the top-right corner and the big **play** button in the top-left corner. By clicking on this button, we can preview the selected animation. This lets us detect those errors in motion that we talked about earlier, and just generally make sure that the animation is what we want.

The target's animations

So, now that the description is all out of the way, let's actually make something with it. We start by setting up the animations for the target.

Time for action – setting up target's animations

Using the knowledge we just gained, we can now set up our target's animations.

1. For starters, if you missed or skipped it earlier, be sure to import the `Target.blend` and `Target.png` files to the `Targets` folder. Also, on the **Rig** page of the import settings, set the **Animation Type** attribute to **Generic** and the **Root Node** attribute to **Bone_Arm_Upper**.

2. We need a total of six animations. By clicking on the + button in the **Clips** section, you can add four more animations. If you have added too many, click on the - button to remove the extra clips.

3. All of these clips should have a **Source Take** drop-down list of **Default Take** and all of the **Bake into Pose** options should be checked, because the target isn't going to be moving from its starting location.

4. First, let's create our idle animations. Select the first clip and rename it to `Idle_Retract`. Because it is a mechanical object, we can get away with a really short animation; so short that we are just going to use the first frame. Set the starting frame to `0.9` and the ending frame to `1`.

5. We also need to turn on **Loop Pose** because idle animations are of course looping.

6. The extended idle animation is created in almost exactly the same manner. Select the second clip and rename it to `Idle_Extend`. The starting frame here is `14` and the ending frame is `14.1`. Also, this animation needs to loop.

7. Our next two animations are for when the target extends and retracts. They are going to be called `Extend` and `Retract`, so rename the next two clips. The `Extend` animation will start at frame `1` and end at frame `13`. The `Retract` animation starts at frame `28` and ends at frame `40`. Neither of these will loop.

8. The last two animations also will not loop. They are for when we shoot the targets. There is one for being shot in the front and one for being shot from behind. The `Hit_Front` animation will be from frame `57` to frame `87`. The `Hit_Back` animation will be from frame `98` to frame `128`.

9. Once all of the changes are made, be sure to click on **Apply** or they will not be saved.

What just happened?

We set up the animations that will be used by our targets. There were six in total. They may not seem like much now, but the next section would be lost without them.

State machines

In order for us to control these new animations in Unity, we need to set up a state machine. A state machine is just a fancy object that keeps track of what an object can do, and how to transition between those things. Think of it in terms of a builder from a Real Time Strategy game. The builder has a walk state that is used when moving to the next construction site. When it gets there, it switches to a build state. If an enemy shows up, the builder will enter a run away state until the enemy is gone. Finally, there is an idle state for when the builder is doing nothing. In Unity, these are called Animator Controllers when working with animations and Mecanim.

Time for action – creating the target state machine

The use of a state machine allows us to focus more on what the target is doing, while letting Unity handle the *how it is going to do it* part.

1. Creating an Animator Controller is simple and done just as we have been doing for our scripts and materials. The option is second from the bottom of the **Create** menu. Create one in the `Targets` folder and name it `TargetController`.

2. Double-click on `TargetController` to open a new window.

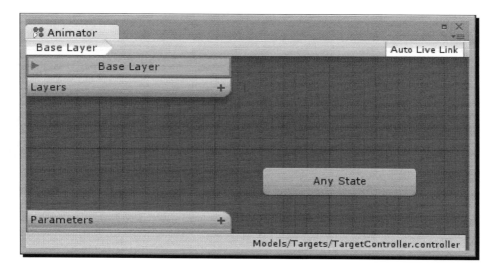

3. The **Animator** window is where we edit our state machines.

    □   At the top-left corner of the window, there is a breadcrumb trail as you might find on a website that lets us see where we are in the state machine at a glance.

    □   The **Auto Live Link** button in the top-right controls our ability to see the state machine's update in real time with the game. This is useful for debugging transitions and controls for the character.

    □   Underneath the breadcrumb trail, there are a list of layers and a button for adding new layers. Every state machine will have at least the **Base Layer**. Adding additional layers would allow us to blend state machines. Say we have a character that walks around normal when at full health. When his health drops below half, he starts to limp. If the character has only ten percent of his health left, he starts to crawl. This would be achieved through the use of layers.

- ❑ At the bottom-left corner of the window, there is the **Parameters** list. Clicking on the **+** button will add a new parameter to the list. These parameters can be Boolean, float, vector, and integer values. The transitions between states are most often triggered by changes in the parameters. Any scripts working with the state machine can modify these values.

- ❑ Finally, that green box in the center with **Any State** on it that allows a character to transition from any action to a specific one. When a character's health drops below zero, we want them to go to the death state. The **Any State** box would hold this transition, and it would be able to pull the character out of any other state and put them in the death state.

4. To create a new state, right-click on the grid that is inside our **Animator** window. Mouse over **Create State** and select **Empty**. This creates a new empty state for our state machine. Normally new states are gray but, because this is the first state in our machine it is orange, which is the color of the default state.

5. Every state machine will start in its default state. Click on the state to select it, and we can take a look at it in the **Inspector** window.

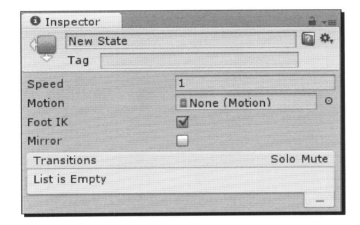

- ❑ At the top, there is a text field for changing the name of the state.

- ❑ Below that, you can add a tag for organizational purposes.

- ❑ Next, there is a **Speed** field. This field controls the speed of the animation.

- ❑ The **Motion** field is where we will add connections to the animation clips that we created earlier.

- ❑ The **Foot IK** option lets us decide if we want to let part of the animation be calculated with IK. We did not set up any IK for these animations, so we do not need to worry about this option.

- ❑ The last option, **Mirror**, is used to flip the left and right (or x axis) of the animation. If you created a right-hand-waving animation, this option would let you change it to a left-hand-waving animation.

- ❑ Below that, there is the list of transitions that go from this state to another state. These are transitions out of the state, not into it. As you will soon see, a transition in this list appears as the name of the current state with an arrow to the right, followed by the name of the state it is connected to.

- ❑ Checkboxes also appear under the **Solo** and **Mute** labels on the right. These are for debugging transitions between states. Any number of the transitions can be muted at one time, but only one can be soloed at a time. When a transition has been muted, it means that the state machine will ignore it when deciding which transition to make. Checking the solo box is the same as muting all but one of the transitions. It is just a quick way of making it the only active transition.

6. We are going to need one state for each of our target's animations. So, create five more states and rename all six to match the names of the animation clips we created earlier. The default state, the orange one, should be named `Idle_Retract`.

7. In the **Project** window, click on the little triangle to the left of the **Target** model.

- ❑ This expands the model, so that we can see all of the objects that make up that model in Unity. The first group, as indicated by the little thumbnails next to each object, is the raw mesh data. This is followed by an Avatar object; this is what keeps track of the **Rig** setup. Below that, there are the animation clip objects; these are what we are interested in right now. The objects that make up the model are at the bottom of the stack.

8. Select each state in your **Animator** window and pair it with the correct clip by dragging an animation clip from the **Project** window and dropping it on the **Motion** field in the **Inspector** window.

 The thumbnail for animation clips looks like a little play button.

9. Before we can create our transitions, we need a few parameters. Click on the **+** button next to **Parameters** in the bottom-left corner of the window and select **Float** from the menu that appears. A new parameter should now appear in the list.

10. The new field on the left is the name of the parameter; rename this one to `time`. The field on the right is the current value of this parameter. When debugging our state machine, we can modify these values here to trigger changes in the state machine. Any changes made by the scripts while the game is running will also appear here.

11. We need two more parameters. Create two Boolean parameters and rename them to `wasHit` and `inTheFront`. These will trigger the machine to change to the getting hit states, while the `time` parameter will trigger the machine to utilize the `extend` and `retract` states.

12. To create a new transition, right-click on a state and select **Make Transition** from the menu that pops up. A transition line is now connected from the state to your mouse. To complete the transition creation, click on the state that you wish to connect to. There is an arrow on the line, indicating the direction of the transition.

    1. We need a transition from `Idle_Retract` to `Extend`.

    2. We also need a transition from `Extend` to `Idle_Extend`.

    3. `Idle_Extend` needs three transitions, one each going to `Retract`, `Hit_Front`, and `Hit_Back`.

    4. `Retract`, `Hit_Front`, and `Hit_Back` need a transition going to `Idle_Retract`.

Use the following diagram for reference. If you create a transition or state that you do not want, select it and click on the *Delete* key on your keyboard to remove it.

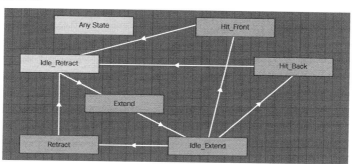

13. If you click on one of the transition lines, then we can take a look at its settings.

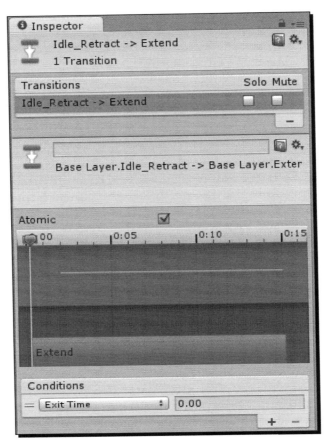

- At the top of the **Inspector** window, we have the same indicators of which states we are transitioning between that we had in the state, the name of the state the transition starts in followed by an arrow, and finally the name of the state the transition ends in.

- Underneath the familiar **Transitions** list, there is a text field where we can give our transitions specific names. This would be useful if we had several different types of transitions between the same two states.

- Directly under the field, there is a more exact path-based indication of which states the transition is between.

❑ The **Atomic** checkbox allows us to decide whether or not a transition can be interrupted. If **Atomic** is checked, it cannot be interrupted.

In the example about the **Any State** option and the death state, perhaps we were shot while pulling out a sword, going from an idle state to an attack state. That transition cannot be atomic, if we are to avoid the weirdness of completing our sword draw before falling over dead.

❑ Next is a timeline block that lets us preview the transition between animations. Dragging the little flag left and right, we can watch the transition in the **Preview** window below. The top half of this block holds wave forms that indicate the movement contained in an animation. The bottom half shows the states as boxes that overlap where the transition actually occurs. Either of these boxes can be dragged to change the length of the transition.

Because our two idle animations are of negligible length, this can't be seen in our setup normally. If you temporarily create a transition between the extend and retract states, it would be visible.

❑ Lastly, we have a **Conditions** list. Using the parameters we set up, we can create any number of conditions here that must be met before this transition can take place.

The default condition is **Exit Time**. This means that, when the first state reaches a certain percentage of the way through its animation, as defined by the float field to the right, it will start transitioning into the next state. For half of our transitions, this is what we want. The other half, namely anything that exits our idle states, need to be based on our parameters.

There is also another **Preview** window at the bottom of the **Inspector** panel. It functions just like the one for the animation import settings page, but this one plays the transition between the two relevant animations.

14. Select the transition between the Idle_Retract state and Extend state. We want the targets to randomly pop up. This will be controlled by a script changing the time parameter.

15. Click on Exit Time under the **Conditions** list to bring up the list of parameters and select time from the list.

16. In order to turn a float value into a conditional statement, we need to compare it with another value. That is why we got a new drop-down button of comparison options when we selected the parameter. A float value will be either greater than or less than the value on the right. Our time will be counting down, so select **Less** from the list and leave the value at zero.

17. Change the conditions for the transition between the `Idle_Extend` and `Retract` states to be the same.

18. For the transition between the `Idle_Extend` state and `Hit_Front` state, we will use both of the Boolean parameters that were created. Select the transition and click on the + button under **Conditions** to add a second condition.

19. For the first condition, select **wasHit** and select **inTheFront** for the second condition.

20. A Boolean is either true or false. In the case of the transitions, it needs to know which of those values it is waiting for. For this transition, both should be left as true.

21. Next, set up the conditions for the transition between `Idle_Extend` and `Hit_Back`, just as you did for the previous transition. The difference being that false needs to be selected from the drop-down list next to the `inTheFront` conditional.

What just happened?

We created a state machine that will be used by our targets. By linking each state to an animation and connecting them all with transitions, the target will be able to switch between animations. This transitioning is controlled through adding conditionals and parameters.

Time for action – scripting the target

We only need one more piece before we can finish putting the target together.

1. That piece is a script. Create a new script in our `Scripts` folder and name it `Target`.

2. First, in order to interact with our state machine, we need a reference to the `Animator` component. It is the component that you removed from the tank and the city. The `Animator` component is what ties all of the pieces of animation together.

```
public Animator animator;
```

3. It is followed by two float values that will dictate the range of time, in seconds, that our targets will sit in their idle states.

```
public float maxIdleTime = 10f;
public float minIdleTime = 3f;
```

4. Next, we have three values that will hold the ID numbers of the parameters that we need to change. It is technically possible to just use the names of the parameters to set them, but using the ID number is much faster.

```
private int timeId = -1;
private int wasHitId = -1;
private int inTheFrontId = -1;
```

5. The last two variables will hold the ID numbers of the two idle states. We need these for checking which state we are in. All of the IDs are initially set to -1 as a dummy value, we set them to their actual values with the following function:

```
private int idleRetractId = -1;
private int idleExtendId = -1;
```

6. The `Awake` function is a special function in Unity that is called on every script at the beginning of the game. Its purpose is initialization before the game gets underway, perfect for initially setting our ID values. For each ID, we make a call to the `Animator.StringToHash` function. This function calculates the ID number of the parameter or state that we give it the name of. The state names also need to be prefixed with `Base Layer`. This is because Unity wants us to be specific when it is possible to have several different layers with states that are named the same thing. It is also very important that the name here exactly matches the name in the **Animator** window. If it does not, IDs will not match, errors will occur, and the script will not function correctly.

```
public void Awake() {
   timeId = Animator.StringToHash("time");
   wasHitId = Animator.StringToHash("wasHit");
   inTheFrontId = Animator.StringToHash("inTheFront");
   idleRetractId = Animator.StringToHash("Base Layer.Idle_
Retract");
   idleExtendId = Animator.StringToHash("Base Layer.Idle_Extend");
}
```

7. To make use of all of these IDs, we turn to our very good friend—the `Update` function. At the beginning of the function, we use the `GetCurrentAnimatorStateInfo` function to figure out which state is the current one. We send it a zero because it wants to know the index of the layer we are inquiring about, of which we only have the one. The function returns an object with the info about the current state, and we grab the `nameHash` value (also known as the ID value) of this state right away and set our variable to it.

```
public void Update() {
   int currentStateId = animator.GetCurrentAnimatorStateInfo(0).
nameHash;
```

8. The next line of code is a comparison with our idle state IDs to figure out if we are in one of those states. If we are, we call upon the SubtractTime function (which we will write in a moment) to reduce the time parameter.

```
if(currentStateId == idleRetractId || currentStateId ==
idleExtendId) {
   SubtractTime();
}
```

9. If the target is not currently in one of its idle states, we start by checking to see if we were hit. If so, the hit is cleared using the ClearHit function and the time parameter is reset using the ResetTime function. Both functions will also be written in a moment. Finally, we check to see if our timer had dropped below zero. If that is the case, we again reset the timer.

```
else {
   if(animator.GetBool(wasHitId)) {
      ClearHit();
      ResetTime();
   }

   if(animator.GetFloat(timeId) < 0) {
      ResetTime();
   }
}
}
```

10. In the SubtractTime function we use the GetFloat function of our Animator component to retrieve the value of a float parameter. By sending it our timeId variable, we can receive the current value of the time parameter. Like we did with the tank, we then use Time.deltaTime to keep in pace with our frame rate and subtract time from the timer. Once done, we need to give the state machine the new value, which is done with the SetFloat function. We tell it which parameter to change by giving it an ID value, and we tell it what to change it to by giving it our new time value.

```
public void SubtractTime() {
   float curTime = animator.GetFloat(timeId);
   curTime -= Time.deltaTime;
   animator.SetFloat(timeId, curTime);
}
```

11. The next function to create is ClearHit. This function uses SetBool from the Animator component to set Boolean parameters. It functions just as the SetFloat function. We just give it an ID and a value. In this case, we are setting both of our Boolean parameters to false so that the state machine no longer thinks it has been hit.

```
public void ClearHit() {
  animator.SetBool(wasHitId, false);
  animator.SetBool(inTheFrontId, false);
}
```

12. The last function for the script is `ResetTime`. This is another quick function. First, we use the `Random.Range` function to get a random value. By passing it a minimum and maximum value, our new random number will be between them. Finally we use the `SetFloat` function to give the state machine the new value.

```
public void ResetTime() {
  float newTime = Random.Range(minIdleTime, maxIdleTime);
  animator.SetFloat(timeId, newTime);
}
```

What just happened?

We created a script to control the state machine of our target. For comparing states and setting parameters, we gathered and used IDs. For now, do not worry about when the hit states are activated. It will be made clear in the following section when we finally make the tank shoot.

Creating the prefab

Now that we have the model, animations, state machine, and script, finally it is time to create the target and turn it into a prefab.

Time for action – creating the target

We have all the pieces; the next step is to put them together.

1. Start by dragging the **Target** model from the **Project** window to the **Hierarchy** window. This creates a new instance of the `target` object.

2. By selecting the new `target` object, we can see that it already has an `Animator` component attached; we just need to add a reference to `AnimatorController` that we created. Do this by dragging `TargetController` from the **Project** window and dropping it on the Animator component's **Controller** field, just as with all the other object references we have set up so far.

3. Also, we need to add the `Target` script to the object and connect a reference to the `Animator` component in its relevant field.

4. The last thing to do to the target object is to add a collider to actually receive our cannon shots. Unfortunately, because the `target` object uses bones and a rig to animate, it is not as simple as adding a collider directly to the mesh we will be shooting at. Instead, we need to create a new empty `GameObject`.

5. Rename it `TargetCollider`, and make it a child of the target's `Bone_Target` bone.

6. Add a `MeshCollider` component to the new `GameObject`.

7. Now, we need to provide it with some mesh data. Find the `Target` mesh data in the **Project** window, underneath the **Target** model. Drag it to the **Mesh** value of the `MeshCollider` component. This causes a green cylinder to appear in the **Scene** view. This is our collision, but it is actually not on the target.

 The many objects in the **Project** window can be easily told apart by the little symbol that sits next to each. The symbol for a mesh is a gray and blue grid.

8. Use the **Transform** component to set the GameObject's position to 4 for the **X** value and 0 for both **Y** and **Z**. The rotation needs to be changed to 0 for **X**, -90 for **Y** and 90 for **Z**.

9. As we made the changes, you probably noticed that the font of everything that was new or changed became bold. This is to indicate that something is different with this prefab instance when compared to the original. Remember, models are essentially prefabs; their problem is that we cannot directly make changes such as adding scripts. To make this target into a new prefab, simply drag it from the **Hierarchy** window and drop it on the `Prefabs` folder in the **Project** window.

10. With this spiffy new prefab created, populate the city with it.

11. In placing all of these targets, you probably noticed that they are a little large. Instead of editing each target individually or even all of them as a group, we only have to make a change to the original prefab. Select the `Target` prefab in the **Project** window. The **Inspector** window displays the same information for a root prefab object as it does for any other object in the scene. With our prefab selected, half the scale and all of the instances already in the scene will automatically be updated to match. We can also make changes to the min and max idle times and have it affect the whole scene.

What just happened?

We just finished creating the targets for our tank. By making use of Unity's prefab system, we are also able to duplicate the target throughout our game and easily make changes that affect them all.

If you wanted one of the targets to be larger than all of the others, you could change it in the scene. Any changes made to a prefab instance are saved, and they take precedence over changes made to the root prefab object. Also, when looking at an instance in the **Inspector** window, there will be three new buttons at the top of the window. The **Select** button selects the root prefab object in the **Project** window. **Revert** will remove any unique changes made to this instance, whereas the **Apply** button updates the root object with all the changes that were made in this instance.

Have a go hero – more targets

Using all that you have learned about animations and state machines, your challenge here is to create a second type of target. Play around with different movements and behaviors. Perhaps, create one that transitions from waving around to standing still.

Ray tracing to shoot

Play the game now; it is pretty cool. We have our drivable tank and textured city. We even have fancy animated targets. We are just missing one thing: how do we shoot? We need to make one more script and we can shoot targets to our heart's content.

Time for action – simple shooting

With the addition of one more object and a single script, we can start shooting at our targets.

1. First, we need to add an empty `GameObject` to our tank. Rename it to `MuzzlePoint` and make it a child of the cannon's pivot point object. Once done, position it at the end of the cannon so the blue arrow points away from the tank, along the same direction as the cannon. This will be the point where our bullets will come from.

2. We also need something to indicate where we are shooting. The explosions are covered in future chapters, so choose **Sphere** from the **Create Other** menu and rename it `TargetPoint`.

3. Set the sphere's scale to `0.2` for each axis and give it a red material. This way it can be more easily seen, without being completely obtrusive.

4. Remove the `SphereCollider` component from `TargetPoint`. The `SphereCollider` has to be removed because we don't want to shoot our own target indicator.

5. Now, create a new script and call it `FireControls`.

6. This should start to look familiar to you. We start with variables to hold references to our muzzle and targeting objects that we just created. They are followed by an `OnGUI` function that draws a button in the bottom-right corner of the screen, just above where we drew the turret control buttons. If the button is pressed, we call upon the `Fire` function that we will create next.

```
public Transform muzzlePoint;
public Transform targetPoint;

public void OnGUI() {
  Rect fire = new Rect(Screen.width - 70, Screen.height - 220, 50,
50);
  if(GUI.Button(fire, "Fire")) {
    Fire();
  }
}
```

7. The `Fire` function starts by defining a variable that will hold the detailed information about what was shot. It is followed by an `if` statement that checks the `Physics.Raycast` function. The `Raycast` function works just like shooting a gun. We start with a position (the muzzle point's position) pointing in a specific direction (forward relative to the muzzle point) and get out what was hit. If we hit something, the `if` statement evaluates to true; otherwise it is false and we would skip ahead. When we do hit something, we first move our target point to the point that was hit. We then use the `SendMessage` function to tell what we hit that it was hit. The `SendMessage` function is only available for `GameObjects` and `MonoBehaviours`, and our `Target` script is on the root object for the target, hence the `hit.transform.root.gameObject` in order to get at the `GameObject` that was hit. The `SendMessage` function takes the name of a function and tries to find it on the `GameObject` to which the message was sent. We are also providing it with a value, `hit.point`, to give to the function that should be found. The `SendMessageOptions.DontRequireReceiver` part of the line keeps the function from throwing an error if it is unable to find the desired function. The last part of our `Fire` function occurs if we didn't hit anything. We send our target point back to the world origin, so the player can tell that they missed everything.

```
public void Fire() {
  RaycastHit hit;
  if(Physics.Raycast(muzzlePoint.position, muzzlePoint.forward,
out hit)) {
    targetPoint.position = hit.point;
    hit.transform.root.gameObject.SendMessage("Hit", hit.point,
SendMessageOptions.DontRequireReceiver);
  }
```

```
      else {
        targetPoint.position = Vector3.zero;
      }
    }
```

8. The last thing to do is to add the `Hit` function to the end of our `Target` script. We start the function by getting the current state ID, just as we did earlier in the script. However, this time we check only against our extended idle ID. If they do not match, we use return to exit the function early. We do this because we don't want to let the player shoot any targets that are down or in mid transition. If our state is correct, we continue by telling the animation that we were hit using the `SetBool` function.

```
public void Hit(Vector3 point) {
  int currentStateId = animator.GetCurrentAnimatorStateInfo(0).
nameHash;
  if(currentStateId != idleExtendId) return;
  animator.SetBool(wasHitId, true);
```

9. The rest of the `Hit` function figures out which side the target was hit on. To do this, we first had to convert the point that we received from world space into local space. The `InverseTransformPoint` function from our **Transform** component does this nicely. We then do a check to see where the shot came from. Because of the way the target is constructed, if the shot was positive on the x axis, it came from behind. Otherwise, it came from the front. Either way, we set the `inTheFront` parameter from our state machine to the proper value. Then we give the player some points by incrementing the static variable that we created on our `ScoreCounter` script, way back at the beginning of the chapter.

```
Vector3 localPoint = transform.InverseTransformPoint(point);
  if(localPoint.x > 0) {
    animator.SetBool(inTheFrontId, false);
    ScoreCounter.score += 5;
  }
  else {
    animator.SetBool(inTheFrontId, true);
    ScoreCounter.score += 10;
  }
}
```

10. Finally, be sure to add the new `FireControls` script to the tank. Also, you need to connect the references to the `MuzzelPoint` and `TargetPoint` objects.

What just happened?

We created a script that allows us to fire the cannon of our tank. The method of using ray tracing is the simplest and most widely used. In general, bullets fly too fast for us to see them. Ray tracing is like this, that is; it is instant. However, this method does not take gravity, or anything else that might change the direction of a bullet, into account.

Have a go hero – better GUI

Now that all of the buttons and components are in place, make them look better. Use the skills you gained from the previous chapter to style the GUI and make it great. Perhaps you could even manage to create a directional pad for the movement.

Summary

And, that is it! The chapter was long and we learned a lot. We imported meshes and set up a tank. We created materials so that color could be added to a city. We also animated some targets and learned how to shoot them down. It was a lot and it is time for a break. Play the game, shoot some targets, and gather those points. The project is all done and ready to be built to your device of choice. The build process is the same as both of the previous projects, so have fun!

The next chapter is about special camera effects and lighting. We will be learning about lights and their types. Our Tank Battle game will expand through the addition of a skybox and several lights. We will also take a look at distance fog. With the addition of shadows and lightmaps, the city we will battle in really starts to become interesting and dynamic.

4
Setting the Stage – Camera Effects and Lighting

In the previous chapter, you learned about the basic building blocks of any game: meshes, materials, and animations. We created a Tank Battle game that utilized all of these blocks.

In this chapter, we will expand upon the Tank Battle game. We will start with the addition of a skybox and distance fog. The exploration of camera effects continues with a target indicator overlay that uses a second camera. The creation of a turbo boost effect for the tank will round out our look at camera effects. Continuing with a look at lighting, we will finish off our tank environment with the addition of lightmaps and shadows.

In this chapter, we will cover the following topics:

- ◆ Skyboxes
- ◆ Distance fog
- ◆ Using multiple cameras
- ◆ Adjusting the field of view
- ◆ Adding lights
- ◆ Creating lightmaps
- ◆ Adding cookies

We will be directly piggybacking off the project from *Chapter 3, The Backbone of Any Game – Meshes, Materials, and Animation*. So, open it in Unity and we will get started.

The camera effects

There are many great camera effects that you should add to give your game the last great finishing touch. In this chapter, we will be covering a few options that are easy to add. These will also give our tank game a great finished look.

Skyboxes and distance fog

When a camera renders a frame of a game, it starts by clearing the screen. By default, cameras in Unity do this by coloring everything in solid blue. All of the game's meshes are then drawn on top of this blank screen. Blue is rather boring for an exciting battle of tanks. So, lucky for us, Unity allows us to change the color. But, pink is not better than blue, so we have to change the method of clearing the screen. This is where the skybox comes in. A skybox is just a fancy word for the series of images that form the background sky of any game. Distance fog works in conjunction with the skybox by easing the visual transition between models and background.

Time for action – adding a skybox and distance fog

The very first thing we need is a skybox, obviously. We could create our own; however, Unity provides us with several excellent ones that will fit our needs just fine.

1. At the top of the Unity Editor, select **Assets** followed by **Import Package**. About half way down this list, select **Skyboxes**.

2. After a little bit of processing, a new window will pop up. A package in Unity is just a compressed group of assets that have already been set up in Unity. This window displays the contents and allows us to selectively import them. We want them all, so just click on **Import** in the bottom-right corner of this window.

3. A new folder, Standard Assets, will be added to the **Project** window. This contains a folder, Skyboxes, which contains various skybox materials. Select any one of these. You can see in the **Inspector** window that they are normal materials that make use of the Skybox shader. They each have six images, one for each direction.

4. To add the skybox of your choice to the game, first make sure you have the correct scene loaded. If you do not, simply double-click on it in the **Inspector** window. This is necessary because the settings we are about to change are specific to each scene.

5. Go to the top of the Unity Editor and select **Edit**, followed by **Render Settings**. The new group of settings will appear in the **Inspector** window.

6. At the moment we are concerned with the value that is fifth from the bottom, **Skybox Material**. Just drag-and-drop the skybox material into the **Skybox Material** slot and it will be automatically updated. The change can be viewed in the **Game** window.

7. To add distance fog, we also adjust it in **Render Settings**. To turn it on, simply click on the **Fog** checkbox.

8. The next setting, **Fog Color**, allows us to pick a color for the fog. It is good to pick a color that is close to the general color of the skybox.

9. **Fog Mode** is a drop-down list of options that dictate the method Unity will use to calculate the distance fog. For nearly all cases, the default of **Exp2** is suitable.

10. The next three settings, **Fog Density**, **Linear Fog Start**, and **Linear Fog End**, all determine how much fog there is and how close it starts. **Fog Density** is used for the **Exponential** and **Exp2** fog modes while the others are used for the **Linear** fog mode. Settings that put the fog at the edge of sight are generally good.

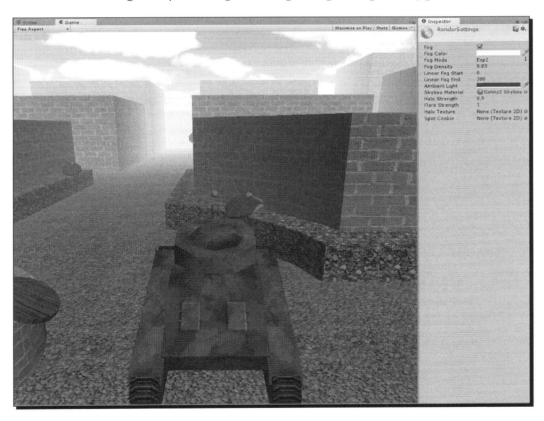

What just happened?

We imported several skyboxes and added them to the scene. The distance fog settings were also turned on and adjusted. Now, our scene has started to look like a real game.

Target indicator

Another camera effect that is rather interesting is the use of multiple cameras. A second camera could be used for making a 3D GUI, a minimap, or perhaps a security camera pop-up. In this next section, we will be creating a system that will point at targets that are nearby. Using a second camera, we will make it appear above the player's tank.

Time for action – creating the pointer

We are going to start by creating an object that will point at targets. We will be making a prefab that can be used repeatedly. However, you will need a model for the player to see. We will use a pie-slice type mesh. The size isn't particularly important; we will be adjusting the scale later. Let's perform the following steps to create the pointer:

1. Once you have created and imported your mesh, add it to the scene.

2. Create an empty `GameObject` and rename it to `IndicatorSlice`.

3. Make your mesh a child of `IndicatorSlice` and position it so that it points along the GameObject's z axis. `IndicatorSlice` will be centered in our indicator. Each slice that is created will have its z axis pointing in the direction of a target.

4. Now, we need to create a new script that will control our indicator. Create a new script called **TargetIndicator** in the **Project** window.

5. We start this script off with a pair of variables. The first will hold a reference to the target that this indicator piece will point at. The indicator is also going to grow and shrink based on how far away the target is. The second variable will control the distance at which the indicator will start to grow.

```
public Transform target;
public float range = 25;
```

6. The next function will be used to set the `target` variable when the indicator piece is created.

```
public void SetTarget(Transform newTarget) {
   target = newTarget;
}
```

7. The last set of code goes in the `LateUpdate` function. The `LateUpdate` function is used so the indicator pieces can point at a target after our tank moves in the `Update` function. We start the function with a check to make sure the target variable has a value. If it is null, the indicator slice is destroyed. The `Destroy` function can be used to remove any object that exists from the game. The `gameObject` variable is automatically provided by the `MonoBehaviour` class and holds a reference to the `GameObject` that the script component is attached to. Destroying it will also destroy everything that is a child of (or attached to) it.

```
public void LateUpdate() {
   if(target == null) {
     Destroy(gameObject);
     return;
   }
```

8. The next bit of code sets the scale of the indicator slice. As you can see in the following code snippet, the first line of code uses `Vector3.Distance` to determine how far the two positions are from each other. The next code line determines the vertical scale, y axis, of the slice. It does so by using a bit of carefully applied math and the `Mathf.Clamp01` function. This function limits the supplied value to be between zero and one. The last line of code sets the indicator slice's local scale. By adjusting the local scale, we can easily control how big the whole indicator is by just changing the scale of the parent object.

```
float distance = Vector3.Distance(transform.position, target.
position);
float yScale = Mathf.Clamp01((range - distance) / range);
transform.localScale = new Vector3(1, yScale, 1);
```

9. One last set of code for this script. The `transform.LookAt` function is just a fancy, automatic way of rotating a `GameObject` so its z axis points to a specific spot in the world. However, we want all of the indicator slices to lay flat on the ground and not pointing into the air at any targets that might be above us. So, we collect the target's position. By setting the variable's Y value to the position of the slice, we ensure that the slice remains flat. That last line, of course, closes off the `LateUpdate` function.

```
Vector3 lookAt = target.position;
lookAt.y = transform.position.y;
transform.LookAt(lookAt);
}
```

10. That is the last code for this script. Return to Unity and add the `TargetIndicator` script to the `IndicatorSlice` object in the scene.

11. To finish off the indicator, create a prefab of it.

12. Lastly, delete the `IndicatorSlice` object from the scene. We will be creating slices dynamically when the game starts. That requires the prefab, but not the one in the scene.

What just happened?

We created a prefab of the object we will be using to indicate the direction of targets. The script that was created and attached will rotate each instance of the prefab to point at the target. It will also adjust the scale to indicate how far the target is from the player.

Time for action – controlling the indicator

We now need to create a script that will control the indicator slices. This will include creating new slices as they are needed. Also, the `GameObject` it is attached to will act as a center point for the indicator slices, that we just created, to rotate around.

1. Create a new script and name it `IndicatorControl`.

2. We start this script off with a pair of variables. The first will hold a reference to the prefab that was just created. This will allow us to spawn instances of it whenever we desire. The second is a static variable, meaning it can be easily accessed without a reference to the component that exists in the scene. It will be filled when the game starts with a reference to the instance of this script that is in the scene.

```
public GameObject indicatorPrefab;
private static IndicatorControl control;
```

3. This next function will be used by the targets. Soon, we will be updating the target's script to call this function at the beginning of the game. The function is static, just like the variable, and starts by checking to see whether there is a reference to any object in it. If it is empty, equal to null, `Object.FindObjectOfType` is used to attempt to fill the variable. By telling it what type of object we want to find, it will search in the game and try to find one. This is relatively a slow process and should not be used often, but we use this process and the variable so that we can always be sure that the system can find the script. The second part of the `CreateSlice` function checks to make sure our static variable is not empty. If so, it then tells the instance to create a new indicator slice and passes it to the target.

```
public static void CreateSlice(Transform target) {
  if(control == null) {
    control = Object.FindObjectOfType(typeof(IndicatorControl))
as IndicatorControl;
  }

  if(control != null) {
    control.NewSlice(target);
  }
}
```

4. One more function for this script. The `NewSlice` function does as its name implies, it creates new indicator slices when called. It does this by first using the `Instantiate` function to create a copy of the `GameObject` that is passed to it. The second line of the function makes the new slice a child of the control's transform. The next line just zeroes out the local position of the new slice. This way it will be centered properly after it is created. The last line uses the slice's `SendMessage` function to call the `SetTarget` function that we created previously and passes it the desired target object.

```
public void NewSlice(Transform target) {
  GameObject slice = Instantiate(indicatorPrefab) as GameObject;
  slice.transform.parent = transform;
  slice.transform.localPosition = Vector3.zero;
  slice.SendMessage("SetTarget", target);
}
```

5. Now that the script is created, we need to use it. Create an empty `GameObject` and name it `IndicatorControl`.

6. The new `GameObject` needs to be made a child of your tank, followed by having its position set to zero on each axis.

7. Add the script we just created to `IndicatorControl`.

8. Finally, with the `GameObject` selected, add the reference to the `IndicatorSlice` prefab. Do this by dragging the prefab from the **Project** window to the proper slot in the **Inspector** window.

What just happened?

We created a script that will control the spawning of our target indicator slices. The `GameObject` we created at the end will also allow us to control the size of the whole indicator with ease. We are almost done with the target indicator.

Time for action – working with a second camera

If you were to play the game now, it would still look no different. This is because the targets do not yet make the call to create the indicator slices. We will also be adding that second camera in this section as we finish off the target indicator.

1. Start by opening the `Target` script and adding the following line of code to the end of the `Awake` function. This line tells the `IndicatorControl` script to create a new indicator slice for this target.

    ```
    IndicatorControl.CreateSlice(transform);
    ```

2. On playing the game now, you can see the indicator in action. However, it is probably too large and certainly appears inside the tank. A bad solution would be to move the `IndicatorControl` object until the whole thing appears above the tank. However, when explosions occur and things start flying through the air, they will obscure the target indicator all over again. A better solution is to add a second camera. Do so now by selecting **GameObject** from the top of the Unity Editor, followed by **Create Other**, and finally **Camera**.

3. Additionally, make the camera a child of `Main Camera`. Be sure to set the new camera's position and rotation values to zero.

4. By default, every camera in Unity is given a variety of components: **Camera**, **Flare Layer**, **GUI Layer**, and **Audio Listener**. Besides the **Camera** component, the others are generally unimportant to every other camera, and there should only be one **Audio Listener** component in the whole of the scene. Remove the excess components from the camera, leaving just the **Camera** component.

5. Before we do anything else with the camera, we need to change the layer that the `IndicatorSlice` prefab is on. Layers are used to cause selective interaction between objects. They are used primarily for physics and rendering. First select the prefab in the **Project** window.

6. At the top of the **Inspector** window is the **Layer** label with a drop-down list that reads **Default**. Click on the drop-down list and select **Add Layer...** from the list.

7. A list of layers will now appear in the **Inspector** window. These are all the layers used in the game. The first few are reserved for use by Unity; hence, they are grayed out. The rest are for our use. Click on the right-hand side of **User Layer 8** and name it **Indicator**.

8. Select the `IndicatorSlice` prefab again. This time select the new **Indicator** layer from the **Layer** drop-down list.

9. Unity will ask if we want to change the layer of all the child objects as well. We would want the whole object rendered on this layer, so select **Yes, change children** and we will be able to do so.

10. Now, back to our second camera. Select it and take a look in the **Inspector** window.

11. The first attribute of the **Camera** component is **Clear Flags**. This list of options dictate what the camera will fill the background with before drawing all of the models in the game. The second camera does not block out everything drawn by the first camera. We select **Depth only** from the **Clear Flags** drop-down list. This means that, instead of putting the skybox in the background, it will leave what was already rendered and just draw new things on top.

12. The next attribute, **Culling Mask**, controls which layers are rendered by the camera. The first two options, **Nothing** and **Everything**, are for deselection and quick selection of all of the layers. For this camera, deselect all other layers, so that only the **Indicator** layer has a check next to it.

13. The last thing to do is to adjust the scale of IndicatorControl so that the target indicator is not too large or small.

What just happened?

We created a system to indicate the direction of potential targets. To do this, we used a second camera. By adjusting the layers in the **Culling Mask** attribute, we can make a camera render only a part of a scene. Also, by changing the **Clear Flags** attribute to **Depth only**, the second camera can draw on top of what was drawn by the first camera.

Have a go hero – adjusting the position

It is possible to change where the indicator is drawn by moving the camera. If you were to instead move the `IndicatorControl` object, it will change how the distance from and direction to targets are calculated. Move and angle the second camera so that there is a more pleasing view of the target indicator.

When you were moving the second camera or when you use the boost from the next section, you probably noticed that the target indicator can still be seen in the tank. Adjust the main camera so that it does not render the target indicator. This is done very similarly to how we made the second camera only render the target indicator.

Turbo boost

The last camera effect we will be looking at in this chapter is a turbo boost. It is going to be a button on the screen that will propel the player forward rapidly for a short amount of time. The camera effect comes in because a simple adjustment to the **Field of View** attribute can make it look as if we are going much faster. A similar method is used by movies to make the car chases look even faster.

Time for action – using the boost effect

We will only be making a single script in this section. It will move the tank in a similar manner to the `ChassisControls` script we created in the last chapter. The difference is, we won't have to hold down a button for the boost to work. Let's get to it.

1. Start by creating a new script and calling it `TurboBoost`.

2. To start the script off, we need four variables. The first is a reference to `CharacterController`. We need this for movement. The second is how fast we will be moving while boosting. The third is how long, in seconds, we will be boosting. The last is used internally for whether or not we can boost and when we should stop.

    ```
    public CharacterController controller;
    public float boostSpeed = 50;
    public float boostLength = 5;
    public float startTime = -1;
    ```

3. The next bit of code returns to our good friend, the OnGUI function. Here we are just drawing a button on the screen, the same as we did several times before. If the button is pressed, it calls the StartBoost function that we will be writing in a moment.

```
public void OnGUI() {
    Rect turboRect = new Rect(10, Screen.height - 220, 75, 75);
    if(GUI.Button(turboRect, "Turbo"))
        StartBoost();
}
```

4. The StartBoost function is pretty simple. It checks to see if the startTime variable is less than zero. If it is, the variable is set to the current time as provided by Time.time. Being less than zero means that we are not currently boosting.

```
public void StartBoost() {
    if(startTime < 0)
        startTime = Time.time;
}
```

5. The last function we are going to use is the Update function. It begins with a check of startTime to see if we are currently boosting. If we are not boosting, the function is exited early. The next line of code checks to make sure we have our CharacterController reference. If the variable is empty, then we can't make the tank move.

```
public void Update() {
    if(startTime < 0) return;
    if(controller == null) return;
```

6. The next line of code should look familiar. This is the line that makes the tank move.

```
controller.Move(controller.transform.forward * boostSpeed * Time.
deltaTime);
```

7. The following few lines of code actually apply the camera effect. First is a check to see whether we are in the first half-second of the boost. If we are, we transition the camera by adjusting the fieldOfView value. The Camera.main value is just a reference provided by Unity to the main camera used in the scene. The Mathf. Lerp function takes a starting value and moves it towards a goal value based on a third value between zero and one. Using this, the camera's fieldOfView is moved towards our goal over the half-second. The second half of this set of code checks for the last half-second of our boost and uses the same method to transition the fieldOfView value back to the default.

```
if(Time.time - startTime < 0.5f)
    Camera.main.fieldOfView = Mathf.Lerp(Camera.main.fieldOfView,
130, (Time.time - startTime) * 2);
```

```
else if(Time.time - startTime > boostLength - 0.5f)
   Camera.main.fieldOfView = Mathf.Lerp(Camera.main.fieldOfView,
60, (Time.time - startTime - boostLength + 0.5f) * 2);
```

8. The last bit of code checks to see whether we are done boosting. If so, `startTime` is set to negative one to indicate that we can start another boost. That last curly brace, of course, closes off the `Update` function.

```
if(Time.time > startTime + boostLength)
   startTime = -1;
}
```

9. We are almost done. Add the script to your tank and connect the `CharacterController` reference.

10. Try it out.

What just happened?

We created a turbo boost. The same method of movement used in the last chapter moves the tank here. By adjusting the **Field of View** attribute of the camera, we make it look like the tank is moving even faster.

Have a go hero – styling and control

The easy and obvious challenge here is to style the button. To spice it up, try changing it so there is a label while boosting and a button when not boosting. The label and button could each have their own style.

Another thing you might notice while playing the game is that you can still turn while boosting. Try adding a check to the `ChassisControls` script to lock the controls, if we are boosting. You are going to need to add a reference to the `TurboBoost` script.

For an added, extra challenge try adding a cooldown to the boost. Make it so the player can't constantly use the boost. Also, try canceling the boost if the tank runs into something. This is a big one, so you will start off with a hint: take a look at `OnControllerColliderHit`.

Lights

Unity provides a variety of light types for brightening the game world. They are **Directional Light**, **Spotlight**, **Point Light**, and **Area Light**. Each of them projects light in a different way and are explained in detail as follows:

- **Directional Light**: This functions very much like the sun. It projects all of its light in a single direction. The position of the light does not matter, only the rotation. Light is projected over the entirety of the scene in one direction. This makes it perfect for initially adding light to a scene.

- **Spotlight**: This functions just like the ones on a stage. Light is projected in a cone-like shape in a specific direction. Because of this, it is also the most complex light type for the system to calculate. Unity has made significant improvements in how it calculates lights, but overuse of these lights should be avoided.

- **Point Light**: This is the primary light type that will be used in your games. It emits light in every direction. This functions just like a light bulb.

- **Area Light**: This is a special-use light. It emits light in a single direction from a plane. Think of it as the big neon sign used to advertise a hotel or restaurant. Because of their complexity, these lights can only be used when baking shadows. There are too many calculations for them to be used when the game is running.

The next obvious question when talking about lights concerns shadows, especially real-time shadows. While real-time shadows add a lot to a scene and are technically possible on any platform, they are very expensive. On top of that, they are a Unity Pro feature. All in all, that makes them a bit too much for your average mobile game.

On the other hand, there are perfectly viable alternatives that do not cost nearly as much and often look more realistic than real-time shadows. The first is for your environment. In general, the environment in a game never moves and never changes within a specific scene. For this, we have lightmaps. They are extra textures that contain shadow data. Using Unity you can create these textures while making your game. Then, when the game is running, they are automatically applied and your shadows appear. This however does not work for dynamic objects (anything that moves).

For dynamic objects we have cookies. These are not your grandmother's cookies. In lighting, a cookie is a black and white image that is projected onto meshes in the game. This is similar to shadow puppets. The shadow puppets use a cutout to block a part of the light, whereas cookies use black and white images to tell the light where it can cast its light.

Cookies can also be used to create other nice effects, both static and dynamic, such as cloud cover that pans across the scene. Perhaps light projecting out from a cage. Or, you could use them for making the uneven focus point of a flashlight.

Time for action – adding more lights

Adding additional lights to the scene is rather simple. Also, as long as one sticks to point lights, the cost to render them stays low.

1. At the top of the Unity Editor, select **GameObject**, followed by **Create Other**, and lastly **Point Light**.

2. With the new light selected, there are a few attributes that we are concerned about in the **Inspector** window.

   - **Range**: This is how far light will be emitted from the object. The light emitted from this point is brightest at the center and fades to nothing as it reaches the extent of the range. The range is additionally represented as a yellow wire sphere in the **Scene** view.

   - **Color**: This is simply the color of the light. By default, it is white; however, any color can be used here. This setting is shared between all light types.

   - **Intensity**: This is the brightness of the light. The greater the intensity of the light, the brighter the light will be at its center. This setting is also shared between all light types.

3. Create and position several more lights, arranging them along the streets to add some more interest to the environment.

4. Using *Ctrl + D* will duplicate the selected object. This can greatly speed up the creation process.

5. While adding these lights, you probably noticed one of their major drawbacks. There is a limit to how many lights will affect a surface in real time. It is possible to somewhat get around this by using more complex meshes. The better option is to use lightmaps, which we'll be seeing in the next section.

6. At the top of the Unity Editor again, select **GameObject**, followed by **Create Other**, and this time select **Spotlight**.

7. Again, select the new light and take a look at it in the **Inspector** window.

    ❑   **Spot Angle**: This is unique to this type of light. It dictates how wide a cone the light emits. Together with **Range**, it is represented by a yellow wire cone in the **Scene** view.

8. Add a few spotlights around the fountain in the center of our tank battle city.

9. Having so many objects in a scene starts to clutter the **Hierarchy** window, making it hard to find anything. To organize it, you can use empty GameObjects. Create one and name it PointLights.

10. By making all of your point lights children of this empty GameObject, the **Hierarchy** window becomes significantly less cluttered.

What just happened?

We added several lights to the game. By changing the lights of the colors, we make the scene much more interesting to look at and play in. However, a drawback of the lighting system is revealed. The city we are using is very simple and there is a limit to the number of lights that can affect a plane at one time. While the look of our scene is still improved, much of the impressiveness is stolen by this drawback.

Lightmaps

Lightmaps are great for complex lighting setups that would be too expensive or simply won't work at runtime. They also allow you to add detailed shadows to your game world without the expense of real-time shadows. However, it will only work for objects that do not move over the course of a game.

Time for action – creating a lightmap

Lightmaps are a great effect for any game environment, but we need to explicitly tell Unity which objects will not move and then use lightmaps.

1. The first thing to do is make our environment meshes static. To do this start by selecting a piece of your city.

2. In the top-right corner of the **Inspector** window to the right of the object name field are a checkbox and a **Static** label. Checking this box will make the object static.

3. Make all of the city's meshes static.

 Instead of selecting each checkbox one by one, if you have any sort of grouping (as we just did for the lights), this step can be completed much faster.

   1. Select the root object of your city, the one that is the parent to all the pieces of our city, the buildings, and streets.

   2. Now go and select the **Static** checkbox.

   3. On the new pop-up, select **Yes, change children** to cause all of the subobjects to become static as well.

4. Any mesh that is either not unwrapped or has UV positions outside the normalized UV space will be skipped when Unity generates a lightmap. In the **Model Import Settings** window, there is an option to have Unity automatically generate lightmap coordinates, **Generate Lightmap**. If you are using `TankBattleCity` for your environment, this option should be turned on now.

5. Go to the top of the Unity Editor and select **Window** followed by **Lightmapping**, near the bottom.

6. Most of your time will be spent on the **Bake** page looking at this window. Select **Bake** at the top of the window to switch to it.

7. **Mode** dictates what types of lightmaps will be rendered by the system. To save on processing speed and file size, select **Single Lightmaps** from the **Mode** drop-down list to the right. This means that only a **Far** set of lightmaps is created rather than both **Near** and **Far**. Using **Dual Lightmaps** also requires special shaders that you won't use most of the time.

8. **Quality** is a set of presets that dictates how good the lightmaps look. **High** is obviously the best and **Low** is the fastest to process. For our purposes, **Low** will look good enough and should be selected.

9. **Resolution** is how much space an object will take up on a single lightmap. To the right of the input field, it reads texels per world unit. A texel is just a fancy type of pixel used for lightmaps. It is the number of pixels a single unit of space in the world will take up on the lightmap. A setting of 30 here will maintain the desired level of quality while making the whole thing run faster.

10. At the bottom of the page is a **Bake Scene** button. Clicking on this button will start the render process. A loading bar will appear in the bottom-right corner of Unity so you can monitor the progress.

    1. If you are still adjusting lights and settings and desire to see what a portion of the game will look like, start by selecting the meshes you wish to see.

    2. Next, click on the little arrow to the right of the **Bake Scene** button.

    3. From the new drop-down list, select **Bake Selected**. This will run an identical process to **Bake Scene**, except it will only be for the selected objects rather than the entire scene.

 Be warned, this process will likely take a while. Especially as the complexity of the environment and the number of lights increases, this will take longer and longer to run. And, unless you have a superior computer, there isn't much you can do in Unity while it is running.

11. If you clicked on the button and realized you made a mistake, don't fret. After **Bake Scene** is selected, the button changes to **Cancel**. At this time it is possible to select it and stop the process from continuing. However, once the textures have been created and Unity starts to import them, there is no stopping it.

12. To the left of **Bake Scene** is **Clear**. This button is the quickest and easiest way to delete and remove all of the lightmaps that are currently being used in the scene. This cannot be undone.

13. In order to add shadows to your buildings, select **Directional Light** in your scene and take a look at the **Inspector** window.

14. From the **Shadow Type** drop-down list, select **Soft Shadows**. This simply turns shadows on for this light. It also turns on real-time shadows for this light, if you are using Unity Pro. The more lights with shadows turned on, the more expensive they become to render.

15. When all of your lights and settings match your desires, select **Bake Scene** and gaze in wonder at the now beautiful scene before you.

What just happened?

We added lightmaps to our game world. The length of time it takes to just process this step makes it difficult to make minor tweaks. However, our lighting has vastly improved with a few clicks. While before the lights were broken by the meshes, we now have smooth patches of color and light.

Have a go hero – reason and speed

When playing a game, there is only one light that people will not question the source of: the Sun. Every other light looks weird if a source cannot be seen. Create a mesh and add it to the game to give the lights you are using a reason. This could be something along the lines of torches, or lamp posts, or even glowing alien goo balls. Whatever they end up being, having them adds that touch of completeness that makes the difference between an alright OK-looking game and a great-looking game.

As a second challenge, take a look at your lightmap's quality. Play with the various quality settings we discussed to see what the differences are. Also, find out how low the resolution can go before you notice any pixelation. Can the settings go even lower when running on the smaller, mobile device screens? Go find out.

Cookies

Cookies are a great way to add interest to the lights in your game. They use a texture to adjust how the light is emitted. This effect can cover a wide range of uses from sparkling crystals to caged industrial lights and, in our case, headlights.

Time for action – applying headlights

By giving our tank headlights, we give the player the ability to control the light in their world. Using cookies, we can make them look more interesting than just circles of light.

1. Start by creating a **Spotlight**.

2. Position the light in front of the tank and pointing away.

3. In the **Inspector** window, increase the value of the **Intensity** attribute to three. This will make our headlights bright like real headlights.

4. Now we need some cookie textures. At the top of the Unity Editor, select **Assets**, followed by **Import Package**, and lastly **Light Cookies**.

5. On the new window, select **Import** and wait for the loading bar to finish.

6. We now have a few options to choose from. Inside the `Standard Assets` folder, a new folder was created, `Light Cookies` that contains the new textures. Drag `Flashlight` from the **Project** window and drop it onto the **Cookie** field on the **Spotlight** in the **Inspector** window. It is as simple as that to add a cookie to a light.

7. To finish it off, duplicate the light for the second headlight and make them both children of the tank. What good is having headlights if they don't come with us?

What just happened?

We created a pair of headlights for our tank using cookies. This is exactly how many other games, especially horror games, create flashlight effects.

Have a go hero – adding a switch

Try making a script that will allow the player to turn the headlights on and off. It should be a simple button that toggles the lights. Take a look at the enabled variable that is supplied as part of the light.

As a simpler challenge, create a lamp that sits on the turret of the tank. Give it a light as well. With this, the player can point a light to where they are shooting and not just in the direction their tank is pointing.

Blob shadow

Blob shadows are a simpler and cheaper method for adding a shadow to a character. They have been around since the dawn of time. A normal shadow is a solid, dark projection of an object onto another surface. The contours of the shadow exactly match the contours of the object. This becomes expensive to calculate when characters start to move around randomly.

A blob shadow is a blot of black texture underneath a character or an object. It usually does not have a clearly definable shape and never matches the contours of the object it is meant to be the shadow of. The blob shadow also, generally, does not change sizes. This makes it significantly easier to calculate, making it the shadow of choice for many generations of video games. That also means it is a better option for our mobile devices where processing speed can quickly become an issue.

Time for action – a tank with a shadow

We are going to add a blob shadow to our tank. Unity has already done the bulk of the work for us; we just need to add it to the tank.

1. We start this one off by importing Unity's blob shadow. Go to the top of the Unity Editor, select **Assets**, **Import Package**, and finally **Projectors**.

2. Select **Import** in the new window and take a look in the **Project** window for a new folder called `Projectors` created under `Standard Assets`.

3. Drag the `Blob Shadow Projector` prefab from the **Project** window to the scene and position it above the tank.

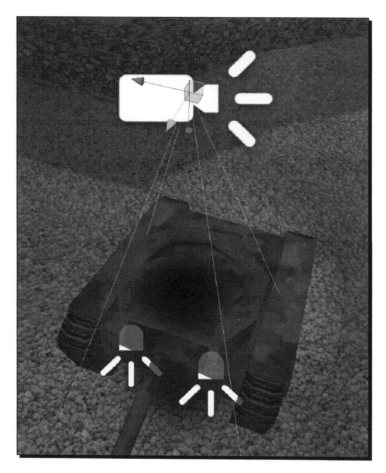

4. Unfortunately, the shadow is appearing on top of our tank. To fix this, we need to again make use of layers. So, select the tank.

5. From the **Layer** drop-down list, select **Add Layer...**.

6. Click on the right-hand side of **User Layer 9** and give it the name `PlayerTank`.

7. Select your tank once more, but select `PlayerTank` from the **Layer** drop-down list this time.

8. When the new window pops up, be sure to select **Yes, change children** to change the layer of the whole tank. If you don't, the blob shadow may appear on some parts of the tank while not on other parts.

9. Now, select `Blob Shadow Projector` from the **Hierarchy** window.

> The blob shadow is created by the **Projector** component.
> This component functions in a similar manner to the **Camera** component. However, it puts an image on the world rather than turning the world into an image and putting it on your screen.

10. Take a look at the **Inspector** window. The value we are concerned with right now is that of **Ignore Layers**. Right now it is set to **Nothing**.

11. Click on **Nothing** and select `PlayerTank` from the **Layers** drop-down list. This will make the projector ignore the tank and only make the blob shadow appear underneath it.

12. The next step is to change the size of the shadow to roughly match the size of the tank. Adjust the value of the **Field of View** attribute until the size is about right. A value of about 70 seems to be a good place to start from.

13. The final step is to make `Blob Shadow Projector` a child of the tank. We need to be able to bring our shadow with us; we don't want to lose it.

What just happened?

We gave our tank a shadow. Shadows are great for making objects, and especially characters, look like they are actually touching the ground. The blob shadow that we used is better than real-time shadows because it is processed faster.

Have a go hero – making it square

The texture that the blob shadow came with is round but our tank is mostly square. Try creating your own texture for the blob shadow and use that. Some sort of rectangle should work well.

If you managed to add your own texture to the blob shadow, then how about taking a look at that cannon? The cannon sticks out of our tank and ruins its otherwise square profile. Use a second blob shadow, attached to the turret, to project a shadow for the cannon. The texture for it will also have to be a rectangle-type shape.

Summary

At this point, you should be well and truly familiar with camera effects and lights.

In this chapter, we started with a look at using multiple cameras. We then played around with a turbo boost camera effect. The chapter continued with the lighting of our city. The lights improved greatly when we made use of lightmaps. We finished it off with a look at cookies and blob shadows for use with some special lighting effects.

In the next chapter, will see the creation of enemies for our game. We will use Unity's pathfinding system to make them move around and chase the player. After this, the player is going to need to be much more active if they hope to keep their points.

5
Getting Around – Pathfinding and AI

In the previous chapter, we learned about camera and lighting effects. We added a skybox, lights, and shadows to our Tank Battle game. We created lightmaps to make our scene dynamic. We took a look at cookies by giving our tank headlights. We also took a look at projectors by creating a blob shadow for the tank. A turbo boost was also created for the tank. By adjusting the viewing angle of the camera, we were able to make the tank look as if it is going much faster than it really is. When we finished, we had a dynamic and exciting-looking scene.

This chapter is all about the enemy. No longer will the player be able to just sit in one place to gather points. We will be adding an enemy tank to the game. By using Unity's NavMesh system, the tank will be able to do pathfinding and chase the player. Once found, the tanks will shoot and reduce the player's score.

In this chapter, we will be covering the following topics:

- NavMesh
- NaveMeshAgent
- Pathfinding
- Chase and attack AI
- Spawn points

We will be adding modifications to the Tank Battle game from *Chapter 4, Setting the Stage – Camera Effects and Lighting*, so open it up and we can begin.

Understanding AI and pathfinding

AI is, as you might have guessed, **artificial intelligence**. In the broadest sense this is anything an inanimate object might do to appear to be making decisions. You are probably most familiar with this concept from video games. When a character, not controlled by the player, selects a weapon to use and a target to use it on, this is AI.

In its most complex form, AI attempts to mimic full human intelligence. However, there is still far too much happening incredibly fast for this to truly succeed. Video games do not need to reach nearly this far. We are primarily concerned with making our characters appear intelligent, but still conquerable by our players. Usually, this means not allowing characters to act on more information than a real player might have. Adjusting how much information characters have and can act on is a good way to adjust the level of difficulty in a game.

Pathfinding is a subset of AI. We use it all the time, though you have probably never realized it. Pathfinding is, as the word suggests, the act of finding a path. Every time you need to find your way between any two points, you are doing pathfinding. As far as our characters are concerned, the simplest form of pathfinding is to follow a straight line to the goal point. Obviously, this method works best on an open plain, but tends to fail when there are any obstacles in the way. Another method is to overlay the game with a grid. Using the grid, we can find a path that goes around any obstacles and reaches our target.

An alternative method of pathfinding, and perhaps the one most often chosen, makes use of a special navigation mesh, or NavMesh. This is just a special model that is never seen by the player but covers all of the area that a computer character can move around in. It is then navigated in a similar way to the grid, the difference being that the triangles of the mesh are used rather than the squares of the grid. This is the method we will be using in Unity. Unity provides a nice set of tools for creating the NavMesh and utilizing it.

The NavMesh

Creating the navigation mesh in Unity is very simple. The process is similar to the one we used for making lightmaps. We just mark some meshes to be used, adjust some settings in a special window, and hit a button. So, load up the Tank Battle game in Unity, if you haven't already done so, and we can get started.

Time for action – creating the NavMesh

Unity can automatically generate a NavMesh from any meshes that exist in a scene. To do so, the mesh must first be marked as static, just as we did for lightmaps. However, we do not want or need to be able to navigate the roofs of our city, so we make use of a special list of settings for dictating what type of static each object will be:

1. Select the city from the **Hierarchy** window and click on the down arrow to the right of **Static** in the **Inspector** window and we can take a look at the options available for static objects as follows:

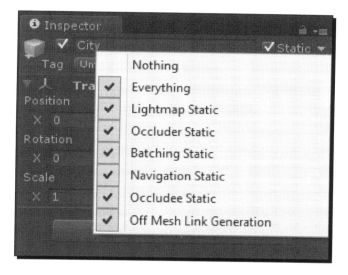

- ❑ **Nothing**: This option is used to quickly deselect all the other options. If all the others are unchecked, this one will be checked.

- ❑ **Everything**: Using this option, you can quickly select all the other options. When all of them are checked, this one will also be checked. The checkbox next to the **Static** label in the **Inspector** window performs the same function as checking and unchecking the **Everything** checkbox.

- ❑ **Lightmap Static**: This option needs to be checked, when working with lightmaps, in order for them to work. Any mesh that does not have this checked will not be lightmapped.

- **Occluder Static**: This is an option for working with occlusion. **Occlusion** is a method of runtime optimization that involves only rendering objects that can actually be seen whether or not they are within the camera's view space. An **Occluder** is an object that will block other objects from being seen. It works in conjunction with the **Occludee Static** option. The best object choices for this option are large and solid.

- **Batching Static**: This is another option for runtime optimization. Batching is the act of grouping objects together before rendering them. It greatly increases the overall render speed of a game.

- **Navigation Static**: This is the option we are primarily concerned with at this point. Any mesh that has this option checked will be used when calculating the NavMesh.

- **Occludee Static**: As mentioned a moment ago, this option works in conjunction with **Occluder Static** for the good of occlusion. An Occludee is an object that will be obscured by other objects. When covered by an Occluder, this object will not be drawn.

- **Off Mesh Link Generation**: This option also works with the NavMesh calculation. An Off Mesh Link is a connection between two parts of the NavMesh that aren't physically connected, such as the roof and the street. Using a few settings in the **Navigation** window and this option, the links are automatically generated.

2. In order to make the NavMesh work properly, we need to change the settings so that only the streets of the city can be navigated. When was the last time you saw a tank jump to or fall from the roof of a building? So, we need to change the **Static** options so that only the streets have **Navigation Static** checked. This can be done in one of the following two ways:

   - The first way is to go through and uncheck the option for each object we want changed.

   - The second is to uncheck **Naviagation Static** for the top-level object in the **Hierarchy** window and, when Unity asks if we want to make the change for all children objects, reply with a yes. Then, go to just the objects that we want to navigate and recheck the option.

3. Now, open the **Navigation** window by going to Unity's toolbar and clicking on **Window** followed by **Navigation** at the bottom of the menu. The following screenshot displays the window where all the work of making the NavMesh happens:

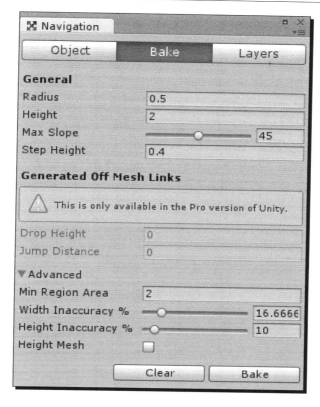

4. This window consists of three pages and a variety of settings:

- When an object is selected, the settings will appear on the **Object** page. The two checkboxes correspond directly with the **Static** options of the same name that we set a moment ago. The drop-down list in **Navigation Layer** lets us use different layers for different parts of our NavMesh. These layers can be used to affect the pathfinding calculation. For example, a car can be set to only travel on a road layer and the human can follow the sidewalk layer.

- The **Bake** page is the one we are interested in; it is full of options to change how the NavMesh is generated.

  Radius: This should be set to the size of the average character. It is used to keep characters from walking too close to the walls.

  Height: This is the height of your characters. Using this, Unity can calculate and remove the areas that are too low for them to pass. Anything lower than this value is deemed too small.

Max Slope: Anything steeper than this value is ignored when calculating NavMesh.

Step Height: When making use of stairs, one must use this value. This is the maximum height of a stair that a character can step on.

Drop Height: This is the height from which characters can fall. With it, paths will include jumping off ledges, if it is faster to do so. As you can tell from the screenshot, this is a Unity Pro-only feature.

Jump Distance: Using this value, characters can jump across gaps in NavMesh. This value represents the longest distance that can be jumped. As you can tell from the screenshot, this is a Unity Pro only feature.

Min Region Area: If parts of the NavMesh are too small, anything smaller than this value, they will not be used in the final NavMesh.

Width Inaccuracy %: When doing the NavMesh calculations, Unity makes use of a number of approximations. This is not entirely accurate, but it is fast. This value represents how much inaccuracy is allowed for the horizontal.

Height Inaccuracy %: This is the same as the previous settings, the difference being that it works for the vertical.

Height Mesh: With this option checked, the original height information is maintained in NavMesh. Unless you have a special need of it, this option should remain off. It takes the system longer to calculate and requires more memory to store.

❑ The third page, **Layers**, allows us to adjust the cost of movement for each of our layers. Essentially, how difficult is it to move through different parts of our game world. With cars, we could adjust the layers, so it is twice as costly for them to move through the field as it is to move along the road.

At the bottom of the window, we have two buttons:

Clear: This button removes the previously created NavMesh. After using this button, you will need to re-bake the NavMesh before you can make use of pathfinding again.

Bake: This button starts the work and creates the NavMesh.

5. Our city is very simple, so the default values will suit us well enough. Hit **Bake** and watch the progress bar in the bottom-right corner. Once it is done, a blue mesh will appear. This is the NavMesh and, of course, represents all of the area that a character can move through.

6. There is one last thing we need to do. Our NavMesh is just right but, if you look closely, it goes through the fountain in the center of the city. It would just be wrong if enemy tanks start driving through the fountain. To fix this, start by selecting the mesh that forms the wall around the fountain.

7. In the toolbar of Unity, click on **Component**, followed by **Navigation**, and finally **NavMeshObstacle**. This simply adds a component that tells the navigation system to go around when finding a path. Because we had the wall already selected, the new component is already sized to fit. You can see it represented as a wire cylinder in the **Scene** view.

What just happened?

We created the NavMesh. We made use of the **Navigation** window and the **Static** options to tell Unity which meshes to use when calculating the NavMesh. The Unity team put a lot of work into making this process quick and easy.

Have a go hero – creating extra obstacles

Remember, in *Chapter 3*, *The Backbone of Any Game – Meshes, Materials, and Animation*, when the challenge was to create obstacles for the player, you were encouraged to create additional meshes, such as tank traps and rubble. It would be a bad idea to let the enemy tanks drive through these, as well. So, have a go at turning these into obstacles for the navigation system. This will be done just as with the fountain.

The NavMeshAgent component

You might be thinking that it is all well and good that we have a NavMesh, but there are no characters to navigate it. In this section, we will start the creation of our enemy tank.

Time for action – creating the enemy

We will need to import and do a little setup on a second tank, before we can do any AI type programming:

1. Select `Tanks_Type03.png` and `Tanks_Type03.blend` from the starting assets for the chapter and import them to the `Tanks` folder under the `Models` folder.

2. Once Unity has finished importing, select the new tank in the **Project** window and take a look at it in the **Inspector** window.

3. This tank has no animations, so the **Animation Type** can be set to **None** and **Import Animation** can be unchecked from the **Rig** and **Animations** pages respectively.

4. Drag the tank from the **Project** window to the **Scene** window; any clear patch of street will work just fine.

5. For starters, rename the model in the **Scene** view to `EnemyTank`.

6. Now, we need to change the parenting of the tank so the turret can turn and the cannon will follow, just as we did for the player's tank. To do that, create an empty **GameObject** and rename it to `TurretPivot`.

7. Position `TurretPivot` to be at the base of the turret.

8. In the **Hierarchy** window, drag-and-drop `TurretPivot` onto `EnemyTank` to make `EnemyTank` the parent.

9. Still in the **Hierarchy** window, make the cannon and turret mesh objects children of `TurretPivot`. When Unity asks whether you are sure that you want to break the prefab connection, be sure to click on **Yes**.

10. The tank is a little large, so adjust the **Scale Factor** of the tank's Import Settings in the **Inspector** window to `0.6` to give us a tank that is about the size of the player's.

11. In order for the tank to be able to navigate our new NavMesh, we need to add a **NavMeshAgent** component. First, select `EnemyTank` in the **Hierarchy** window and then go to the toolbar of Unity; click on **Component**, followed by **Navigation**, and then click on **NavMeshAgent**. In the **Inspector** window, we can see the new component and the settings associated with it, as shown in the following screenshot:

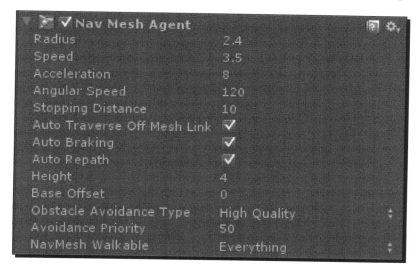

- **Radius**: This is simply how big the agent is. Working in conjunction with the **Radius** value we set in the **Navigation** window, this keeps the object from walking partly in the walls.

- **Speed**: The **NavMeshAgent** component automatically moves the connected object when it has a path. This value dictates how fast to follow the path in units per second.

- **Acceleration**: This is the maximum speed that the agent will accelerate with.

- **Angular Speed**: This is the degrees per second that the agent can turn. A person would have a very high angular speed, while a car's angular speed would be low.

- **Stopping Distance**: This is how far away from the target destination the agent will start to slow down and stop.

- **Auto Traverse Off Mesh Link**: With this checkbox checked, the agent will use the Off Mesh Links when pathfinding, such as jumping gaps and falling off ledges.

- **Auto Braking**: With this checkbox checked, the agent will stop as soon as it reaches the destination, rather than overshooting, because of the irregular frame rate.

- ❑ **Auto Repath**: If the path that was found is incomplete for any reason, this checkbox allows Unity to automatically try to find a new one.

- ❑ **Height**: This setting affects the cylinder that appears in the editor, around the agent. It simply sets the height of that cylinder.

- ❑ **Base Offset**: This is the vertical offset of the colliders that are attached to the agent.

- ❑ **Obstacle Avoidance Type**: This is how much effort the agent will put in to find a smooth path around obstacles. The higher the quality, the more work is done.

- ❑ **Avoidance Priority**: This value dictates who has the right of way. An agent with a high value will go around an agent with a low value.

- ❑ **NavMesh Walkable**: Remember those layers that were mentioned earlier when discussing the **Navigation** window? This is where we can set which layers the agent is able to traverse. Only the layers in this list that are checked will be used for pathfinding.

12. Now that we understand the settings, let's use them. For the enemy tank, a value of 2.4 for the **Radius** and 4 for the **Height** will work well. You should be able to see another wire cylinder in the **Scene** window, this time around our enemy tank.

13. The last thing to do is to turn `EnemyTank` into a prefab. Do this just as we did with the targets, by dragging it from the **Hierarchy** window and dropping it on the `Prefabs` folder in the **Project** window.

What just happened?

We created an enemy tank. We also learned about the settings for the **NavMeshAgent** component. However, if you try to play the game now, nothing will appear to happen. This is because the **NavMeshAgent** component is not being given a destination. We will solve that in the next section.

The chase

Our next task is to make our enemy tank chase the player around. We will need two scripts. The first will simply advertise the player's current position. The second will use that position and the **NavMeshAgent** component that we set up earlier to find a path to the player.

Time for action – the player is over here

With a very short script, we can easily allow all our enemies know the location of the player:

1. Start by creating a new script in the `Scripts` folder of the **Project** window. Name it `PlayerPosition`.

2. This script will start with a single static variable. This variable will simply hold the current position of the player. Because it is static, we will be able to easily access it from the rest of our scripts.

   ```
   public static Vector3 position = Vector3.zero;
   ```

3. For the next lines of code, we make use of the `Start` function. This function is automatically called when a scene is first loaded. We use it so that the `position` variable can be filled and used as soon as the game starts.

   ```
   public void Start() {
     position = transform.position;
   }
   ```

4. The last segment of code simply updates the `position` variable in every frame to the player's current position. We also do this in the `LateUpdate` function so that it is done after the player has moved. The `LateUpdate` function is called at the end of every frame. With that, the player is able to move during the `OnGUI` and `Update` functions and their position is updated later.

   ```
   public void LateUpdate() {
     position = transform.position;
   }
   ```

5. The last thing to do with this script is to add it to the player's tank. So, return to Unity and drag-and-drop the script from the Project window to the tank to add it as a component, just as we have done with all our other scripts.

What just happened?

We created the first script needed for our chase AI. This script simply updates a variable with the player's current position. We will make use of it in our next script, where we will make the enemy tank move around.

Time for action – chasing the player

Our next script will control our simple chase AI. Because we are making use of the **NavMesh** and **NavMeshAgent** components, we can leave nearly all the difficult portions of pathfinding to Unity:

1. Again, create a new script. This time name it `ChasePlayer`.

2. The first line for this script simply holds a reference to the **NavMeshAgent** component that we set up earlier. We need access to this component in order to move the enemy.

   ```
   public NavMeshAgent agent;
   ```

3. The last segment of code first makes sure that we have our **NavMeshAgent** reference and then updates our goal destination. It uses the `PlayerPosition` script's variable, that was set up earlier, and the `SetDestination` function from the **NavMeshAgent**. Once we tell the function where to go, the **NavMeshAgent** component does all the hard work of getting us there. We are updating our goal destination in the `FixedUpdate` function because we do not need to update the destination in every frame. Updating too often could cause a serious lag if there are a whole lot of enemies. The `FixedUpdate` function is called at regular intervals and is slower than the frame rate, so it is perfect.

   ```
   public void FixedUpdate() {
     if(agent == null) return;

     agent.SetDestination(PlayerPosition.position);
   }
   ```

4. We now need to add the script to our enemy tank. Select the `prefab` in the **Project** window, and drag-and-drop the script in the **Inspector** panel, underneath the **NavMeshAgent** component.

5. Be sure to connect the reference, as we have done previously. Drag the **NavMeshAgent** component to the **Agent** value in the **Inspector** window.

6. Play the game now to try it out. Wherever the enemy starts, it finds its way around all the buildings and makes it to the player's position. As you drive around, you can watch the enemy follow. However, the enemy tank ends up going through our tank. Also, we can drive through it.

7. The first step to fixing it is to add some colliders. Add a **Box Collider** component from underneath **Physics** in the **Component** menu to the turret, chassis, and each of the **TreadCase** objects. Neither the cannon nor the treads need colliders. The tread casings already cover the area of the treads, and the cannon is too small a target to be shot at properly.

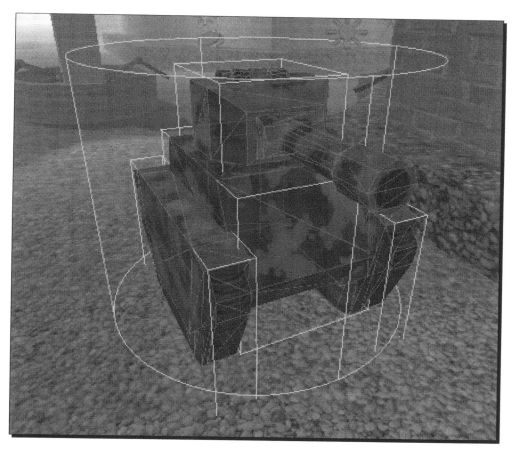

 If you are making any of these changes in the **Scene** view, be sure to click on the **Apply** button in the **Inspector** window to update the root prefab object.

8. The last thing to change is the **Stopping Distance** property on the **NavMeshAgent** component. When the tanks fight, they move into range and start firing. They do not try to occupy the same space as the enemy, unless that enemy is small and squishy. By setting **Stopping Distance** to 10 we are able to replicate this behavior.

What just happened?

In this section, we created a script that causes a **NavMeshAgent** component, in this case our enemy tank, to chase the player. We added colliders to stop us from driving through the enemy. And, we adjusted the **Stopping Distance** to give us a better tank behavior.

Have a go hero – adding shadow

Try adding a blob shadow to the enemy tank. This will give it a better visual sense of being grounded. You can just copy the one that was made for the player's tank.

Being attacked

What fun is a game without a little conflict; the nagging choice, the fight to the death, the doom of the cosmos? Every game needs some form of conflict to drive the player towards seeking a resolution. Our game will become a battle for points. Before, it was just shoot some targets and get some points.

Now, we will make the enemy tank shoot at the player. Every time the enemy scores a hit, we will reduce the player's score by a few points.

Time for action – getting ready to fire

The enemy will shoot in a similar manner to how the player fires, but we will use some basic AI to control the direction and firing speed, replacing the player's input controls:

1. We will start this off with a new script called `ShootAtPlayer`. Create it in the `Scripts` folder.

2. As with all our other scripts, we start this one out with two variables. The first variable will hold the last position the enemy tank was at. It will not be shooting if the tank is in motion, so we need to store that last position to see if we have moved. The second variable will be the maximum speed at which we can move and shoot. If the tank moves faster than this, it will not fire.

   ```
   private Vector3 lastPosition = Vector3.zero;
   public float maxSpeed = 1f;
   ```

3. The next two variables dictate how long it takes the tank to ready a shot. It is unrealistic to be shooting the player in every single frame. So, we use the first variable to adjust the length of time it takes to ready a shot, and the second to store when the shot is ready.

   ```
   public float readyLength = 2f;
   private float readyTime = -1;
   ```

4. The next variable is how fast the turret can rotate. While the tank is readying its shot, the turret will not be rotating to point at the player. That gives the player an opportunity to move out of the way. However, we need a speed to keep the turret from snapping to face the player after shooting.

   ```
   public float turretSpeed = 45f;
   ```

5. The last two variables here hold references to other parts of the tank. The `turretPivot` variable, of course, is the pivot of the turret that we will be rotating. The `muzzlePoint` variable will be used as the point from where our cannon is fired. These will be used in the same manner as the ones for the player's tank.

   ```
   public Transform turretPivot;
   public Transform muzzlePoint;
   ```

6. For the first function of the script, we will make use of the Update function. It starts by calling a function that will check to see whether it is possible to fire the cannon. If we can fire, we perform some checks on our readyTime variable. If it is less than zero, we have not yet begun to ready our shot and call a function to do so. Otherwise, if it is less than the current time, we have finished the preparation and call the function to fire the cannon. If we are unable to fire, we first call a function to clear any preparations and then rotate the turret to face the player.

```
public void Update() {
  if(CheckCanFire()) {
    if(readyTime < 0) {
      PrepareFire();
    }
    else if(readyTime <= Time.time) {
      Fire();
    }
  }
  else {
    ClearFire();
    RotateTurret();
  }
}
```

7. Next, we will create our CheckCanFire function. The first part of code checks to see if we have moved too fast. First, we use Vector3.Distance to see how far we have moved since the last frame. By dividing the distance by the length of the frame, we are able to determine the speed with which we moved. Next, we update our lastPosition variable with our current position, so it is ready for the next frame. Finally, we compare the current speed with the maxSpeed. If we moved too fast in this frame, we are unable to fire and return a result of false.

```
public bool CheckCanFire() {
  float move = Vector3.Distance(lastPosition, transform.position);
  float speed = move / Time.deltaTime;

  lastPosition = transform.position;

  if(speed > maxSpeed) return false;
```

8. For the second half of the `CheckCanFire` function, we check to see if the turret is pointed at the player. First, we find the direction to the player. Given any point in space and subtracting the second point's location from it, will give us the direction from the second point to the first as a vector. We then flatten the direction by setting the y value to 0. This is done because we do not want to be looking up or down at the player. Then, we use `Vector3.Angle` to find the angle between the direction to the player and our turret's forward direction. Finally, we compare the angle to a low value to determine whether we are looking at the player, and return the result.

```
  Vector3 targetDir = PlayerPosition.position - turretPivot.
position;
    targetDir.y = 0;

    float angle = Vector3.Angle(targetDir, turretPivot.forward);

    return angle < 0.1f;
}
```

9. The `PrepareFire` function is quick and easy. It simply sets our `readyTime` variable to the time in the future when the tank will be done preparing its shot.

```
public void PrepareFire() {
    readyTime = Time.time + readyLength;
}
```

10. The `Fire` function starts by making sure that we have a `muzzlePoint` reference to shoot from.

```
public void Fire() {
    if(muzzlePoint == null) return;
```

11. The function continues with the creation of a `RaycastHit` variable to store the result of our shot. We use `Physics.Raycast` and `SendMessage`, just as we did in the `FireControls` script, to shoot at anything and tell it that we hit it.

```
RaycastHit hit;
if(Physics.Raycast(muzzlePoint.position, muzzlePoint.forward, out
hit)) {
    hit.transform.gameObject.SendMessage("RemovePoints", 3,
SendMessageOptions.DontRequireReceiver);
}
```

12. The `Fire` function finishes by clearing the fire preparations.

```
    ClearFire();
}
```

13. The `ClearFire` function is another quick function. It sets our `readyTime` variable to be less than zero, indicating that the tank is not preparing to fire.

```
public void ClearFire() {
   readyTime = -1;
}
```

14. The last function for the script is `RotateTurret`. It begins by checking the `turretPivot` variable and canceling the function should the reference be missing. It is followed by the finding of the flat direction that points at the player, just as we did earlier. Next, we create the `step` variable to hold how much we can move this frame. We use `Vector3.RotateTowards` to find a vector that is closer to pointing at our target than the current forward direction is. Finally, we use `Quaternion.LookRotation` to create a special rotation that points our turret in the new direction.

```
public void RotateTurret() {
   if(turretPivot == null) return;

   Vector3 targetDir = PlayerPosition.position - turretPivot.
position;
   targetDir.y = 0;

   float step = turretSpeed * Time.deltaTime;

   Vector3 rotateDir = Vector3.RotateTowards(turretPivot.forward,
targetDir, step, 0);
   turretPivot.rotation = Quaternion.LookRotation(rotateDir);
}
```

15. Now, returning to Unity, create an empty **GameObject** and rename it to `MuzzlePoint`.

16. Position `MuzzlePoint` as we did for the player, at the end of the cannon.

17. Make `MuzzlePoint` a child of the cannon and zero out any **Y** rotation that might be on it, in the **Inspector** window.

18. Next, add our new `ShootAtPlayer` script to the enemy tank. Additionally, connect the references to the `TurretPivot` and `MuzzlePoint` variables.

19. Finally, for the enemy tank, hit the **Apply** button in the **Inspector** window to update the prefab.

20. If you play the game now, you will see the enemy rotating to point at you, but your score never decreases. This is because of two issues. First, the tank is slightly floating. It doesn't matter where in the world you place it, when playing the game, the tank will slightly float. This is because of the way the NavMeshAgent component functions. The fix is simple, just set the **Base Offset** to -0.3 in the **Inspector** window. This tricks the system and puts the tank on the ground.

21. The second reason the score isn't changing is because the player is missing a function. Open the ScoreCounter script.

22. We will be adding the RemovePoints function. Given an amount, this function simply removes that many points from the player's score.

```
public void RemovePoints(int amount) {
   score -= amount;
}
```

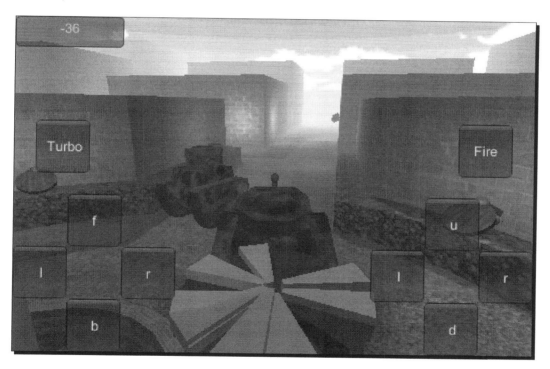

What just happened?

We gave the enemy the ability to attack the player. The new `ShootAtPlayer` script checks first to see whether the tank has slowed down and whether the cannon is trained on the player. If so, it will take regular shots at the player to reduce their score. The player is going to need to keep moving and aim at targets fast, if they hope to be left with any points at the end of the game.

Have a go hero – player feedback

Unless you are paying close attention to your score, it is difficult to tell when you are being shot at. We will be working with explosions in a future chapter but, even so, the player needs some feedback to tell what is going on. Most games will flash a red texture on the screen when the player is hit, whether or not there are any explosions. Try creating a simple texture and drawing it on the screen for half a second when the player is hit.

Attacking the enemy

Players tend to become frustrated quickly when faced with an enemy they are unable to fight against. So, we are going to give our player the ability to hurt and destroy the enemy tank. This will function in a similar manner to the way the targets are shot.

Time for action – giving it a weakness

The easiest way to weaken our enemies is to give them some health that is reduced when they are shot, and to destroy them when they run out of health:

1. We start by creating a new script and naming it `Health`.

2. This script is rather short and starts with a single variable. This variable will keep track of the remaining health of the tank. By setting the default value to 3, the tank will be able to survive three hits before being destroyed.

   ```
   public int health = 3;
   ```

3. This script also contains only one function, `Hit`. As in the case of the targets, this function is called by the `BroadcastMessage` function when the player shoots at it. The first line of the function reduces `health` by one point. The next line checks to see if `health` is below zero. If it is, the tank is destroyed by calling the `Destroy` function and passing it the `gameObject` variable. We also give the player a handful of points.

   ```
   public void Hit() {
     health--;
   ```

```
    if(health <= 0) {
      Destroy(gameObject);
      ScoreCounter.score += 5;
    }
  }
}
```

4. It really is just that simple. Now, add the new script to the `EnemyTank` prefab in the **Project** window, and it will update all the enemy tanks that you currently have in the scene.

5. Try it out. Add a few extra enemy tanks to the scene and watch them follow you around and disappear when you shoot them.

What just happened?

We gave the enemy tank a weakness, health. By creating a short script, the tank is able to track its health and detect when it has been shot. Once the tank runs out of health, it is removed from the game.

Have a go hero – coloring the enemy

We now have two targets to shoot at: the animated ones and the tank. However, they are both indicated with red slices. Try to make the ones that point at tanks be a different color. You will have to make a duplicate of the `IndicatorSlice` prefab and change the `IndicatorControl` script so that it can be told which type of slice to use when the `CreateSlice` and `NewSlice` functions are called.

As a further challenge, the moment we give a creature some health, players want to be able to see how much damage they have done to it. There are two ways you could do this. First, you could put a cluster of cubes above the tank. Then, each time the tank loses health, you delete one of the cubes. The second option is a little more difficult, drawing the bar in the GUI and changing its size based on the remaining health. To make the bar stay above the tank as the camera moves around, take a look at `Camera.WorldToScreenPoint`, in the documentation.

Spawning

Having a limited number of enemies in the game, at the beginning, is not suitable for our game to have lasting fun. Therefore, we need to make some spawn points. As tanks are destroyed, these will issue forth new tanks to keep the player on their toes.

Time for action – creating spawns

The script we will be creating in this section will keep our game world populated with all the enemies our player might want to destroy:

1. We need another new script for this section. Once created, name it `SpawnPoint`.

2. This script begins simply with a few variables. The first variable will hold a reference to our `EnemyTank` prefab. We need it so we can spawn duplicates.

    ```
    public GameObject tankPrefab;
    ```

3. The second variable tracks the spawned tank. When it is destroyed we will create a new one. Using this variable we prevent the game from becoming overwhelmed with the enemy. There will only be as many tanks as spawn points.

    ```
    private GameObject currentTank;
    ```

4. The third variable is for setting a distance from the player, to prevent spawning tanks on top of the player. If the player is outside this distance, a new tank can be spawned. If they are within, a new tank will not be spawned.

    ```
    public float minPlayerDistance = 10;
    ```

5. The first function we will use is `FixedUpdate`. It will start by checking a function to see whether it needs to spawn a new tank. If it does, it will call the `SpawnTank` function to do so.

    ```
    public void FixedUpdate() {
      if(CanSpawn())
        SpawnTank();
    }
    ```

6. Next, we create the `CanSpawn` function. The first line of the function checks to see whether we already have a tank and returns `false` if we do. The second line uses `Vector3.Distance` to determine how far away the player currently is. The last line compares that distance to the minimum distance away that the player needs to be before we can spawn anything and returns the result.

    ```
    public bool CanSpawn() {
      if(current != null) return false;
    ```

```
  float currentDistance = Vector3.Distance(PlayerPosition.
position, transform.position);
  return currentDistance > minPlayerDistance;
}
```

7. The last function, SpawnTank, starts by checking to make sure the tankPrefab reference has been connected. It can't continue if there is nothing to spawn. The second line uses the Instantiate function to create a duplicate of the prefab. In order to store it in our variable, we use as GameObject to make it the proper type. The last line moves the new tank to the spawn point's position. We don't want the tanks appearing in random locations.

```
public void SpawnTank() {
  if(tankPrefab == null) return;

  currentTank = Instantiate(tankPrefab) as GameObject;
  currentTank.transform.position = transform.position;
}
```

8. Return to Unity, create an empty **GameObject**, and rename it to SpawnPoint.

9. Add the SpawnPoint script that we just created, to it.

10. Next, with the spawn point selected, connect the prefab reference by dragging the EnemyTank prefab from the Prefabs folder and dropping it on the appropriate value.

11. Now, turn the SpawnPoint object into a prefab, by dragging-and-dropping it from the **Hierarchy** window and into the Prefabs folder.

12. Finally, populate the city with the new points. Positioning one in each corner of the city will work well.

What just happened?

We created spawn points for the game. Each point will spawn a new tank. When a tank is destroyed, a new one is created at the spawn point. Feel free to build the game and try it out on your device. This section and chapter are now complete and ready for wrap up.

Have a go hero – two for one

Having one spawn point per tank is great, until we want many tanks. Or, we desire them to all spawn in the same location. Your challenge here is to make a single spawn point track multiple tanks. If any one of the tanks is destroyed, a new one should be created. You will definitely need an array to keep track of all the tanks. Also, implement a delay for the spawn. We don't want it spawning multiple tanks on top of each other.

Now that you have all the knowledge and tools that you need, as a further challenge, try creating other types of enemy tanks. Experiment with size and speed. They can also have different strengths, or give more points when destroyed. Perhaps there is a tank that actually gives the player points when shooting at them. Play around and have some fun with it.

Pop Quiz – understanding enemies

Q1. Probably the most common act performed in games is shooting with guns. We have done it a couple of times now. Do you remember what function we use to determine where and what our bullet might hit?

1. `Input.mousePosition`
2. `Transform.position`
3. `Physics.Raycast`

Q2. We will need a great many enemies running around for us to shoot at. Do you remember which function we use to make them move around our NavMesh?

1. `CharacterController.Move`
2. `NavMeshAgent.SetDestination`
3. `NavMesh.CalculatePath`

Q3. Finally, all these enemies will have to be spawned again and again. Do you remember what function we use to spawn these enemies?

1. `Instantiate`
2. `Destroy`
3. `Start`

Summary

In this chapter, we learned about NavMeshes and pathfinding. We also did a little work with AI. It was perhaps among the simplest types of AI but chase behaviors are highly important to all types of games. To utilize all of this, we created an enemy tank. It chased the player and shot at them to reduce their score. To give the edge back to the player, we gave health to the enemy tanks. The player can now shoot the enemy tanks as well as the targets for points. But, we also created some spawn points. Every time a tank was destroyed a new one will be created. In terms of general game play, our Tank Battle game is pretty much complete.

In the next chapter, we will be creating a new game. In order to explore some of the special features of the mobile platform, we will create a Space Fighter game. Nearly all the buttons will be removed from the screen, in favor of new control methods. We will be turning the device's tilt sensors into our steering method. And, we will have to touch enemies and targets to shoot at them. We will also take a look at a different methods of spawning to give the player an endless amount of space to fly through.

6
Specialties of the Mobile Device – Touch and Tilt

In the previous chapter, we learned about Pathfinding and AI. We expanded our Tank Battle game to include enemy tanks. We created points for them to spawn at, and made them shoot at the player. Utilizing Unity's pathfinding system, we made the tanks chase the player. Also, the player was given the ability to destroy the tanks. Once destroyed, the player receives some points and a new enemy tank is spawned.

In this chapter, we start working on a new game as we explore some of the specialties of the mobile device. We will be creating a Space Fighter game. The player will take control of a space ship and blast enemy ships, mines, and asteroids for points. To steer their ship, the player will have to tilt the mobile device. To shoot, the player will touch the screen where they want their laser blast to hit.

In this chapter, we will be covering the following topics:

◆ Touch controls
◆ Tilt controls

We will be creating a new project for this chapter, so start up Unity and we will begin.

Setting up

As with every project, we need a little bit of preparation work in order to prepare our development environment. Don't worry, the setup for this chapter is simple and straightforward.

Time for action – creating the project

Let's get started. The first step is, of course, to start Unity and create a new project. Naming the project Ch6_SpaceFighter will work well:

1. Once Unity has finished initializing, this is a perfect opportunity to set our build settings. Open the **Build Settings** window, select **Android** from the list of platforms, and hit **Switch Platform** to change the target platform.

2. While at the **Build Settings** window, select **Player Settings** to open the player settings in the **Inspector**. Adjust the **Company Name**, **Product Name**, and especially the **Bundle Identifier**.

3. We need to create a few folders to keep the project organized. The Scripts, Models, and Prefabs folders should be created in the **Project** window.

4. We now need to import the assets for this project. We are going to need a space ship for the player, an enemy space ship, an explosive mine, and some asteroids. Luckily, all of these have already been prepared and are available with the starting assets for this chapter. Import PlayerShip.blend, PlayerShip.png, EnemyShip.blend, EnemyShip.png, Asteroid.blend, Asteroid.png, SpaceMine.blend, and SpaceMine.png to the Models folder that you just created.

What just happened?

We just finished the setup for this chapter's project. Once again, a little bit of effort at the beginning of the project will save time and frustration later. Especially, as a project grows in size, the organization done at the beginning becomes most important.

Controlling with tilt

Modern mobile devices possess a broad variety of internal sensors for detecting and providing information about the surrounding world. Though you may not have thought of them in such a way, you are certainly most familiar with the microphone and speaker that are required for making calls. There is a Wi-Fi receiver for connecting to the Internet and a camera for taking pictures. Your device almost certainly has a magnetometer to work with your GPS to provide directions.

The sensor we are interested in right now is the **gyroscope**. This sensor detects local rotation of the device. In general, it is used to determine the orientation of the device. We are going to use it to steer our ship. When the user tilts their device left and right, their space ship will turn to the side. When the device is tilted up and down, the ship will go up and down.

Time for action – steering the space ship

To steer our ship, we will need to create a single script and apply it to our ship:

1. To start this off, create a new script and name it `TiltSteering`.

2. As with all of our other scripts, we will begin this one with a few variables. The first two variables control the speed with which the ship will rotate as the device is tilted. The second two are going to be used to limit the rotation of the ship. These will determine how tight a circle the player's ship can turn in.

   ```
   public float horizRotateSpeed = 7f;
   public float vertRotateSpeed = 3f;

   public float horizMax = 60f;
   public float vertMax = 45f;
   ```

3. Next, we will make use of the `Update` function. We start out by creating a variable to store the ship's current rotation. Next, we have to adjust the rotation. When working with Euler rotations, Unity adjusts values to be between zero and 360. This way, the values are never negative. Anything below zero simply wraps around and starts counting down from 360; anything above 360 wraps back to start counting up from zero again. We need the negative values. So, if the parts of the rotation are above 180, we subtract 360 to determine their negative values. Also, we are not making adjustments to the z component because the ship will not be rotating around its forward axis.

   ```
   public void Update() {
     Vector3 rotation = transform.eulerAngles;

     if(rotation.y > 180f) rotation.y -= 360f;
     if(rotation.x > 180f) rotation.x -= 360f;
   ```

4. Next, we apply the accelerometer measurement. When the device is held horizontally, with the home button on the right and the screen towards the user, the x component holds the rotation of the device while it is facing the user. The z component holds the rotation of the screen being tilted up and down. The components are multiplied by their respective speeds and are added to the rotation. The y rotation controls pointing left and right while the x component controls pointing up and down. However, the z acceleration is the opposite of how the ship should rotate, so we take the negative.

```
rotation.y += Input.acceleration.x * horizRotateSpeed;
rotation.x += -Input.acceleration.z * vertRotateSpeed;
```

5. After the acceleration is applied, we need to limit the rotations so that the ship is not rotated too far. We use the `Mathf.Clamp` function to limit the rotation components between the negative of the max and the max of the relevant values.

```
rotation.y = Mathf.Clamp(rotation.y, -horizMax, horizMax);
rotation.x = Mathf.Clamp(rotation.x, -vertMax, vertMax);
```

6. Finally, we apply the rotation to the ship's transform and close off the function for the script.

```
    transform.eulerAngles = rotation;
}
```

7. In order to make use of our new script, we need to do some setup for the player's ship. Start by creating an empty **GameObject** and setting its position to zero. Rename it to `PlayerShipPivot`. This will allow us to control the movement and appearance of the player's ship independently.

8. Drag your `PlayerShip` model from the **Project** window and drop it on the pivot point we just created. Be sure to center your ship on the point and rotate it to face forward along the z axis.

9. You can now add the script to the pivot point.

10. This is the point when it is especially important to have Unity Remote. With your device attached and Unity Remote running, you can hold it up and steer the ship. Feel free to adjust the rotation speeds and limits until you find the settings that feel natural to control.

11. We will need to be able to see past the ship, so that we can later shoot at targets we are flying towards. Adjust the position of the camera so the ship is centered horizontally and a little below center.

12. The scene also needs to be slightly lit. The light in deep space tends to be very general, so we can get away with just adjusting the ambient light. Click on **Edit** in the menu bar of Unity, and then click on **Render Settings**. By setting the **Ambient Light** to white, our scene will be bright enough to see everything.

13. Once all the settings are in place, be sure to save the scene. Name it `SpaceFighter`.

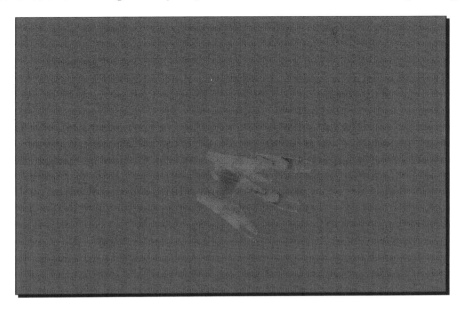

What just happened?

We made use of the accelerometer to provide steering control of a spaceship. By measuring how the player is tilting their device, we are able to rotate the ship accordingly. We did not make the ship actually move, but just rotated it in place. We will come to understand why in a little bit.

Making things move in space

Your first instinct to make the ship move would be probably to just change the position of the ship. However, things get weird when objects are really far from the world origin. In programming, there are actually limits on the size of the number that a variable can hold. This limit causes the rendering system to begin failing when the vertex positions become too large, resulting in the model being distorted beyond recognition. Admittedly, we are talking about positional values in the hundreds of thousands and beyond. However, say the player were to just fly straight for a long time; eventually, they could reach this distance of distortion.

As a potential solution, we could force the player to turn, or stop their forward progress, or wrap their position so they continue flying from the opposite side of a finite space. However, it is so much more fun to fly through an infinite space. We can achieve this by leaving the player's ship in place and moving everything else around it. As a new space is entered, new enemies and objects can be spawned to fill the space. Old objects and enemies that are too far away can be destroyed by removing them where the player won't see. This would give the illusion of an infinite amount of space.

Time for action – flying asteroids

The first objects we will be avoiding in our infinite space will be asteroids:

1. To make the asteroids work, we will first need to make the player ship's rotation and speed available for the asteroids to use. To do this, we need to create a new script and call it `PlayerShip`.

2. Again, this script starts with a group of variables. The first is the speed of the player's ship. The asteroids and other objects in the space will use it to move around the player. The second variable will hold a reference to the `TiltSteering` script that we created earlier. This will give us access to the ship's rotational speed. The last variable is a static variable that will hold a reference to the instance of this script that exists in the scene. This will allow other scripts to access the information stored by this script. We call the `use` variable to indicate to other scripts that this is the instance they should access.

   ```
   public float speed = 10f;
   public TiltSteering tilt;

   private static PlayerShip use;
   ```

3. Next, we make use of the `Awake` function. This function is automatically called at the beginning of the game, making it perfect for initialization. We are using it to simply set the `use` variable that we created earlier to the current instance of the script.

   ```
   public void Awake() {
     use = this;
   }
   ```

4. The next function is for providing other scripts with the player's current rotation. Being static, any script can call it at any time. The function first checks to see whether a reference is available to the current instance of the script. If it cannot be found, a neutral rotation, `Quaternion.identity`, is returned. Otherwise, the rotation of the transform that the script instance is attached to is returned.

```
public static Quaternion GetRotation() {
  if(use == null) return Quaternion.identity;

  return use.transform.rotation;
}
```

5. The `Rotate` function here is for faking the movement of the player. This function takes the transform that is passed to it and moves and rotates it to make it look like it is the player that has moved through space. As with the previous `GetRotation` function, it first checks for a reference to the player and does nothing if there isn't one.

```
public static void Rotate(Transform other) {
  if(use == null) return;
```

6. To rotate the asteroid, and anything else, around the player's position, its current position needs to be multiplied by the mirror of the player's current rotation. To do that, we need to adjust the rotation so that it can be mirrored properly. The Euler angles of the player's rotation are stored in a variable for manipulation. We then shift the values that are greater than 180, just as we did earlier. The rotation is then scaled by the player ship's rotation speed. Finally, it is multiplied by the frame speed to keep it in time.

```
Vector3 euler = use.transform.eulerAngles;
if(euler.x > 180f) euler.x -= 360f;
if(euler.y > 180f) euler.y -= 360f;
euler.Scale(new Vector3(use.tilt.vertRotateSpeed, use.tilt.
horizRotateSpeed, 0));
euler *= Time.deltaTime;
```

7. We turn the negative Euler rotation, which is the mirrored rotation, back into a Quaternion and store it in a variable for use.

```
Quaternion mirror = Quaternion.Euler(-euler);
```

8. The mirrored rotation is then multiplied by the passed object's position, updating the position to be rotated around the player as if they were turning. The player's rotation is then multiplied by a forward-facing vector, the player's speed, and finally the frame speed. This is all subtracted from the object's current position in order to imitate the player's forward movement. Finally, the passed object's rotation is multiplied by the mirrored rotation to change its orientation. Altogether, this fakes the movement of the player.

```
other.position = mirror * other.position;
other.position -= playerRotation * Vector3.forward * use.speed *
Time.deltaTime;
other.rotation *= mirror;
```

9. Add the script to the `PlayerShipPivot` object that was created previously. Be sure to connect the `TiltSteering` reference.

10. Next, we need to make use of that script by creating another. Name it `Asteroid`. This script will control an asteroid as it flies through space and the player is forced to avoid it.

11. The first two of the variables for this script are used for determining a random speed at which the asteroid will fly through space. The third variable will hold the random speed. The final variable will hold the random direction in which the asteroid is flying through space.

```
public float minSpeed = 5f;
public float maxSpeed = 10f;

private float speed = 1f;
private Vector3 direction = Vector3.forward;
```

12. Next, we again make use of the `Awake` function for initialization. Any point that lies on the surface of a sphere with a radius of one is essentially a vector that points in a random direction. Therefore, we use `Random.onUnitSphere` to find a random direction for the asteroid to go. It is followed by the use of `Random.Range` and the first two variables to determine a random speed for the asteroid to travel.

```
public void Awake() {
    direction = Random.onUnitSphere;
    speed = Random.Range(minSpeed, maxSpeed);
}
```

13. The last function for this script is `LateUpdate`. We need the asteroid to move after the player's ship has updated its rotation; that is why we use this function. The first line of the function uses the `GetRotation` function that we created for the `PlayerShip` script and stores it in a variable for use.

```
public void LateUpdate() {
    Quaternion playerRotation = PlayerShip.GetRotation();
```

14. Next, we make a call to the `PlayerShip.Rotate` function, passing it the asteroid's transform, so that the asteroid can be moved to fake the player's movement.

```
PlayerShip.Rotate(transform);
```

15. The next line of code rotates the asteroid's movement direction by the player's rotation, again making a change that fakes the player's movement. The position is again updated with the asteroid's own movement in the adjusted direction.

```
direction = playerRotation * direction;
transform.position += direction * speed * Time.deltaTime;
```

16. The function and the script finishes with a check to see if the asteroid is too far away from the player. We do this by checking `sqrMagnitude` of the asteroid's position. The length of a vector is its magnitude. For positional vectors, this is the distance from the center point. The `sqrMagnitude` is the square of the vector's magnitude. This is much faster to calculate and just as easy for comparison. We just need to compare it to the square of the desired value. In this case a max distance of about 300, whose square is 100,000, will work well for our needs. If you remember from math class, 1e5 is the same as a one with five zeros behind it, which is 1 million. Finally, if the asteroid is too far away, it is destroyed.

```
    if(transform.position.sqrMagnitude > 1e5) Destroy(gameObject);
}
```

17. In order to test this script, we need an asteroid prefab. To create it, start off by adding the `Asteroid` model to the scene and deleting two of the three meshes.

18. Add the script to the model and drag it to the `Prefabs` folder, turning it into a prefab.

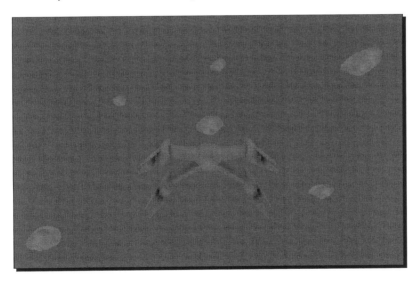

What just happened?

We created two scripts and a prefab. The first script is used by the player's ship to relay information about its rotation and speed to other scripts. The second script controls the motion of asteroids in the game world. Because of the weirdness in the model's behavior when subjected to extreme distances, the player never actually moves. The game world and all of the objects in it are instead moved around the player. Finally, we created an asteroid prefab. Try adding several prefabs to the scene and try them out. You can fly in, out, and around them even though your ship never actually moves.

Adding space collisions

Flying around, you probably noticed that you can fly straight through the asteroids. To make it possible for the player to hit them, we need to add some collision to the player's ship and the asteroid. This is similar to what was done for the Tank Battle game. We will be going into more detail about how the collision works in the next chapter, but we will need to make use of the **Rigidbody** component. It provides access to Physics calculations and allows us to group colliders to make more complex collision shapes.

Time for action – adding collisions

We need to add some collision capabilities to our space objects, so that they can crash into each other and be shot at properly:

1. Let's start by giving collision to the asteroid. Do this by first selecting the mesh for the asteroid and adding a **MeshCollider** component. This will later let us shoot at the asteroid.

2. Next, select the same object that holds our Asteroid script component. Add a **SphereCollider** component to the object and adjust the **Radius** to be a little larger than the asteroid. This collider will detect when the asteroid has collided with the player.

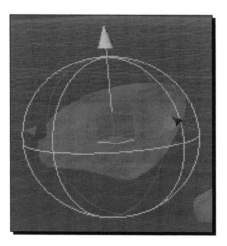

3. The **SphereCollider** needs to have the **Is Trigger** checkbox checked. We are not checking the true collision, just an approximate one. With this checkbox checked, objects will no longer be stopped by the collider, but instead trigger an event in script when an object enters the collider volume. When the player enters the collider, it will be close enough that we can assume and act as if it has collided.

4. When you are satisfied with the changes, be sure to apply them to the prefab. Otherwise, the other asteroids will not be updated and collidable.

5. To detect when the player has entered the new trigger area, we need to add a short function to the `Asteroid` script. We add a `OnTriggerEnter` function to the end of the script. This function is automatically called by the Physics system when one collider enters another. The collider that is passed to it is the one that it collided with. However, the function only works if at least one of the objects has a **Rigidbody** component attached. We will be covering it in detail in *Chapter 7, Throwing Your Weight Around – Physics and a 2D Camera*, but the Rigidbody component is what actually connects an object into Unity's Physics engine, giving our scripts access to the `OnTrigger` and `OnCollision` groups of functions. We will be adding this to the player's ship. When the function is called, it simply destroys the asteroid.

```
public void OnTriggerEnter(Collider other) {
    Destroy(gameObject);
}
```

6. Next, we need to add collision to the the player's ship. Start by adding that **Rigidbody** component to the **PlayerShipPivot** GameObject that we created earlier.

7. Be sure to check the **Is Kinematic** checkbox of the new component. This tells the Physics system that we want to control the object's motion through the script. If it was not checked, the ship would begin to fall as soon we start playing the game.

8. One of the features of a **Rigidbody** component is that it treats all colliders on child objects in the **Hierarchy** as a part of a single collision shape. This way, we are able to build a complex collision shape using several simple and faster process colliders. By creating an empty **GameObject** and adding the simple colliders, we size and position them to cover the player's ship. Be sure to make the collider objects children of the ship's pivot point.

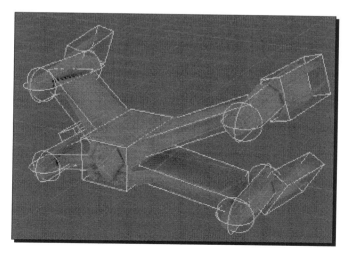

What just happened?

We added collision to the asteroids and the player's ship. This gives the player the ability to crash into and destroy the asteroids. We are utilizing a trigger collider to approximate collision with the asteroid. Also, we make use of the **Rigidbody** component, allowing our ship to collide with other things in the scene. Additionally, this gives us the advantage of being able to build a complex collision shape out of the simple colliders that are provided by Unity. Although it is technically possible to just use a **MeshCollider** to exactly match the shape of the ship, it is not recommended. The **Rigidbody** and **MeshCollider** components do not mix well. Also, several simple colliders are much faster for the computer to calculate than a single **MeshCollider**.

Have a go hero – adding points

It is great that we can make the player ship collide with the asteroids, but it doesn't mean much in terms of a game. There is no penalty for the collision. This challenge is for you to implement a scoring system similar to the one we used for the Tank Battle game from the previous chapters. When the player collides with asteroids, subtract points from the score. Use the `SendMessage` function on the other collider from the `OnTriggerEnter` function. Don't just subtract points when the trigger is entered, because (as you will find out later) the asteroids will not be colliding only with the player.

Creating the enemy

Flying around space with a handful of asteroids is great, but it doesn't make for much of a fight. That is why we are going to add an enemy spaceship that will chase and shoot at the player. We have no mesh to use for pathfinding, so we cannot use the techniques we learned in the previous chapter. However, there are no buildings in space to navigate around, so the chasing of the player will be much simpler.

Time for action – adding an enemy ship

To make our enemy ships, we will need a script to turn our enemy ship into a prefab:

1. The first thing we need to do is create a new script and call it `EnemyShip`. This script will control the movement and shooting of the enemy ships.

2. The script starts off with several variables. The first two define the speed with which the ship moves forward and how fast it turns.

```
public float moveSpeed = 8f;
public float turnSpeed = 0.5f;
```

3. The next three variables are for controlling the shooting of the ship. First is the rate at which bullets are fired. It is followed by the range that the ship has to be within to fire at the player. Third is a holder for how long it has been since the last bullet was fired. This will work with the rate of fire to dictate when the ship can fire again.

```
public float fireRate = 1.5f;
public float fireRange = 60f;
private float fireTime = 0;
```

4. The last two variables will hold a reference to the bullet prefab that will be fired and the point from which the bullet will be released. This is similar to how we made the enemy tanks shoot in the previous chapter. The difference is that space games tend to have a lot of laser blasts flying around that force the player to dodge.

```
public GameObject bullet;
public Transform muzzlePoint;
```

5. In the `Update` function, we will do the work of actually shooting. It starts by tracking how long it has been since a bullet was last fired. Then we check to see if it has been long enough since the last firing in order to fire again, and exit the function if it is not. The third line of code in the function checks the range. This is done in exactly the same way as we checked to see if the asteroids moved too far away from the player. Next, we check to make sure the ship is pointed at the player. This is done in the same way as we did when the enemy tanks were to shoot at the player. A comparison of the forward direction is done with the direction to the player to check the angle. If it is pointing close enough at the player, the ship can start shooting. The shooting is done with a call to the `Instantiate` function. By passing it the `muzzlePoint` variable's position and rotation, the new bullet is automatically rotated. A separate script will be handling the movement of the bullet. Finally, the time since the ship last fired is reset to zero.

```
public void Update() {
  fireTime += Time.deltaTime;
  if(fireTime < fireRate) return;

  if(transform.position.sqrMagnitude > fireRange * fireRange)
return;

  if(Vector3.Angle(transform.forward, -transform.position) > 10)
return;

  Instantiate(bullet, muzzlePoint.position, muzzlePoint.rotation);
  fireTime = 0;
}
```

6. The next function is the `LateUpdate` function. We are going to use this function just as we did for the asteroid. The first line of code just calls out to the `PlayerShip` script to have the ship rotated and moved to fake the player's movement.

```
public void LateUpdate() {
  PlayerShip.Rotate(transform);
```

7. The next line of code applies movement to the ship. The process is similar to how we made the enemy turrets rotate to face the player in the previous chapter. The `step` variable is used to dictate how fast the ship turns towards the player. We use the `Slerp` function to change the ship's current rotation towards the target rotation. In this case, the rotation is the one that looks at the player. Lastly, the ship is moved forward. Altogether, this results in movements similar to how a car turns.

```
float step = turnSpeed * Time.deltaTime;
Quaternion toPlayer = Quaternion.LookRotation(-transform.
position);
transform.rotation = Quaternion.Slerp(transform.rotation,
toPlayer, step);
transform.position += transform.forward * moveSpeed * Time.
deltaTime;
```

8. The last code snippet for the function and the script is the check to see if the ship is too far away. It is exactly the same as the one used by the asteroid.

```
  if(transform.position.sqrMagnitude > 1e5) Destroy(gameObject);
}
```

9. Before we can put our enemy ship together, we need to make one more short script. Create a new script and name it `Bullet`. As you might guess, this is the script that will control the movement of the enemy bullets.

10. This script starts with a single variable, that is, how fast the bullet will move through space.

```
public float speed = 20f;
```

11. Next, we make use of the `LateUpdate` function again. This function first uses `PlayerShip.Rotate` to reposition the bullet, just as with all the other objects in the game world. It then moves forward with speed. Last, it does the check for being out of range.

```
public void LateUpdate() {
  PlayerShip.Rotate(transform);

  transform.position += transform.forward * speed * Time.
deltaTime;
```

```
    if(transform.position.sqrMagnitude > 1e5) Destroy(gameObject);
}
```

12. The last function for the script, `OnTriggerEnter`, works just like the one for the asteroid. If the bullet makes contact with a ship, it will destroy itself.

```
public void OnTriggerEnter(Collider other) {
  Destroy(gameObject);
}
```

13. Now that we have our scripts, the next step is to create the enemy ship and bullet prefabs. To create the bullet, start by navigating to **GameObject | Create Other | Sphere**.

14. Rename the new sphere to `Bullet` and scale it to about half of its original size.

15. Next, add the `Bullet` script to the object and be sure to check the **Is Trigger** checkbox in its **SphereCollider** component. Without that box checked, the bullet won't work properly.

16. Finally, drag the object to the `Prefabs` folder to turn it into a prefab.

17. Next, we need to make the enemy ship. Start by creating an empty **GameObject** and renaming it to `EnemyShipPivot`.

18. Add a copy of the `EnemyShip` model to the scene and make it a child of the pivot point we just created. Be sure to rotate it to face forward along the z axis, and position it to be centered on the pivot point.

19. Next, use simple colliders and empty **GameObject** to create a collision shape for the ship. This is exactly like what we did for the player's ship. Be sure to make all of the colliders children of the enemy ship's pivot point.

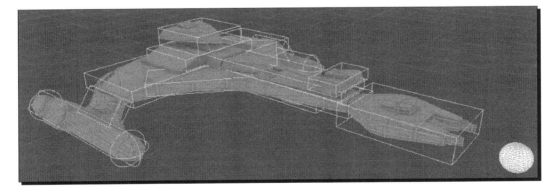

20. We need to create a muzzle point and position it in front of the enemy ship. Do it just as we did for the tanks. Be sure to also make it a child of the ship's pivot point.

21. Now, add the `EnemyShip` script and a **Rigidbody** component to the pivot point.

22. Almost done. Drag the muzzle point from the **Hierarchy** window and drop it on the appropriate slot in the script component in the **Inspector**. Also, drag-and-drop the **Bullet** prefab from the **Project** window to the waiting slot.

23. Finally, make the ship into a prefab by dragging it from the **Hierarchy** window to the `Prefabs` folder.

24. Add a couple of extra ships to the scene and try it out.

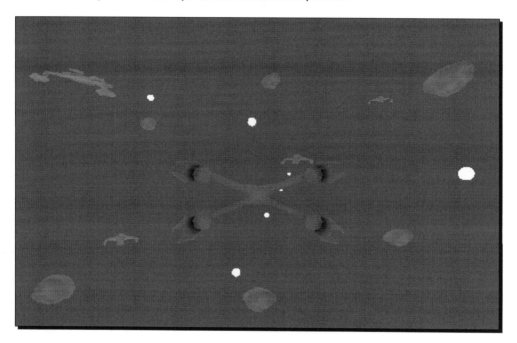

What just happened?

We created an enemy space ship. The ships will fly after the player and begin shooting when within range. Like the asteroids, they move around the player to fake the player's movement. However, instead of moving in a random direction, the enemy ships turn towards the player. By slowing down how fast the ships can turn, they move in arcs rather than pivoting quickly in place. Also, because of the **Rigidbody** component attached to the enemy ships, they can collide with the asteroids that are in the scene.

Have a go hero – skybox and fog

Now that we have several objects flying around in space, it is a good idea to make the scene look a little better. For our Tank Battle game, we added a skybox to make the scene look like it is actually on a planet. However, we are flying around in space. The challenge is for you to find or make a skybox that looks like outer space. Also, adding some distant fog will obscure objects as they move too far away from the player. If the fog is black, it will look like the objects are swallowed by the blackness of deep space.

Controlling with touch

Now that we have several objects flying around in our space scene, including some that will shoot at the player, we should give the player the ability to do more than just dodge. One of the most obvious features of the modern mobile device is the touch screen. The devices use the electrical conductivity of the user's finger and many tiny contact points to determine the location that is being touched. Unity provides us with easy access to the touch inputs. By combining the input with ray casts, as we did for making the tanks fire, we can determine which object in the 3D space was touched by the user. For us, this means we can give the player the ability to shoot at and destroy the objects in space.

Time for action – touch to shoot

For making use of the touch inputs, we will need to add a single script to our player's ship:

1. To give the player the ability to shoot, we need to first create a new script and call it `TouchShoot`.

2. This script begins with a single variable. A `LayerMask` is used to selectively hit objects with a raycast. There are essentially a lot of layers that should be hit. This one will be used to determine what the player can or cannot shoot.
   ```
   public LayerMask touchMask = -1;
   ```

3. The `Update` function is the only function in this script. It starts with a loop. The `Input` class provides us with the `touchCount` value, which is simply a counter for how many fingers are currently touching the device screen.
   ```
   public void Update() {
     for(int i=0;i<Input.touchCount;i++) {
   ```

4. As we progress through the loop, we use the `Input.GetTouch` function to access information about each touch. This line of code checks the phase of the touch. Every touch has five potential phases: **Began**, **Moved**, **Stationary**, **Ended**, and **Cancelled**:

```
if(Input.GetTouch(i).phase == TouchPhase.Began) {
```

   - **Began**: This phase of touch is when the user first touches the screen.
   - **Moved**: This phase of touch is when the user moves his/her finger across the screen.
   - **Stationary**: This phase of touch is the opposite of the previous phase; it is when the finger is not moving across the screen.
   - **Ended**: This phase of touch is when the finger is lifted off the screen. This is the normal way for a touch to complete.
   - **Cancelled**: This phase of touch is when an error occurs while tracking the touch. This phase tends to occur most often when a finger is touching the screen, but not moving for too long. The touch system is not perfect, so it assumes it missed the finger being lifted off the screen and just cancels it.

5. Next, we create a pair of variables. The first is a `Ray`, which is just a container for storing a point in space and a directional vector. The `ScreenPointToRay` function is specially provided by the camera for converting touch positions from the 2D space of the screen to the 3D space of the game world. As with our tanks, the second is a holder for what was hit by our raycast.

```
Ray ray = Camera.main.ScreenPointToRay(Input.GetTouch(i).
position);
RaycastHit hit;
```

6. The last step for the function is to call the `Raycast` function. We pass the ray, and the tracking variable to the function. Next, we have to give it a distance, and finally the `LayerMask`. If an object is hit, it is destroyed. Also, there are several curly braces required to close off the if statements, loop, and function.

```
        if(Physics.Raycast(ray, out hit, Mathf.Infinity, touchMask))
    {
        Destroy(hit.transform.gameObject);
    }
  }
 }
}
```

7. To try the script out, simply add it to the **PlayerShipPivot** GameObject. Be careful. At this point, if you were to touch the player's ship while testing, it would be destroyed.

8. In order to fix this issue, we need to create a new layer. Start by going to the menu bar of Unity and clicking on **Edit | Project Settings | Tags**. This is just a second path to the same location where we created layers for the Tank Battle game.

9. Click on the right of **User Layer 8** and input `Player` in the field. This will create the new layer.

10. Select the **PlayerShipPivot** object in the **Hierarchy** window.

11. In the top-right corner of the **Inspector** window, select the layer we just created from the **Layers** drop-down list.

12. When Unity asks whether you want to change the children objects as well, confirm that you do.

13. For the `TouchShoot` script, deselect the new layer from the **Touch Mask** list. This will allow the player to shoot everything but themselves.

14. There is one last thing we need to do. Go to the menu bar of Unity and click on **Edit | Project Settings | Physics**. This opens a new set of controls in the **Inspector** window that adjust how the Physics engine runs.

15. At the moment, we only care about the **Raycasts Hit Triggers** checkbox. Uncheck it. If we don't, the players will hit the trigger volume that is around the asteroid when they shoot, rather than the asteroid itself. It is not so great an issue for the asteroids. But, if we were to create something, such as an explosive mine, the trigger volume would be much larger. That would make it very odd-looking for shooting at the mine.

What just happened?

We gave the player the ability to shoot when they touch the screen. By looping through the list of touches, the player is able to use more than one finger for shooting at targets. The special `ScreenPointToRay` function provided by the camera allows us to change 2D screen touches into 3D game world interactions. By making use of the `LayerMask`, we also prevent the player from shooting and destroying themselves.

Have a go hero – healthy ships

The challenge here is to give the enemy ships some health. When we created the enemy tanks in the previous chapter, we caused them to take a few shots from the player before they would be destroyed. Do the same thing here for the enemy ships.

Spawning in space

So far, we have created a space game that allows the player to fly infinitely through space. The player never actually moves; instead, the objects in the scene move around it to fake the movement. We have asteroids that will fly in a random direction through space. We also created enemy spaceships that fly after the player and shoot at them. Finally, we have the ability to shoot at and destroy the objects in the scene. However, at this point we can quickly run out of things to shoot at. Either they get too far away, or we destroy them. To fix this, we will now create a system that will randomly spawn all that we have created around the player.

Time for action – creating a space spawn

Our last script will populate our space and will be attached to the player's ship, since it is the center of the game world:

1. To fill our space with the objects, we need to create another script. Name it `SpaceSpawn`.

2. We start it out with two variables. These two define the space within which the new objects will be spawned. They will be created outside the minimum range but within the maximum range.

    ```
    public float minRange = 200f;
    public float maxRange = 300f;
    ```

3. Next, we have two variables for controlling the frequency at which objects should be spawned. These will work the same as the ones we used for making the enemy ships shoot at the player.

    ```
    public float frequency = 0.3f;
    private float spawnTime = 0;
    ```

4. The final variable for this script, is an array. It is simply a list of all of the objects that can be spawned. We will be filling it in a little bit, when we return to Unity to set it up.

    ```
    public GameObject[] spawnList = new GameObject[0];
    ```

5. `Update` is once again our function of choice for the script. We start it off by making sure that there is something in the list to be spawned. If there are no objects to be spawned, there is no point in continuing.

    ```
    public void Update() {
      if(spawnList.Length <= 0) return;
    ```

6. Next, we track how long it has been since the last spawn and check to see if it has been long enough to spawn once more. Again, this works just like the shooting of the enemy ships.

```
spawnTime += Time.deltaTime;
if(spawnTime < frequency) return;
```

7. Now, we need to figure out where to spawn the next object in space. To do this, we first use `Random.onUnitSphere` to find a random direction. Next, we find a random distance that lies within our min and max ranges. Finally, they are multiplied together to give us a position.

```
Vector3 direction = Random.onUnitSphere;
float distance = Random.Range(minRange, maxRange);
Vector3 position = direction * distance;
```

8. To pick a random object, we use `Random.Range` and pass the length of the list of objects to it. This will give us the index of one of the slots of the list. The following line of code makes sure that there is an object in the slot. If there isn't, we cannot spawn it.

```
int index = Random.Range(0, spawnList.Length);
if(spawnList[index] == null) return;
```

9. Next, we actually spawn the object using our good friend, the `Instantiate` function. We pass the object we randomly selected, the position we found, and finally, a random rotation to the `Instantiate` function. As a result, the object is created in the scene and set into place.

```
Instantiate(spawnList[index], position, Random.rotation);
```

10. Finally, we subtract the `frequency` variable from our time tracker to finish off the function and the script. This will cause a spawn to occur on every frequency tick without losing any time.

```
    spawnTime -= frequency;
}
```

11. We now return to Unity to set up the script. Add it to the `PlayerShipPivot` object. It will work as well here as anywhere else.

12. To fill the list, just drag your prefabs from the **Project** window and drop them on **Spawn List** in the **Inspector** window. The little triangle to the left of the field will let you expand the list and see what is currently in it. If you want to adjust the chances of the various objects appearing, just change how many of them are in the list. There is nothing keeping you from putting nine references to the asteroid prefab into the list and a single reference to the enemy ship prefab, to give the ship a one in 10 chance of being spawned. Whatever you choose, use the list to set the object chances and include at least one of each obstacle we have created.

13. Finally, test it out. Hit play and fly around to see the objects spawn and fly around.

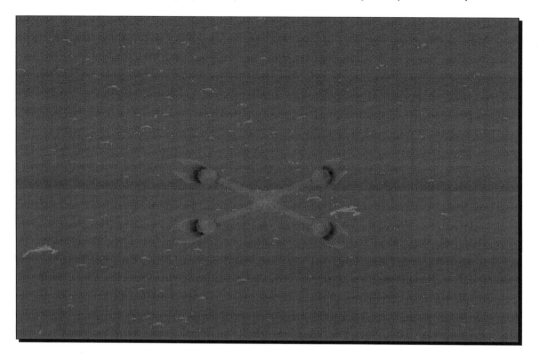

What just happened?

We created a system for spawning objects randomly in space. First, we tracked time in the same way as we did for making the enemy ships shoot at the player. Next, we found a random direction and the range with which we determined a position. After that, the system selects a random object from the list and finally spawns it. In order to adjust the chances of any single object appearing, we just adjust how often it appears in the list of objects to be spawned, relative to the other objects in the list.

Have a go hero – more to spawn and shoot

Included in the starting assets for this chapter are two more asteroid meshes and a mine. Using these, you can create more objects to be spawned in the game. The mine can also be created with a much larger trigger volume. This would allow it to explode when ships get close, not just hit it. If you were additionally inclined, you could at least make the asteroids randomly pick a scale when they are spawned. This would give the appearance of even greater variety in the asteroids, even though there are only a few.

Also, try creating another ship or several other ships. Perhaps one is a transport ship and it flees from the player. A hard one would be a ship that splits into two smaller ships when destroyed. Or, just recreate your favorite space ships from your favorite sci-fi media. In this game, the universe is the limit.

For the Tank Battle game, we created a turbo boost button for getting the player across the city quickly. It is also useful for fleeing enemies. Implement it for the space fighter. It would be useful for catching enemies and dodging bullets.

Pop Quiz – understanding Android components

Modern mobile devices have many parts that perform a huge variety of functions. Knowing what they are and how they work together is the first step towards being able to use them. Are the following statements true or false?

Q1. The magnometer and accelerometer work together to give position on a map.

1. True
2. False

Q2. The gyroscope detects rotation and movement of the device.

1. True
2. False

Q3. 2D positions on the touch screen can be translated into 3D positions in the game.

1. True
2. False

Q4. What line of code will allow us to translate the user's touch to a 3D position in the game?

1. `Camera.main.ScreenPointToRay(Input.GetTouch(0).position)`
2. `Input.GetMouseButton(0)`
3. `Camera.main.WorldToScreenPoint(Input.GetTouch(0).position)`

Q5. What line of code will give us the device's acceleration?

1. `Input.gyro`
2. `Input.compass`
3. `Input.acceleration`

Summary

In this chapter, we learned about the specialties of the modern mobile device. We created a Space Fighter game to try it out. We gained access to the device's accelerometer to detect when it is rotated. This gave our spaceship the ability to be steered. We also made use of the touch screen to give a player the ability to shoot enemies in the game. Because we wanted an infinite amount of space to fly through, we had to make it all without the player moving. Instead, everything else moves around the player, faking the player's movement. It also required a system that continuously spawned new enemies and obstacles around the player, allowing us to keep flying and finding new things to play with.

In the next chapter, we will be taking a short break from our Space Fighter game. Almost certainly the most popular mobile game on the market, Angry Birds is a distinct and not uncommon type of game. In order to learn about Physics in Unity and the possibility of a 2D-style game, we will be making an Angry Birds clone. We will also take a look at Parallax scrolling to create a pleasing background. Before you know it, we will be creating all of the Angry Birds levels that you always wished you could play.

7
Throwing Your Weight Around – Physics and a 2D Camera

In the previous chapter, we learned about the special features of a mobile device and how to create touch and tilt controls. We also created a Space Fighter game to use these new controls. The steering of the ship was done by tilting the device and shooting by touching the screen. Using some special movement tricks, we gave the player an infinite amount of space to fly and enemies to fight.

In this chapter, we take a short break from the Space Fighter game to explore Unity's physics engine. We will also take a look at options for creating a 2D game experience. To do all of this, we will be recreating one of the most popular mobile games on the market, Angry Birds. We will use physics to throw birds and destroy structures. We will also take a look at the creation of a level-selection screen.

In this chapter, we will be covering the following topics:

◆ Unity Physics
◆ Parallax scrolling
◆ Isometric camera
◆ Level selection

We will be creating a new project for this chapter, so start up Unity and let's begin!

2D games in a 3D world

Perhaps the most underrealized thing when developing games is the fact that it's possible to create 2D-style games in a 3D game engine such as Unity. As with everything else, it comes with its own set of advantages and disadvantages, but the choice can be well worth it for generating a pleasing game experience. The foremost of the advantages is that one can use 3D assets for the game. This allows dynamic lighting and shadows to be easily included. However, if using a 2D engine, any shadow would need to be painted directly into the assets and you would be hard-pressed to make it dynamic. On the disadvantage side is the use of 2D assets in the 3D world. It is completely possible to use them, but large file sizes become necessary to achieve the desired detail and keep it from appearing pixelated. Most 2D engines, however, make use of vector art that will keep the image's lines smooth as it is scaled up and down. Also, one is able to use normal animations for the 3D assets, but frame-by-frame animation is generally required for any 2D asset. Altogether, the advantages have outweighed the disadvantages for many developers, creating a large selection of great looking 2D games that you may never realize were actually made in a 3D game engine. Now, we shall design another game by recreating the highly popular Angry Birds.

Time for action – preparing the world

Let's get started with preparing the world for the Angry Birds game:

1. To start it all off, we need to create a new project in Unity. Naming it `Ch7_ AngryBirds` will work well. Be sure to change the target platform to **Android** and set the **Bundle Identifier** to an appropriate value.

2. Next, import the starting assets for this chapter and create some folders to keep everything organized.

3. In Unity, it is very easy to turn a game from 3D to 2D. Simply select the **Main Camera** object that is by default present in every new scene, find the **Projection** value, and select **Orthographic** from the drop-down list.

 Every camera has two options for how to render the game. **Perspective** renders everything utilizing the distance from the camera, imitating the real world; objects that are farther away from the camera are drawn smaller than objects that are closer. **Orthographic** renders everything without this consideration; objects are not scaled based on their distance from the camera.

4. Initially, the amount of the scene that the camera views is far too large. To change this, set the **Size** value to 5. This reduces the amount of space the camera will render. This value will keep us focused on the action as the game is played.

5. To make the camera properly usable, set its **Position** to 10 for the **X** axis, 3 for the **Y** axis, and 0 for the **Z** axis. Also, set its **Rotation** for the **Y** axis to -90. Everything is going to be positioned along the z axis, so our camera needs to be set to watch the axis and be far away enough so that it is not in the action.

6. Next, we are going to need a ground. So, go to the menu bar of Unity and click on **GameObject**, followed by **Create Other**, and finally, click on **Cube**. This will suit well enough as a simple ground.

7. To make it look a little like a ground, create a green material and apply it to the **Cube**.

8. The ground cube needs to be large enough to cover the whole of our field of play. To do this, set its **Scale** to 5 for the **X** axis, 10 for the **Y** axis, and 100 for the **Z** axis. Also, set its **Position** to 0 for the **X** and **Y** axes, and 30 for the **Z** axis. Since nothing will be moving along the x axis, the ground only needs to be large enough for the other objects that will be in our scene to land on. It does, however, need to be wide and tall enough to keep the camera from seeing the edges.

9. Right now, the ground looks rather dark due to the lack of light. From the menu bar of Unity, click on **GameObject**, followed by **Create Other**, and lastly click on **Directional Light** to add some brightness to the scene. It should be positioned to shine on the side of the cube that faces the camera.

10. Next, we need to keep all of the objects that will be flying around the scene from straying too far and causing problems. To do this, we need to create some trigger volumes. The simplest way to do this is to create three more cubes. Position one at each end of the ground object and the last cube at about 50 units above. Then, scale them to form a box with the ground. Each should be no thicker than a single unit, and they need to be five units deep, the same as the ground. Next, remove their **Mesh Renderer** and **Mesh Filter** components. This removes the visible box, while leaving the collider volume. To change them to trigger volumes, check the **Is Trigger** checkbox on each **Box Collider** component.

11. To make the volumes actually keep objects from straying too far, we need to create a new script. Create it and name it GoneTooFar.

12. This script has a single, short function, OnTriggerEnter. We use it to destroy any object that might enter the volume. This function is used by Unity's physics system to detect when an object has entered a trigger volume. We will go into more detail later but, for now, know that one of the two objects, either the volume or the object entering it, needs a **Rigidbody** component. In our case, everything we might want to remove when they enter the trigger will have a **Rigidbody** component.

```
public void OnTriggerEnter(Collider other) {
  Destroy(other.gameObject);
}
```

13. Finally, return to Unity and add the script to the three trigger-volume objects.

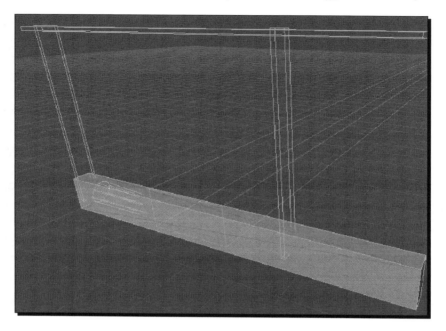

What just happened?

We did the initial setup for our 2D game. By changing our camera view to **Orthographic**, the view switches from a 3D game to a 2D one. We also created a ground and some trigger volumes for our scene. Together, these will keep our birds and anything else from straying too far.

Physics

In Unity, physics simulation primarily focuses on the use of the **Rigidbody** component. When the **Rigidbody** component is attached to any object, it will be taken over by the physics engine. The object will fall with gravity and bump into any object that has a collider. In our scripts, making use of the `OnCollision` function and the `OnTrigger` function requires a **Rigidbody** component to be attached to at least one of the two interacting objects. However, a **Rigidbody** component can interfere with any specific movement we might cause the object to take. Every **Rigidbody**, though, can be marked as kinematic, meaning the physics engine will not move it. The **CharacterController** component that we used for our tank is a special, modified **Rigidbody**. In this chapter, we will be making heavy use of the **Rigidbody** component to tie all of our birds, blocks, and pigs into the physics engine.

Building blocks

For our first physics objects, we will create the blocks that the pig castles are built out of. We will be creating three types of blocks: wood, glass, and rubber. With these few simple blocks, we will be able to easily create a large variety of levels and structures to smash with birds.

Time for action – creating planks

Each of the blocks we will be creating will be largely similar:

1. First, we will create the plank of wood. To do this, we need another cube. Rename it `Plank_Wood`.

2. Set the plank's **Scale** to 2 for the **X** and **Y** axes, and `0.25` for the **Z** axis. Its scale on the y and z axis define its size as seen by the player. The scale on the x axis makes sure that it will be hit by other physics objects in the scene.

3. Next, create a new material using the `plank_wood` texture and apply it to the cube.

4. To convert this new wood plank into a physics object, add a **Rigidbody** component. Make sure your plank is selected, go to the menu bar of Unity and click on **Component**, followed by **Physics**; finally, click on **Rigidbody**.

5. We need to keep the plank from moving along the x axis and out of alignment with our other physics objects as well as keeping it from rotating to show its other sides to the player. To do this, we make use of the **Constraints** group of checkboxes on the **Rigidbody** component. Check the checkbox for the **X** axis next to **Freeze Position** and the **Y** and **Z** checkboxes next to **Freeze Rotation**. These will keep the object from moving in ways we don't want it to.

6. To make the plank function properly within our game, we need to create a new script and name it `Plank`.

7. This script begins with a bunch of variables. The first two are for tracking the health of the plank. We need to separate the total amount of health from the current health, so we will be able to detect when the object has been reduced to half health. At that point, we will make use of our next three variables to change the object's material to one that shows damage. The last variable is used when the object runs out of health and is destroyed. We will use it to increase the player's score.

```
public float totalHealth = 100f;
private float health = 100f;

public Material damageMaterial;
```

```
public Renderer plankRenderer;
private bool didSwap = false;

public int scoreValue = 100;
```

8. For the script's first function, we use `Awake` for initialization. We make sure the object's current health is the same as its total health, and we make sure the `didSwap` flag is set to `false`.

```
public void Awake() {
  health = totalHealth;
  didSwap = false;
}
```

9. Next, we make use of the `OnCollisionEnter` function. This is a special function, triggered by the **Rigidbody** component, that gives us information about what the object collided with and how. We use this information to find `collision.relativeVelocity.magnitude`. This is the speed at which the objects collided, and we use it as damage to reduce the current health. Next, the function checks to see if the health has been reduced to half and calls the `SwapToDamaged` function if it has. By using the `didSwap` flag, we make sure the function will only be called once. Finally, for the function, it checks to see if the health has dropped below zero. If it has, the object is destroyed and we call the `LevelTracker` script, which we will soon be making, to add to the player's score.

```
public void OnCollisionEnter(Collision collision) {
  health -= collision.relativeVelocity.magnitude;

  if(!didSwap && health < totalHealth / 2f) {
    SwapToDamaged();
  }

  if(health <= 0) {
    Destroy(gameObject);
    LevelTracker.AddScore(scoreValue);
  }
}
```

10. Finally for the script, we have the `SwapToDamaged` function. It starts by setting the `didSwap` flag to `true`. Next, it checks to make sure the `plankRenderer` and `damageMaterial` variables have references to other objects. Ultimately, it uses the `plankRenderer.sharedMaterial` value to change to the damaged looking material.

```
public void SwapToDamaged() {
  didSwap = true;
```

```
    if(plankRenderer == null) return;
    if(damageMaterial == null) return;

    plankRenderer.sharedMaterial = damageMaterial;
}
```

11. Before we can add our `Plank` script to our objects, we need to create the `LevelTracker` script that was mentioned earlier. Create it now.

12. This script is fairly short and starts with a single variable. The variable will track the player's score for the level and is `static` so that it can be easily changed as objects are destroyed for points.

```
private static int score = 0;
```

13. Next, we use the `Awake` function to make sure the player starts at zero when beginning a level.

```
public void Awake() {
    score = 0;
}
```

14. Finally for the script, we add the `AddScore` function. This function simply takes the amount of points passed to it and increases the player's score. It is also `static`, so that it can be called by any object in the scene without needing a reference to the script.

```
public static void AddScore(int amount) {
    score += amount;
}
```

15. Back in Unity, we need to create a new material using the `plank_wood_damaged` texture. This will be the material that the script will swap to.

16. Add the `Plank` script to our `Plank_Wood` object. Connect the **Damaged Material** reference to the new material and the **Plank Renderer** reference to the object's **Mesh Renderer** component.

17. As we create different types of planks, we can adjust the **Total Health** value to give them different strengths. A value of 25 works pretty well for the wood planks.

18. Next, create an empty **GameObject** and rename it `LevelTracker`.

19. Add the `LevelTracker` script to the object and it will begin to track the player's score.

20. If you want to see the wood plank in action, position it above the ground and hit the play button. As soon as the game starts, Unity's physics will take over and drop the plank with gravity. If it started out high enough, you will be able to see it switch textures as it loses health.

21. To make the other two planks that we need, select the `Plank_Wood` object and press *Ctrl + D* twice to duplicate it. Rename one to `Plank_Glass` and the other to `Plank_Rubber`.

22. Next, create three new materials. One should be purple for the rubber plank, one should use the `plank_glass` texture for the glass plank, and the last material should use the `plank_glass_damaged` texture for when the glass plank is damaged. Apply the new materials to the proper locations for the new planks.

23. As for the health of the new planks, a value of `15` for the glass and `100` for the rubber will work well.

24. Finally, turn your three planks into prefabs and use them to build a structure for us to knock down. Feel free to scale them to make different-sized blocks, but leave the x axis alone. Also, all of the blocks should be positioned at zero on the x axis and your structure should be centered around about `30` on the z axis.

What just happened?

We created the building blocks we needed for the structures that are going to be knocked down in our game. We used a **Rigidbody** component to tie them into the physics engine. Also, we created a script that keeps track of their health and swaps materials when it drops below half.

Have a go hero – creating a stone block

Wood and glass work well as basic blocks. But, if we are going to make harder levels, we need something a little stronger. Try your hand at making a stone block. Create two textures and materials for it to show its pristine and damaged states.

Physics materials

Physics materials are special types of materials that specifically tell the physics engine how two objects should interact. This does not affect the appearance of an object. It defines the friction and bounciness of a collider. We will use them to give our rubber plank some bounce and the glass plank some slide.

Time for action – sliding and bouncing

Physics materials are quick enough to implement and will allow us to complete this section in four short steps:

1. Physics materials are created like everything else, in the **Project** panel. Right-click inside the **Project** panel and click on **Create | Physic Material**. Create two physic materials and name one `Glass` and the other `Rubber`.

2. Select one of them and take a look at it in the **Inspector** window. Right now, we are only concerned with the first three values. The others are used for more complex situations.

   ❑ **Dynamic Friction**: This property is the amount of friction used when the object is moving. A value of zero is no friction, such as ice, and a value of one is a lot of friction, such as rubber.

   ❑ **Static Friction**: This property functions the same as **Dynamic Friction**, the difference being that it is used when the object is not moving.

   ❑ **Bounciness**: This property is how much of an object's energy is reflected when it hits something or is hit by something. Zero means none of the energy is reflected, while a value of one will reflect all of it.

3. For the `Glass` material, set the two friction values to `0.1` and **Bounciness** to `0`. For the `Rubber` material, set the two friction values to `1` and **Bounciness** to `0.8`.

4. Next, select your `Plank_Glass` prefab and take a look at its **Box Collider** component. To apply your new physics materials, simply drag-and-drop one from the **Project** to the **Material** slot. Do the same for your `Plank_Rubber` prefab and, any time an object hits one of them, the materials will be used to control their interaction.

What just happened?

We created a pair of physics materials. They control how two colliders interact when they run into each other. Using them, we are given control over the amount of friction and bounciness that is possessed by any collider.

Characters

Having a bunch of generic blocks is just the beginning of this game. Next, we are going to create a few characters to add some life to the game. We are going to need some evil pigs to destroy and some good birds to throw at them.

The enemy

Our first character will be the enemy pig. On their own, they don't actually do anything. So, they are really just the wooden blocks we made earlier that happen to look like pigs. To make their destruction the goal of the game, however, we are going to expand our `LevelTracker` script to watch them and trigger a Game Over event if they are all destroyed. We will also expand it to draw the score on the screen and make it save the score for later use. To demonstrate the use of 2D assets in the 3D environment, the pigs are also created as flat textures.

Time for action – creating the pigs

Let's get started with creating the pigs for the Angry Birds game:

1. The pigs are created in a manner similar to that of the the wood planks. Start by creating an empty **GameObject** and naming it `Pig`.

2. Next, create a plane, make it a child of the `Pig` object, and remove its **Mesh Collider** component. We do this because of the rotation the plane will need to face the camera. Being a child of the empty **GameObject** allows us to ignore that rotation when working with the pig.

3. Set the plane's local **Position** to 0 on each axis and set its **Rotation** to 90 on the **X** axis, 270 on the **Y** axis, and 0 on the **Z** axis. This will make the plane face the camera.

4. Now, create two materials. Name one `Pig_Fresh` and the other `Pig_Damage`. From their **Shader** drop-down list, select **Transparent**, followed by **Cutout**, and finally **Soft Edge Unlit**. This allows us to make use of the the texture's alpha channel and provide some transparency.

5. Finish off the materials by adding the `pig_damage` and `pig_fresh` textures to them.

6. To the `Pig` object, add a **Sphere Collider** component, a **Rigidbody** component, and the `Plank` script. We make use of the **Sphere Collider** component, rather than the **Mesh Collider** component the plane came with, because the plane has zero thickness and will, therefore, have many issues colliding with other objects.

7. To complete the pig's creation, apply your material to the plane and connect the references in the `Plank` script. Finally, set the **Constraints** parameters on the **Rigidbody** component just as we did for the other planks.

8. Now, turn the pig into a prefab and add it to your structure. Remember, leave them at zero on the x axis, but feel free to adjust their size, health, and score values to give them some variety.

9. Next, we need to expand the `LevelTracker` script. Open it up and we can add some more code.

10. First, we add some more variables at the beginning of the script. The first one, as its name suggests, will hold a list of all the pigs in our scene. Next is a flag for signaling that the game has ended. And finally, a string for telling the player why the game has ended.

```
public Transform[] pigs = new Transform[0];

private static gameOver = false;
private static string message = "";
```

11. Next, we need to add a line to the `Awake` function. This simply makes sure that the `gameOver` flag is `false` when the level starts.

```
gameOver = false;
```

12. We use the `OnGUI` function to draw a Game Over screen when the game has ended, or for drawing the current score if it is still continuing.

```
public void OnGUI() {
  if(gameOver)
    DrawGameOver();
```

```
    else
      DrawScore();
  }
```

13. The `DrawScore` function takes the current score and uses `GUI.Label` to draw it in the top-right corner of the screen.

```
private void DrawScore() {
    Rect scoreRect = new Rect(Screen.width - 100, 0, 100, 30);
    GUI.Label(scoreRect, "Score: " + score);
}
```

14. The `DrawGameOver` function first uses the `GUI.Box` function to draw a dark box over the whole of the screen, simultaneously drawing the Game Over message on the screen. Next, it draws the player's final score in the middle of the screen. Below that, it draws a button. This button will save the player's current score and load the level-selection screen we will create later. The `Application.LoadLevel` function is used to load any other scene in your game. All of the scenes you intend to load have to be added to the **Build Settings** window found in the **File** menu and can be loaded by using either their name or their index, as used here:

```
private void DrawGameOver() {
    Rect boxRect =  new Rect(0, 0, Screen.width, Screen.height);
    GUI.Box(boxRect, "Game Over\n" + message);

    Rect scoreRect = new Rect(0, Screen.height / 2, Screen.width,
30);
    GUI.Label(scoreRect, "Score: " + score);

    Rect exitRect = new Rect(0, Screen.height / 2 + 50, Screen.
width, 50);
    if(GUI.Button(exitRect, "Return to Level Select")) {
      Application.LoadLevel(0);
      SaveScore();
    }
}
```

15. In the `LateUpdate` function, we call another function to check whether all the pigs have been destroyed if the game is not yet over.

```
public void LateUpdate() {
  if(!gameOver)
    CheckPigs();
}
```

16. Next, we add the `CheckPigs` function. This function loops through the list of pigs to see if they are all destroyed. Should it find one that is still around, it exits the function. Otherwise, the game is flagged as being over and the message is set to tell the player that they succeeded in destroying all of the pigs.

```
private void CheckPigs() {
  for(int i=0;i<pigs.Length;i++) {
    if(pigs[i] != null) return;
  }

  gameOver = true;
  message = "You destroyed the pigs!";
}
```

17. The `OutOfBirds` function will be called by the slingshot we are going to create later, when the player runs out of birds to launch at the pigs. If the game has not yet ended, the function ends the game and sets an appropriate message for the player.

```
public static void OutOfBirds() {
  if(gameOver) return;

  gameOver = true;
  message = "You ran out of birds!";
}
```

18. Finally, we have the `SaveScore` function. Here, we use the `PlayerPrefs` class. It lets us easily store and retrieve small amounts of data, perfect for our current needs. We just need to provide it with a unique key to save the data under. For that, we use a short string combined with the level's index as provided by `Application.loadedLevel`. Next, we use `PlayerPrefs.GetInt` to retrieve the last score that was saved. If there isn't one, the zero that we passed to the function is returned as a default value. Finally, we compare the new score with the old score and use `PlayerPrefs.SetInt` to save the new score if it is higher.

```
private void SaveScore() {
  string key = "LevelScore" + Application.loadedLevel;
  int previousScore = PlayerPrefs.GetInt(key, 0);
  if(previousScore < score)
    PlayerPrefs.SetInt(key, score);
}
```

19. Back in Unity, the pigs need to be added to the `LevelTracker` script's list. With
the `LevelTracker` script selected, drag-and-drop each pig to the `Pigs` value in
the **Inspector** window to add them.

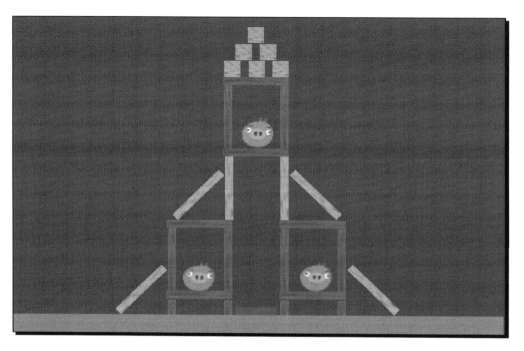

What just happened?

We created the pigs and updated our `LevelTracker` script to track them. The pigs
are really just like the planks of wood, but are spheres instead of boxes. The updated
`LevelTracker` script watches for the instance when all of the pigs are destroyed and
triggers a Game Over screen when they are. It also handles the drawing of the score
while the game is being played and the saving of that score when the level is over.

The ally

Next, we need something to throw at the pigs and their fortification. Here, we will create
the simplest of the birds. The red bird is essentially just a rock. He has no special powers
and nothing particularly special about his code, besides health. You will also notice that
the bird is a 3D model, giving it the shadows that the pigs are missing.

Time for action – creating the red bird

Let's get started with creating the red bird:

1. Although the red bird model is 3D, it is set up in a manner similar to that of the pig. Create an empty **GameObject**, naming it `Bird_Red`, and add the appropriate model from the `birds` model as a child, zeroing out its position. The model should be rotated to align it along the z axis. If turned a little more toward the camera, the player is able to see the bird's face while still giving the impression of looking down the field.

2. Next, give it a **Sphere Collider** component and a **Rigidbody** component, and set the **Constraints** parameters.

3. Now, we need to create a new script named `Bird`. This script will be a base for all of our birds, tracking their health and triggering their special powers when appropriate.

4. It starts with two variables. The first will keep track of the bird's current health. The second is a flag so that the bird will only use its special power once. It is marked as `protected` so the class that extends this script can use it while keeping it from interference from outside the class.

```
public float health = 50;
protected bool didSpecial = false;
```

5. The `Update` function does three checks before activating the bird's special power. First, it checks whether it has already been done, then whether the screen has been touched, and finally whether the bird has a **Rigidbody** component and that it is not being controlled by another script.

```
public void Update() {
  if(didSpecial)
    return;
  if(!Input.GetMouseButtonDown(0))
    return;
  if(rigidbody == null || rigidbody.isKinematic)
    return;

  DoSpecial();
}
```

6. In the case of the red bird, the `DoSpecial` function only sets its flag to `true`. It is marked as `virtual` so that we can override the function for the other birds and make them do some fancier things.

```
protected virtual void DoSpecial() {
  didSpecial = true;
}
```

7. The `OnCollisionEnter` function works just like the one for the planks, subtracting health based on the strength of the collision and destroying the bird if it runs out of health.

```
public void OnCollisionEnter(Collision collision) {
    health -= collision.relativeVelocity.magnitude;
    if(health < 0)
        Destroy(gameObject);
}
```

8. Return to Unity and add the script to the `Bird_Red` object.

9. Complete the bird's creation by turning it into a prefab and deleting it from the scene. The slingshot we will be creating soon will handle the creation of the birds when the game starts.

What just happened?

We created the red bird. It is set up just like our other physics objects. We also created a script to handle the bird's health that is expanded later, when we create the other birds for our game.

Controls

Next, we are going to give the player the ability to interact with the game. First, we will create a slingshot to throw the birds. Following that will be the creation of the camera controls. We will even create a nice background effect to round out the look of our game.

Attacking

To attack the pig fortress, we have our basic bird ammo. We need to create a slingshot to hurl that ammo at the pigs. It will also handle the spawning of the birds at the beginning of the level and automatically reload as birds are used. When the slingshot runs out of birds it will notify the `LevelTracker` script and the game will end. Finally, we will create a script that will keep the physics simulation from going on for too long. We don't want the player forced to sit and watch a pig slowly roll across the screen. So, the script will, after a little while, start damping the movement of the **Rigidbody** components to make them stop rather than keep rolling.

Time for action – creating the slingshot

Most of the slingshot's appearance will actually be an optical illusion:

1. To start off the creation of the slingshot, add the `slingshot` model to the scene and position it at the origin. Apply a light brown material to the `Fork` model and a dark brown one to the `Pouch` model.

2. Next, we need four empty **GameObject**. Make them all the children of the `Slingshot` object.

   ❑ Name the first `FocalPoint` and center it between the fork prongs of the slingshot. This will be the point through which we fire all of the birds.

   ❑ The second is `Pouch`. Make the `pouch` model a child of this object, setting its position to `0.5` on the **X** axis and `0` on the **Y** and **Z** axes. This will make the pouch appear in front of the current bird without having to make a complete pouch model.

   ❑ Third is `BirdPoint`; this will position the bird that is being fired. Make it a child of the `Pouch` point and set its position to `0` on the **X** and **Y** axes and `0.3` on the **Z** axis.

   ❑ Last is `WaitPoint`; the birds waiting to be fired will be positioned behind this point. Set its position to `0` for the **X** axis, `0.5` for the **Y** axis, and `-4` for the **Z** axis.

3. Next, rotate the `Fork` model so that we can see both prongs of the fork. The values of `270` for the **X** axis, `25` for the **Y** axis, and `0` for the **Z** axis will work well.

4. The `Slingshot` script will provide most of the interaction for the player. Create it now.

5. We start it with a group of variables. The first will keep a reference to the damper that was mentioned earlier. The second group keeps track of the birds that will be used in the level. Next is a group of variables that will track the current bird that is ready to be fired. Fourth, we have some variables to hold references to the points we created a moment ago. The `maxRange` variable is the distance from the focal point to which the player can drag the pouch. The last two variables define how powerfully the bird will be launched.

```
public RigidbodyDamper rigidbodyDamper;

public GameObject[] levelBirds = new GameObject[0];
private GameObject[] currentBirds;
private int nextIndex = 0;
public Transform waitPoint;
```

```
public Transform toFireBird;
public bool didFire = false;
public bool isAiming = false;

public Transform pouch;
public Transform focalPoint;
public Transform pouchBirdPoint;

public float maxRange = 3;

public float maxFireStrength = 25;
public float minFireStrength = 5;
```

6. As with our other scripts, we use the `Awake` function for initialization. The `levelBirds` variable will hold references to all of the `bird` prefabs that will be used in the level. We start by creating an instance of each one and storing it in the `currentBirds` variable. The `isKinematic` variable is set to `true` on each bird's **Rigidbody** so that it does not move when it is not in use. Next, it readies the first bird to be fired and, finally, it positions the remaining birds behind the `waitPoint`.

```
public void Awake() {
  currentBirds = new GameObject[levelBirds.Length];
  for(int i=0;i<levelBirds.Length;i++) {
    GameObject nextBird = Instantiate(levelBirds[i]) as
GameObject;
    nextBird.rigidbody.isKinematic = true;
    currentBirds[i] = nextBird;
  }

  ReadyNextBird();
  SetWaitPositions();
}
```

7. The `ReadyNextBird` function first checks to see if we have run out of birds. If so, it calls the `LevelTracker` script to trigger the Game Over event. The `nextIndex` variable tracks the current location of the birds in the list to fire at the player. Next, the function checks to make sure the next slot actually has a bird, incrementing the index and trying for a new bird if it does not have one. If there is a bird available, it is stored in the `toFireBird` variable and made a child of the `BirdPoint` object we created; its position and rotation are zeroed out. Finally, the firing and aiming flags are reset.

```
public void ReadyNextBird() {
  if(currentBirds.Length <= nextIndex) {
    LevelTracker.OutOfBirds();
```

```
      return;
   }

   if(currentBirds[nextIndex] == null) {
      nextIndex++;
      ReadyNextBird();
      return;
   }

   toFireBird = currentBirds[nextIndex].transform;
   nextIndex++;

   toFireBird.parent = pouchBirdPoint;
   toFireBird.localPosition = Vector3.zero;
   toFireBird.localRotation = Quaternion.identity;

   didFire = false;
   isAiming = false;
}
```

8. The `SetWaitingPositions` function uses the position of the `waitPoint` to position all of the remaining birds behind the slingshot.

```
public void SetWaitingPositions() {
   for(int i=nextIndex;i<currentBirds.Length;i++) {
      if(currentBirds[i] == null) continue;
      Vector3 offset = Vector3.forward * (i - nextIndex) * 2;
      currentBirds[i].transform.position = waitPoint.position -
offset;
   }
}
```

9. The `Update` function starts by checking to see if the player has fired a bird and watches the `rigidbodyDamper.allSleeping` variable to see if all of the physics objects have stopped moving. Once they do, the next bird is readied to fire. If we have not fired, the aiming flag is checked and the `DoAiming` function is called to handle the aiming. If the player is neither aiming nor has just fired a bird, we check for touch input and, if the player touches close enough to the focal point, we flag that the player has started aiming.

```
public void Update() {
   if(didFire) {
      if(rigidbodyDamper.allSleeping) {
         ReadyNextBird();
         SetWaitingPositions();
      }
```

```
        return;
    }
    else if(isAiming) {
        DoAiming();
    }
    else {
        if(Input.touchCount <= 0) return;
        Vector3 touchPoint = GetTouchPoint();
        isAiming = Vector3.Distance(touchPoint, focalPoint.position) <
maxRange / 2;
    }
}
```

10. The `DoAiming` function checks to see if the player has stopped touching the screen and fires the current bird when they have. If they have not, we position the pouch at the current touch point. Finally, the pouch's position is limited to keep it within the maximum range.

```
private void DoAiming() {
    if(Input.touchCount <= 0) {
        FireBird();
        return;
    }

    Vector3 touchPoint = GetTouchPoint();

    pouch.position = touchPoint;
    pouch.LookAt(focalPoint);

    float distance = Vector3.Distance(focalPoint.position, pouch.
position);
    if(distance > maxRange) {
        pouch.position = focalPoint.position - (pouch.forward *
maxRange);
    }
}
```

11. The `GetTouchPoint` function uses `ScreenPointToRay` to find out where the player is touching in 3D space. This is just as when we were shooting asteroids but, because this game is 2D, we can just look at the ray's origin and return it with a zero for its x axis value.

```
private Vector3 GetTouchPoint() {
    Ray touchRay = Camera.main.ScreenPointToRay(Input.GetTouch(0).
position);
```

```
    Vector3 touchPoint = touchRay.origin;
    touchPoint.x = 0;
    return touchPoint;
}
```

12. Finally, for this script, we have the `FireBird` function. This function starts by setting our `didFire` flag to `true`. Next, it finds out the direction to fire by finding the direction from the pouch's position to the `focalPoint`. It also uses the distance between them to determine the power to fire the bird with, clamping it between our min and max strengths. Then, it releases the bird by clearing its parent and setting its `isKinematic` flag to `false`. To launch it, we use the `rigidbody.AddForce` function and pass the direction multiplied by the power to it. `ForceMode.Impulse` is also passed to make the force applied once and immediately. Next, the pouch is positioned at the `focalPoint`, as if it were actually under tension. And finally, we call `rigidbodyDamper.ReadyDamp` to start the damping of the `Rigidbody` movement.

```
private void FireBird() {
    didFire = true;

    Vector3 direction = (focalPoint.position - pouch.position).
normalized;
    float distance = Vector3.Distance(focalPoint.position, pouch.
position);
float power = distance <= 0 ? 0 : distance / maxRange;
    power *= maxFireStrength;
    power = Mathf.Clamp(power, minFireStrength, maxFireStrength);

    toFireBird.parent = null;
    toFireBird.rigidbody.isKinematic = false;
    toFireBird.rigidbody.AddForce(direction * power, ForceMode.
Impulse);

    pouch.position = focalPoint.position;

    rigidbodyDamper.ReadyDamp();
}
```

13. Before we can make use of the `Slingshot` script, we need to create the `RigidbodyDamper` script.

14. This script starts with six variables. The first two define how long to wait before the damping movement and how much to damp it by. The next two track whether it can apply the damping and when it will start. Next, is a variable that will be filled with a list of all the rigidbodies that are currently in the scene. Finally, it has the `allSleeping` flag that will be set to `true` when the movement has stopped.

```
public float dampWaitLength = 10f;
public float dampAmount = 0.9f;
```

```
private float dampTime = -1;
private bool canDamp = false;
private Rigidbody[] rigidbodies = new Rigidbody[0];

public bool allSleeping = false;
```

15. The `ReadyDamp` function starts by using `FindObjectsOfType` to fill the list with all of the rigidbodies. It sets when to start damping as the sum of the current time and the wait length. It marks that the script can do its damping and resets the `allSleeping` flag. Finally, it uses `StartCoroutine` to call the `CheckSleepingRigidbodies` function. This is a special way of calling functions to make them run in the background without blocking the rest of the game from running.

```
public void ReadyDamp() {
  rigidbodies = FindObjectsOfType(typeof(Rigidbody)) as
Rigidbody[];
  dampTime = Time.time + dampWaitLength;
  canDamp = true;
  allSleeping = false;

  StartCoroutine(CheckSleepingRigidbodies());
}
```

16. In the `FixedUpdate` function, we first check to see if we can damp the movement and whether it is time to do it. If it is, we loop through all of the rigidbodies, applying our damp to each one's rotational and linear velocity. Those that are kinematic, controlled by scripts, and already sleeping, meaning they stopped moving, are skipped.

```
public void FixedUpdate() {
  if(!canDamp || dampTime > Time.time) return;

  foreach(Rigidbody next in rigidbodies) {
    if(next != null && !next.isKinematic && !next.IsSleeping()) {
      next.angularVelocity *= dampAmount;
      next.velocity *= dampAmount;
    }
  }
}
```

17. The `CheckSleepingRigidbodies` function is special and will run in the background. This is made possible by the `IEnumerator` flag at the beginning of the function and the `yield return null` line in the middle. Together, these allow the function to pause regularly and keep from freezing the rest of the game while it waits for the function to complete. The function starts by creating a check flag and using it to check if all of the rigidbodies have stopped moving. If one is found still moving, the flag is set to `false` and the function pauses until the next frame, when it will try again. When it reaches the end, because all of the rigidbodies are sleeping, it sets the `allSleeping` flag to `true`, so that the slingshot can ready the next bird. It also stops itself from damping while the player is getting ready to fire the next bird.

```
private IEnumerator CheckSleepingRigidbodies() {
  bool sleepCheck = false;

  while(!sleepCheck) {
    sleepCheck = true;

    foreach(Rigidbody next in rigidbodies) {
      if(next != null && !next.isKinematic && !next.IsSleeping())
{
        sleepCheck = false;
        yield return null;
        break;
      }
    }
  }

  allSleeping = true;
  canDamp = false;
}
```

18. Finally, we have the `AddBodiesToCheck` function. This function will be used by anything that spawns new physics objects after the player has fired the bird. It starts by creating a temporary list and expanding the current one. Next, it adds all of the values from the temporary list to the expanded one. Finally, the list of rigidbodies is added after those of the temporary list.

```
public void AddBodiesToCheck(Rigidbody[] toAdd) {
  Rigidbody[] temp = rigidbodies;
  rigidbodies = new Rigidbody[temp.Length + toAdd.Length];

  for(int i=0;i<temp.Length;i++) {
    rigidbodies[i] = temp[i];
  }
```

```
    for(int i=0;i<toAdd.Length;i++) {
      rigidbodies[i + temp.Length] = toAdd[i];
    }
}
```

19. Return to Unity and add the two scripts to the `Slingshot` object. On the `Slingshot` script component, connect the references to the **Rigidbody Damper** component and each of the points. Also, add to the **Level Birds** list as many references to the red bird as you want for the level.

20. To keep objects from rolling back and through the slingshot, create a **Box Collider** component and position it at the stock of the `Fork` model.

21. To finish off the look of the slingshot, we need to create the elastic bands that tie the pouch to the fork. We will do this by first creating the `SlingshotBand` script.

22. The script starts with two variables. One for the point that the band will end at and one to reference the `LineRenderer` that will draw it.

```
public Transform endPoint;
public LineRenderer lineRenderer;
```

23. The `Awake` function makes sure the `lineRenderer` variable has only two points and sets their initial positions.

```
public void Awake() {
  if(lineRenderer == null) return;
  if(endPoint == null) return;

  lineRenderer.SetVertexCount(2);
  lineRenderer.SetPosition(0, transform.position);
  lineRenderer.SetPosition(1, endPoint.position);
}
```

24. In the `LateUpdate` function, we set the `lineRenderer` variable's end position to the `endPoint` value. This point will move around with the pouch, so we need to constantly update the renderer.

```
public void LateUpdate() {
  if(endPoint == null) return;
  if(lineRenderer == null) return;

  lineRenderer.SetPosition(1, endPoint.position);
}
```

25. Return to Unity and create an empty **GameObject**. Name it `Band_Near` and make it a child of the `Slingshot` object.

26. As children of this new point, create a cylinder and a second empty **GameObject**, named `Band`.

27. Give the cylinder a brown material and position it near the prong of the slingshot fork.

28. To the `Band` object, add a **Line Renderer** component found under **Effects** in the **Component** menu. After positioning it in the center of the cylinder, add the `SlingshotBand` script to the object.

29. To the **Line Renderer** under **Materials**, you can put your brown material in the slot to color the band. under **Parameters**. Set the **Start Width** to `0.5` and the **End width** to `0.2` to set the size of the line.

30. Next, create one more empty **GameObject** and name it `BandEnd_Near`. Make it a child of the `Pouch` object and position it inside the pouch.

31. Now, connect the script's references to its line renderer and end point.

32. To make the second band, duplicate the four objects we just created and position them far from the prong of the fork. The end point for this band can just be moved back along the x axis to keep it out of the way of the birds.

33. Finally, turn the whole thing into a prefab so it can be easily reused in other levels.

What just happened?

We created the slingshot that will be used to fire birds. We used techniques we learned in the previous chapter to handle touch input and track the player's finger while they aim and shoot. If you save your scene and position the camera to look at the slingshot, you will notice that it is complete if not entirely playable. Birds can be fired at the pig fortress, although we can only see the destruction from within Unity's **Scene** view.

Watching

The game is technically playable at this point, but it is kind of hard to see what is going on. Next, we will create a system to control the camera. It will allow the player to drag the camera left and right, follow the bird when it is launched and return to the slingshot when everything stops moving. There will also be a set of limits to keep the camera from going too far and viewing things we do not want the player to see.

Time for action – controlling the camera

We will only need one, fairly short script to control and manage our camera:

1. To start and to keep everything organized, create a new empty **GameObject** and name it `CameraRig`. Also, to keep it simple, set its position to zero on each axis.

2. Next, create three more empty **GameObject** and name them `LeftPoint`, `RightPoint`, and `TopPoint`. Set their **X** axis positions to 5. Position the `LeftPoint` to be in front of the slingshot and at 3 on the **Y** axis. The `RightPoint` needs to be positioned in front of the `pig` structure you created. The `TopPoint` can be over the slingshot, but needs to set to 8 on the **Y** axis. These three points will define the limits of where our camera can move when being dragged and following birds.

3. Make all three points, and the `Main Camera` object, children of the `CameraRig` object.

4. Now, we create the `CameraControl` script. This script will control all of the movement and interaction with the camera.

5. Our variables for this script start with a reference to the slingshot; we need this so we can follow the current bird when it is fired. Next are the references to the points we just created. The next group of variables control how long the camera will sit without input before returning to look at the slingshot and how fast it will return. The `dragScale` variable controls how fast the camera actually moves when the player drags their finger across the screen, allowing us to keep the scene moving with the finger. The last group is to control whether the camera can follow the current bird and how fast it can do so.

```
public Slingshot slingshot;

public Transform rightPoint;
public Transform leftPoint;
public Transform topPoint;

public float waitTime = 3f;
private float headBackTime = -1;
private Vector3 waitPosition;
public float headBackDuration = 3f;

public float dragScale = 0.075f;

private bool followBird = false;
private Vector3 followVelocity = Vector3.zero;
public float followSmoothTime = 0.1f;
```

6. In the Awake function, we first make certain the camera is not following a bird and make it wait before heading to look at the slingshot. This allows us to initially point the camera to the pig fortress when the level starts and move to the slingshot after giving the player a chance to see what they are up against.

```
public void Awake() {
  followBird = false;
  StartWait();
}
```

7. The StartWait function sets the time when it will start to head back to the slingshot and records the position that it is heading back from. This allows us to create a smooth transition.

```
public void StartWait() {
  headBackTime = Time.time + waitTime;
  waitPosition = transform.position;
}
```

8. Next, we have the Update function. This one starts by checking whether the slingshot has fired. If it hasn't, it checks to see whether the player has started aiming, signaling that the bird should be followed and zeroing out the velocity if they have. If they have not, the followBird flag is cleared. Next, the function checks whether it should follow and does so if it should, also calling the StartWait function in case this is the frame in which the bird is destroyed. If it should not follow the bird, it checks for touch input and drags the camera if it finds any. The wait is again started in case the player removes their finger in this frame. Finally, it checks to see if the slingshot is done firing the current bird and if it is time to head back. Should both be true, the camera moves back to pointing at the slingshot.

```
public void Update() {
  if(!slingshot.didFire) {
```

```
    if(slingshot.isAiming) {
      followBird = true;
      followVelocity = Vector3.zero;
    }
    else {
      followBird = false;
    }
  }

  if(followBird) {
    FollowBird();
    StartWait();
  }
  else if(Input.touchCount > 0) {
    DragCamera();
    StartWait();
  }

  if(!slingshot.didFire && headBackTime < Time.time) {
    BackToLeft();
  }
}
```

9. The `FollowBird` function starts by making sure there is a bird to follow by checking the `toFireBird` variable on the `Slingshot` script and stops following if a bird is not found. Should there be a bird, the function then determines a new point to move to that will look directly at the bird. It then uses the `Vector3.SmoothDamp` function to smoothly follow the bird. This function works similar to a spring—the farther away it is from its target position, the faster it moves the object. The `followVelocity` variable is used to keep it moving smoothly. Finally, it calls another function to limit the camera's position within those bounding points we set up earlier.

```
private void FollowBird() {
  if(slingshot.toFireBird == null) {
    followBird = false;
    return;
  }

  Vector3 targetPoint = slingshot.toFireBird.position;
  targetPoint.x = transform.position.x;

  transform.position = Vector3.SmoothDamp(transform.position,
targetPoint, ref followVelocity, followSmoothTime);
  ClampPosition();
}
```

10. In the `DragCamera` function, we use the `deltaPosition` value of the current touch to determine how far it has moved since the last frame. By scaling this value and subtracting the vector from the camera's position, the function moves the camera as the player drags across the screen. This function also calls upon the function to clamp the camera's position.

```
private void DragCamera() {
  transform.position -= new Vector3(0, 0, Input.GetTouch(0).
deltaPosition.x * dragScale);
  ClampPosition();
}
```

11. The `ClampPosition` function starts by taking the camera's current position. It then clamps the z position to be between those of the `leftPoint` and `rightPoint` variables' z positions. Next, the y position is clamped between the `leftPoint` and `topPoint` variables' positions. Finally, the new position is reapplied to the camera's transform.

```
private void ClampPosition() {
  Vector3 clamped = transform.position;
  clamped.z = Mathf.Clamp(clamped.z, leftPoint.position.z,
rightPoint.position.z);
  clamped.y = Mathf.Clamp(clamped.y, leftPoint.position.y,
topPoint.position.y);
  transform.position = clamped;
}
```

12. Finally, we have the `BackToLeft` function. It starts by using the time and our duration variable to determine how much progress in returning to the slingshot the camera will have made. It records the camera's current position and uses `Mathf.SmoothStep` on both the z and y axes to find a new position that is the appropriate distance between the `waitPosition` variable and the `leftPoint` variable. Finally, the new position is applied.

```
private void BackToLeft() {
  float progress = (Time.time - headBackTime) / headBackDuration;
  Vector3 newPosition = transform.position;
  newPosition.z = Mathf.SmoothStep(waitPosition.z, leftPoint.
position.z, progress);
  newPosition.y = Mathf.SmoothStep(waitPosition.y, leftPoint.
position.y, progress);
  transform.position = newPosition;
}
```

13. Next, return to Unity and add the new script to the `Main Camera` object. Connect the references to the slingshot and each of the points to finish it off.

14. Position the camera to point at your pig fortress and turn the whole rig into a prefab.

What just happened?

We created the camera rig that will let the player watch all of the action as they play the game. The camera will now follow the birds as they are fired from the slingshot and can now be dragged by the player. By keying off the positions of a few objects, this movement is limited to keep the player from seeing things we don't want them to. If the camera is left idle long enough, it will also return to look at the slingshot.

Have a go hero – more levels

Now that we have all of the pieces needed to make a complete level, we need some more levels. We need at least two more levels. You can use the blocks and pigs to create any level you might want. It is a good idea to keep the pig structures centered at about 30 on the **Z** axis. Also, think about the difficulty of the level while making it, so that you can end up with an easy, medium, and hard level.

A better background

A great feature of many 2D games is a parallax scrolling background. This simply means that the background is created in layers that scroll by at different speeds. Think of it as if looking out the window of your car. The objects that are far away appear to hardly move, while the ones that are near move by quickly. In a 2D game, it gives the illusion of depth and adds a nice touch to the look of the game. For this background, we will be layering several materials on a single plane.

Time for action – creating the parallax background

There is an alternative method of creating and utilizing a second camera, but ours will make use of a single script that additionally allows us to control the speed of each layer:

1. We will start this section with the creation of the `ParallaxScroll` script.

2. This script starts with three variables. The first two keep track of each material and how fast they should scroll. The third keeps track of the camera's last position, so we can track how far it moves in each frame.

   ```
   public Material[] materials = new Material[0];
   public float[] speeds = new float[0];

   private Vector3 lastPosition = Vector3.zero;
   ```

3. In the `Start` function, we record the camera's beginning position. We use `Start` instead of `Awake` here, in case the camera needs to do any special movement at the beginning of the game.

```
public void Start() {
  lastPosition = Camera.main.transform.position;
}
```

4. Next, we use the `LateUpdate` function to make changes after the camera has moved about. It starts by finding the camera's new position and comparing the z axis values to determine how far it moved. Next, it loops through the list of materials. The loop first gathers the current offset of its texture using `mainTextureOffset`. Next, the camera's movement multiplied by the material's speed is subtracted from the offset's x axis to find a new horizontal position. Then, the new offset is applied to the material. Finally, the function records the camera's last position for the next frame.

```
public void LateUpdate() {
  Vector3 newPosition = Camera.main.transform.position;
  float move = newPosition.z - lastPosition.z;

  for(int i=0;i<materials.Length;i++) {
    Vector2 offset = materials[i].mainTextureOffset;
    offset.x -= move * speeds[i];
    materials[i].mainTextureOffset = offset;
  }

  lastPosition = newPosition;
}
```

5. Return to Unity and create six new materials. One for each of the background textures: `sky`, `hills_tall`, `hills_short`, `grass_light`, `grass_dark`, and `fronds`. All of the materials, except for the sky, need to use the **Diffuse** shader under **Transparent** in the **Shader** drop-down list. If they do not, we will not be able to see all of the textures when they are layered.

6. We also need to adjust the **Tiling** of each of these new materials. For all of them, leave the **Y** axis as 1. For the **X** axis, set 5 for the `sky`, 6 for `hills_tall`, 7 for `hills_short`, 8 for `grass_dark`, 9 for `fronds`, and 10 for `grass_light`. This will offset all of the features of the textures so a long pan does not see features regularly lining up.

7. Next, create a new plane. Name it `Background` and remove its **Mesh Collider** component.

8. Position it at -5 on the **X** axis, 7 on the **Y** axis, and 30 on the **Z** axis. Set its rotation to 90 for both the **X** and **Y** axes and 0 for **Z**. Also, set the scale to 10 for the **X** axis, 1 for the **Y** axis, and 1.5 for the **Z** axis. Altogether, these position the plane as facing the camera and filling the background.

9. In the plane's **Mesh Renderer** component, expand the **Materials** list and set the **Size** to 6. Add each of our new materials to the list slots in the order of sky, hills_tall, hills_short, grass_dark, fronds, grass_light. Do the same for the **Materials** list in the **Parallax Scroll** script component.

10. Finally, in the **Parallax Scroll** script component, set the **Size** of the **Speeds** list to 6 and input the following values in the order of 0.03, 0.024, 0.018, 0.012, 0.006, 0. These values will move the materials gently and evenly.

11. Turning the background into a prefab, at this point, will make it easy to reuse later.

What just happened?

We created a parallax scroll effect. This effect will pan a series of background textures, giving the illusion of depth in our 2D game. To easily see it in action, hit play and grab the camera in the **Scene** view, moving it along the z axis to see the background change.

Have a go hero – dark of the night

We have two other levels to add backgrounds to. Your challenge here is to create your own background. Use the techniques you learned in this section to create a night-style background. It could include a stationary moon while everything else scrolls in the shot. For an added trick, create a cloud layer that slowly pans across the screen as well as with the camera and the rest of the background.

The flock variety

There is one last set of assets we need to create for our levels, the other birds. We will create three more birds that each have a unique special ability: a yellow bird that accelerates, a blue bird that splits into multiple birds, and a black bird that explodes. With these our flock will be complete.

To make the creation of these birds easier, we will be making use of a concept called **inheritance**. Inheritance allows a script to expand upon the functions it is inheriting without the need to rewrite them. If used correctly, this can be very powerful and, in our case, will aid in the quick creation of multiple characters that are largely similar.

The yellow bird

First, we will create the yellow bird. Largely, this bird functions exactly as the red bird. However, when the player touches the screen, the bird's speed increases. By extending the `Bird` script that we created earlier, this bird's creation becomes quite simple.

Time for action – creating the yellow bird

Because of the power of inheritance, the script we are creating here consists of only a handful of lines of code:

1. Start by creating the yellow bird in the same way as the red bird, using the `YellowBird` model instead.

2. Instead of using the `Bird` script, we will create the `YellowBird` script.

3. This script needs to extend the `Bird` script, so replace `MonoBehaviour` with `Bird` on line four. It should look similar to the following code snippet:

   ```
   public class YellowBird : Bird {
   ```

4. This script adds a single variable that will be used to multiply the bird's current velocity.

   ```
   public float multiplier = 2f;
   ```

5. Next, we override the `DoSpecial` function and multiply the bird's `rigidbody.velocity` when it is called:

   ```
   protected override void DoSpecial() {
      didSpecial = true;
      rigidbody.velocity *= multiplier;
   }
   ```

6. Return to Unity, add the script to your new bird, and turn it into a prefab. Add some to the list on your slingshot to use the bird in your level.

What just happened?

We created the yellow bird. This bird is simple. It directly modifies its velocity to suddenly gain a boost of speed when the player touches the screen. As you will soon see, we use this same style of script creation to create all of our birds.

The blue bird

Next, we create the blue bird. This bird splits into three birds when the player touches the screen. It will also extend the `Bird` script.

Time for action – creating the blue bird

The blue bird will again make use of inheritance, reducing the amount of code that needs to be written to create the bird:

1. Again, start building your blue bird the same way as the previous two, substituting the appropriate model. You should also adjust the **Radius** of the **Sphere Collider** component to align appropriately with the smaller size of this bird.

2. Next, we create the `BlueBird` script.

3. Again, adjust line four so the script extends `Bird` instead of `MonoBehaviour`.

   ```
   public class BlueBird : Bird {
   ```

4. This script has three variables. The first is a list of prefabs to spawn when the bird splits. Next is the angle difference between each new bird that will be launched. Finally is a value to spawn the birds a little ahead of their current position to keep them from getting stuck inside each other.

   ```
   public GameObject[] splitBirds = new GameObject[0];
   public float launchAngle = 15f;
   public float spawnLead = 0.5f;
   ```

5. Next, we override the `DoSpecial` function and start, as with the others, by marking that we made our special move. Next, it calculates half of the number of birds to spawn and creates an empty list for storing the rigidbodies of the newly spawned birds.

   ```
   protected override void DoSpecial() {
     didSpecial = true;

     int halfLength = splitBirds.Length / 2;
     Rigidbody[] newBodies = new Rigidbody[splitBirds.Length];
   ```

6. The function continues by looping through the list of birds, skipping the slots that are empty. It spawns the new birds at its position, continuing to the next if there is a missing **Rigidbody** component. The new **Rigidbody** component is then stored in the list.

```
for(int i=0;i<splitBirds.Length;i++) {
   if(splitBirds[i] == null) continue;

   GameObject next = Instantiate(splitBirds[i], transform.
position, transform.rotation) as GameObject;
   if(next.rigidbody == null) continue;

   newBodies[i] = next.rigidbody;
```

7. Using `Quaternion.Euler`, a new rotation is created that will angle the new bird along a path split off from the main path. The new bird's velocity is set to the rotated velocity of the current bird. It is then moved forward along its new path to get out of the way of the other birds being spawned.

```
   Quaternion rotate = Quaternion.Euler(launchAngle * (i -
halfLength), 0, 0);
   next.rigidbody.velocity = rotate * rigidbody.velocity;
   next.transform.position += next.rigidbody.velocity.normalized
* spawnLead;
   }
```

8. After the loop, the function uses `FindObjectOfType` to find the slingshot that is currently in the scene. If found, it is changed to track the first new bird spawned as the one that was fired. The new list of rigidbodies is also set to the `rigidbodyDamper` variable to be added to its list of rigidbodies. Finally, the script destroys the bird it is attached to, completing the illusion that the bird has split apart.

```
   Slingshot slingshot = FindObjectOfType(typeof(Slingshot)) as
Slingshot;
   if(slingshot != null) {
      slingshot.toFireBird = newBodies[0].transform;
   slingshot.rigidbodyDamper.AddBodiesToCheck(newBodies);
   }

   Destroy(gameObject);
}
```

9. Before you add the script to your new bird, we actually need two blue birds: one that splits and one that does not. Duplicate your bird and name one `Bird_Blue_Split` and the other `Bird_Blue_Normal`. To the split bird add the new script and to the normal bird add the `Bird` script.

10. Turn both birds into prefabs and add the normal bird to the other's list of birds to be split into.

What just happened?

We created the blue bird. This bird splits into multiple birds when the user taps the screen. The effect actually requires two birds that look identical. One that does the splitting and another that is split into but does nothing special.

Have a go hero – creating a rainbow bird

It is actually possible to add anything we want to spawn to the blue bird's list of things to split into. Your challenge here is to create a rainbow bird. This bird could split into different types of birds, not just blue ones. Or, perhaps it is a stone bird that splits into stone blocks. For an extended challenge, create a mystery bird that picks a bird from its list randomly when it splits.

The black bird

Finally, we have the black bird. This bird explodes when the player touches the screen. As with all the birds discussed previously, it will extend the `Bird` script.

Time for action – creating the black bird

As with the two birds discussed earlier, inheriting from the red bird makes the black bird's creation much easier:

1. As with the others, this bird is initially created in the same way as the red bird, readjusting the **Radius** for its increased size.

2. Again, we create a new script to extend the `Bird` script. This time it is called `BlackBird`.

3. Do not forget to adjust line four to extend the `Bird` script and not `MonoBehaviour`.

```
public class BlackBird : Bird {
```

4. This script has two variables. The first is the size of the explosion and the second is its strength.

```
public float radius = 2.5f;
public float power = 25f;
```

5. Once more we override the `DoSpecial` function, first marking that we did it. Next, we use `Physics.OverlapSphere` to acquire a list of all of the objects that are within the range of the bird's explosion. The function then loops through the list, skipping any empty slots and those without rigidbodies. If the object does exist and has a **Rigidbody** component attached, we call `AddExplosionForce` to simulate the way an explosion's strength against you is reduced the further you are from it. We give the function the explosion's strength, followed by the bird's position and radius. The value 3 is a vertical modifier. It does not interfere with the distance an object is from the explosion but, instead, adjusts the angle the explosion hits it at. This 3 moves the force to below the object, because explosions that throw debris up are cooler than ones that push out. `ForceMode.Impulse` is again used to apply the force immediately. Finally, the function destroys the exploded bird.

```
protected override void DoSpecial() {
  didSpecial = true;

  Collider[] colliders = Physics.OverlapSphere(transform.position,
radius);

  foreach(Collider hit in colliders) {
    if(hit == null) continue;
    if(hit.rigidbody != null)
      hit.rigidbody.AddExplosionForce(power, transform.position,
radius, 3, ForceMode.Impulse);
  }

  Destroy(gameObject);
}
```

6. As with the last two, apply your new script to your new bird and turn it into a prefab. You now have four birds to choose from when selecting the slingshot arsenal for each level.

What just happened?

We created our fourth and last bird, the black bird. This bird explodes when the user touches the screen, throwing anything that might be near into the sky. This can be a fun bird to play around with and effective for destroying your pig forts.

Have a go hero – explosive blocks

Now that you know how to cause explosions, we have another challenge. Create an explosive crate. Extend the `Plank` script to make it. When enough damage is done to the crate, trigger the explosion. For an added challenge, instead of making the crate explode, configure it to throw out a few bombs that explode when they hit something.

Level selection

Finally, we need to create our level selection. From this scene, we will be able to access and start playing all of the levels we created earlier. We will also display the current high scores for each level.

Time for action – creating the level selection

A new scene and a single script will serve us well in managing our level selection:

1. This last section begins by saving your current scene and hitting *Ctrl + N* to create a new one, named `LevelSelect`.

2. For this scene, we need to create a single, short script also named `LevelSelect`.

3. The first and only variable defines the size of the buttons that will appear on screen.

    ```
    public int buttonSize = 100;
    ```

4. The only function is the `OnGUI` function. This function starts with a loop. It will loop through three times for the three levels we should have created earlier. A `Rect` variable is created and initialized to the `buttonSize`. The x and y values are then set to position the buttons in a row, centered on the screen. Next, the current high score for the level is retrieved, using `PlayerPrefs.GetInt` and the same key creation that we used in our `LevelTracker` script. Then, the function creates a string to hold the message that will appear on the button. Finally, the button is drawn and, when clicked, `Application.LoadLevel` is used to load the scene and start the user playing that level.

```
public void OnGUI() {
  for(int i=0;i<3;i++) {
    Rect next = new Rect(0,0, buttonSize, buttonSize);
    next.x = (Screen.width / 2) - (buttonSize * 1.5f) +
(buttonSize * i);
    next.y = (Screen.height / 2) - (buttonSize / 2f);

    int levelScore = PlayerPrefs.GetInt("LevelScore" + (i + 1),
0);
    string text = "Level " + (i + 1) + "\nScore: " + levelScore;

    if(GUI.Button(next, text)) {
      Application.LoadLevel(i + 1);
    }
  }
}
```

5. Return to Unity and add the script to the `Main Camera` object.

6. Finally, open the **Build Settings** and add your scenes to the **Scenes in Build** list. Clicking and dragging on the scenes in the list will let you reorder them. Make sure your **LevelSelect** scene is first and has the index of zero to the right of it. The rest of your scenes can appear in whatever order you desire. But be aware that they will be associated with the buttons in the same order.

What just happened?

We created a level-selection screen. It uses a loop to create a list of buttons associated with the levels in our game. When a button is pressed, `Application.LoadLevel` starts that level. We also made use of `PlayerPrefs.GetInt` to retrieve the high scores for each of the levels.

Have a go hero – adding some style

Here, the challenge is to use GUI styles to make the screen look great. A logo and a background would help a lot. Additionally, take a look at `GUI.BeginScrollView` if you have more than three levels. This function will let the user scroll through a list of levels that is far greater in size than can be easily seen on screen.

Summary

In this chapter, we learned about physics in Unity and recreated the incredibly popular mobile game, Angry Birds. By using Unity's physics system, we are able to make all of the levels that we could ever want to play. With this game, we also explored options for creating a 2D game in a 3D environment. Our birds and slingshot are 3D assets, giving us the ability to light and shade them. The pigs and the background, however, are 2D images, reducing our lighting options, but can allow for some greater detail in the assets. The 2D images were also crucial in the creation of the parallax scrolling effect of the background. Finally, the building's blocks appear to be 2D, but are actually 3D blocks. We also created a level-selection screen. From there, the player can see their high scores and pick any of the levels that we created to play.

In the next chapter, we return to the Space Fighter game we started in the previous chapter. We are going to create and add all of the special effects that finish off a game. We will add the shooting and explosion sound effects that every space game needs. We will also add various particle effects. When ships are shot at, they will actually explode, rather than just disappearing.

8

Special Effects – Sound and Particles

In the previous chapter, we took a short break from our Space Fighter game to learn about physics and 2D games in Unity. We created a clone of Angry Birds. The birds utilized physics to fly through the air and destroy the pigs and their structures. We utilized parallax scrolling to make a pleasing background effect. We also created a level selection screen to load the game's various scenes from.

In this chapter, we return to the Space Fighter game. We are going to add many special effects that will round out the game experience. We start by learning about the controls that Unity provides when working with audio. We move on to add some background music to the game and warning sounds when anything gets too close. Next, we learn about particle systems, creating engine trails for our ship. Finally, we combine the effects of the chapter to create bullet blasts and explosions.

In this chapter, we will be covering the following topics:

- Importing audio clips
- Playing SFX
- Understanding 2D and 3D SFX
- Creating particle systems

Open up your Space Fighter project and we will get started.

Understanding audio

As with other assets, the Unity team has worked hard to make working with audio easy and pain-free. Unity is capable of importing and utilizing a broad range of audio formats, allowing you to keep your files in a format that you can edit in another program.

Import settings

Audio clips have a small assortment of important settings. They let you easily control the type and compression of files.

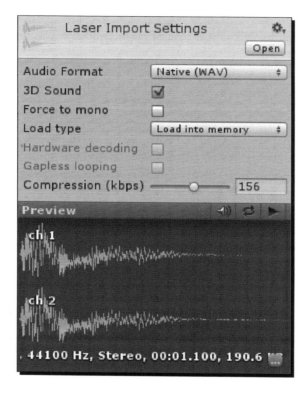

The following are the settings that we have to work with while importing audio clips:

◆ **Audio Format**: This controls whether the file is included in the **Native** format or is **Compressed** in the final game. **Native**, though larger in file size, is best for short sound effects because they can be loaded and played quickly. **Compressed** is better for longer sounds and music. They will have a smaller footprint in the final build.

- **3D Sound**: This checkbox controls whether the file will be played in 2D or 3D. 2D sounds will be played at a constant volume no matter where the player is located—perfect for background music and voice overs. 3D sounds will be adjusted in volume based on their distance from the player—excellent for explosions and gun shots.

- **Force to mono**: This checkbox will cause Unity to change a stereo file to a mono file.

- **Load type**: This controls how the file is loaded when the game is being played.

    - **Load into memory**: This loads a **Native** file directly to the memory to be played.

    - **Stream from disc**: This streams the audio as it is playing, such as streaming music or video from the Web.

    - **Decompress on load**: This removes compression on the file when it is first needed. The overhead for this option makes it a very poor choice for large files.

    - **Compressed in memory**: This only decompresses the file as it is being played. When it is just being held in memory, the file remains compressed.

- **Hardware decoding**: This is only used for iOS devices to reduce processing cost.

- **Gapless looping**: This adjusts the compression method to remove the small pop of silence that some methods can introduce to a file.

- **Compression**: This is the amount of data per second to compress the file to, resulting in a smaller-sized file. It is best to find a value that minimizes the file size while losing the least amount of quality.

Audio Listener

In order to actually hear anything in the game, every scene needs an **Audio Listener** component in it. By default, the `Main Camera` object (included first in any new scene) and any new camera you might create has an **Audio Listener** component attached. There can only be one **Audio Listener** component in your scene at a time. If there is more than one, or you try to play a sound when there isn't one, Unity will fill your console log with complaints. The **Audio Listener** component also gives the precise position for any 3D sound effects to key off.

Audio Source

The **Audio Source** component is like a speaker and controls the settings for playing any sound effect. If the clip is 3D, the position of this object to the **Audio Listener** component and the mode chosen determine the volume of the clip.

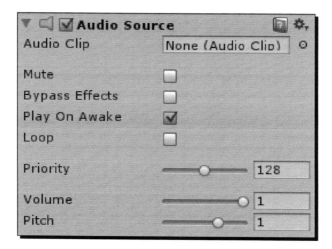

The following are the various settings for an **Audio Source** component:

- **Audio Clip**: This is the sound file that this **Audio Source** component will play by default.

- **Mute**: This is a quick way to toggle the volume of the playing sound on and off.

- **Bypass Effects**: This allows one to toggle any special filters applied to this **Audio Source** component.

- **Play On Awake**: This will cause the **Audio Clip** to immediately start playing when the scene loads or the object is spawned.

- **Loop**: This will cause the playing clip to repeat as it is played.

- **Priority**: This dictates the relative importance of the files being played. **0** is most important and best for music, while **256** is least important. Depending on the system, only so many sounds can be played at once. The list of files to be played starts with the most important and ends when this limit is reached, excluding those with the lowest values if there are more sounds than the limit would allow.

- **Volume**: This decides how loud the clip will be played.

- **Pitch**: This scales the playback speed of the clip.

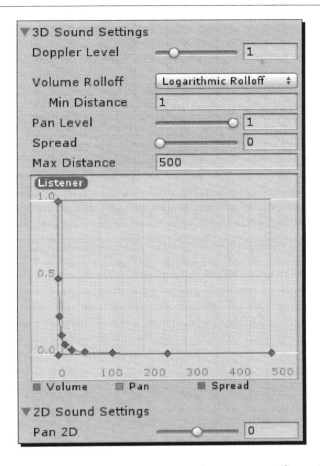

- ◆ **3D Sound Settings**: This contains the group of settings specific to the playing of 3D audio clips. The **Volume**, **Pan**, and **Spread** options can be adjusted using the graph at the end of the group. This allows one to create more dynamic transitions as the player approaches an **Audio Source** component.

  - ❑ **Doppler Level**: This decides how much of the doppler effect to apply to moving sounds.

  - ❑ **Volume Rolloff**: This controls how the volume fades with distance.

    Logarithmic Rolloff: This is a sudden and rapid falloff of the sound at a short distance from the source's center.

    Linear Rolloff: This is an even falloff with distance, the loudest being at the **Min Distance** value and the quietest at the **Max Distance** value.

Custom Rolloff: This allows you to create a custom falloff by adjusting the graph at the end of the group. It is also automatically chosen when the graph is adjusted.

❑ If the **Audio Listener** component is closer than the **Min Distance** value, the audio will be played at the current volume level. Outside this distance, the sound will fall off according to the **Rolloff Mode**.

❑ **Pan Level**: This is the percentage of the 3D effects to be applied to this **Audio Source** component. This affects things such as the falloff and doppler effects.

❑ **Spread**: This adjusts the amount of area in speaker space that the sound covers. It becomes more important when working with more than one or two speakers.

❑ Beyond the **Max Distance** value, the sound will stop transitioning based on the graph at the bottom of the group.

◆ **2D Sound Settings**: This groups the settings that are specific to 2D audio clips.

❑ **Pan 2D**: This adjusts how evenly the sound comes out of each speaker, weighing it towards the left or right speaker

Adding background music

Now that we know about the available audio settings, it is time to put that knowledge into action. We will start by adding some background music. This will have to be a 2D sound effect so we can hear it comfortably no matter where the **Audio Source** component is. We will also create a short script to fade in the music to reduce the suddenness with which sound effects bombard the player.

Time for action – adding background music

Let's get started with a single script to control our background music.

1. We will start by creating a new script and naming it `FadeIn`.

2. This script begins with three variables. The first is the goal volume that the script has to reach. The second is the number of seconds the transition will take. The last is the time when the transition began.

```
public float maxVolume = 1f;
public float fadeLength = 1f;
private float fadeStartTime = -1f;
```

3. Next, we make use of the `Awake` function. It begins by looking at the `audio` variable, which is automatically supplied by Unity, to check for an attached **Audio Source** component. If one cannot be found, the `gameObject` is destroyed and the function is exited.

```
public void Awake() {
  if(audio == null) {
    Destroy(gameObject);
    return;
  }
}
```

4. The `Awake` function ends by setting its volume to `0` and playing it if it isn't already.

```
  audio.volume = 0;

  if(!audio.isPlaying)
    audio.Play();
}
```

5. To cause the transition over time, we use the `Update` function. It will first check to see whether the `fadeStartTime` variable is below zero and set it to the current time if it is. This allows us to avoid the hiccup that can be caused by the initialization of a scene starting.

```
public void Update() {
  if(fadeStartTime < 0)
    fadeStartTime = Time.time;
```

6. The function next checks to see if the transition's time has ended. If it has, the **Audio Source** component's volume is set to `maxVolume` and the script is destroyed to free resources.

```
  if(fadeStartTime + fadeLength < Time.time) {
    audio.volume = maxVolume;
    Destroy(this);
    return;
  }
```

7. Finally, the current progress is calculated by finding the amount of time that has passed since the fade started and dividing it by the length of the transition. The resulting percentage of progress is multiplied by the value of `maxVolume` and applied to the **Audio Source** component's volume.

```
  float progress = (Time.time - fadeStartTime) / fadeLength;
  audio.volume = maxVolume * progress;
}
```

8. Back in Unity, we need to create a new empty `GameObject` and name it `Background`.

9. To this object, add our `FadeIn` script and an **Audio Source** component.

10. If you have not already, create an `Audio` folder in your **Project** panel and import the four sound files included in **Starting Assets** for the chapter.

11. Select the `Background` sound file and uncheck the **3D Sound** checkbox in the import settings.

12. Select your `Background` object in the **Hierarchy** window and drag the `Background` sound to the **Audio Clip** slot.

13. Make sure the **Play On Awake** and **Loop** checkboxes are checked on the **Audio Source** component. The **Volume** option also needs to be set to **0**, all to make the file play throughout the game but make no noise when starting.

What just happened?

We added background music to our game. In order for the sound to be constant and not directional, we utilized the music as 2D sound. We also created a script to fade the music in when the game starts. This eases the transition into the game for the player, preventing a sudden onslaught of sound.

Have a go hero – setting some mood

Background music adds a lot to a game's experience. A horror scene is not nearly as scary without some scary music. Bosses are much less intimidating without their daunting music. Look for some good background music for your other games. Something light and cheery would work nicely for Angry Birds, while a piece that is more industrial and fast-paced would keep hearts racing through the Tank Battle game.

Creating an alarm system

To understand 3D audio effects, we are going to create an alarm system. As objects approach the ship, the alarm will increase in volume. The 3D effect will indicate the direction to the object relative to the ship. This gives the player the needed feedback when they can't see everything around them. There are several ways this effect can be achieved, but this one will demonstrate our ability to adjust the **Audio Source** component over time.

Time for action – warning the player

A single script attached to our objects in space will warn the player as the objects approach.

1. We start by creating a new script and name it `Alarm`.

2. This script starts with a single variable. It will hold the distance value at which the sound will start to fade in.

    ```
    public float warningDist = 100f;
    ```

3. Next, we create the `Update` function. It starts by checking for an **Audio Source** component and exiting the function early if there isn't one. The `audio` variable holds the reference to the attached **Audio Source** component.

    ```
    public void Update() {
      if(audio == null) return;
    ```

4. The function continues by calculating the distance to the player. Because the player never moves, we can just use the position's distance to the origin to make it simpler. We also use `sqrMagnitude`, which is the square of the length of the vector, because it is significantly faster to calculate. If the object is outside the range, the volume is set to `0` and the function is exited.

    ```
    float distance = transform.position.sqrMagnitude;
    if(distance > warningDist * warningDist) {
      audio.volume = 0;
      return;
    }
    ```

5. Finally, we calculate the new volume by dividing the distance by the square of `warningDist` value and subtracting the result from one. This will result in a rounded curve as it approaches maximum volume.

    ```
    float volume = 1 - (distance / (warningDist * warningDist));
    audio.volume = volume;
    }
    ```

6. We now need to add the script to the relevant objects. To both the enemy ship and asteroid prefabs, add the `Alarm` script and an **Audio Source** component.

7. For the **Audio Clip** value, select the `Alarm` clip. Also, make sure both the **Play On Awake** and **Loop** checkboxes are checked.

8. Next, we don't want the alarm to overpower other sounds in our game, so set the **Priority** option to **192**.

9. To keep it from making any noise when the object is spawned, set the **Volume** option to **0**.

10. In order for the script to fully control the **Audio Source** component's volume, expand the **3D Sound Settings** component. Select **Linear Rolloff** for **Volume Rolloff** and **495** for the **Min Distance** option.

What just happened?

We created a script to warn the player when objects get too close. As they approach the player, the volume on their audio source is increased. As they move away from the player, the volume is reduced. By utilizing 3D audio clips, we can direct the player as to where the approaching object is coming from.

Have a go hero – differentiation

It is great that we can tell when objects are coming too close, but we can't tell what it is until we see it. Find some alternate alarm sounds. For each type of object that the player has to contend with, give it a different sound. This way, the player will know whether they need to start pulling some tricky maneuvers to dodge bullets or they are entering an asteroid field and need to fly carefully to avoid a collision.

Understanding particle systems

Particle systems add much to the final look of a game. They can take the form of fire, magic waves, rain, or the great many other effects you can dream up. They are often hard to create well, but are well worth the effort. Keep in mind, especially when working with the mobile platform, that less is more. Larger particles are more effective than a great amount of particles. If your particle system ever contains thousands of particles in a small space or is duplicated on itself to increase the effect, you need to rethink the design and find a more efficient solution.

Particle system settings

Every particle system contains a large variety of components, each with its own settings. Most of the available settings have the option to be **Constant**, **Curve**, **Random Between Two Constants**, and **Random Between Two Curves**. **Constant** will be a specific value. **Curve** will be a set value that changes along the curve over time. The two random settings select a random value between the respective value types. It may seem confusing at first but, as we work through them, they will become more understandable.

As you will be able to see in the images and descriptions that follow, we will work through and gain an understanding of each piece of a particle system.

As you will see in the following screenshot, we will work through and gain an understanding of each piece of a particle system:

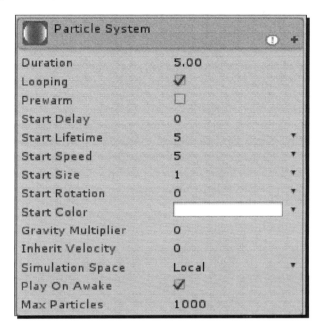

1. The first portion, the **Initial** module, of the particle system holds all the settings used by every emitter in Unity.

    ❑ **Duration**: This is how long the emitter lasts. A looping system will repeat after this amount of time. A non-looping system will stop emitting after this length of time.

    ❑ **Looping**: This checkbox dictates whether or not the system loops.

    ❑ **Prewarm**: This checkbox, if checked, will start a looping system as if it has already had a chance to loop for a while. This is useful in the case of torches that should already be lit, not start when the player enters the room.

    ❑ **Start Delay**: This will stop the particle system from emitting for the given number of seconds when it is initially triggered.

    ❑ **Start Lifetime**: This is the number of seconds an individual particle begins with.

    ❑ **Start Speed**: This is how fast a particle will initially move when spawned.

    ❑ **Start Size**: This dictates how large a particle is when spawned. It is always better to use larger particles rather than more particles.

- **Start Rotation**: This will rotate the emitted particles.
- **Start Color**: This is the color tint of the particles when spawned.
- **Gravity Multiplier**: This gives the particles a greater or lesser amount of the gravity effect.
- **Inherit Velocity**: This will cause particles to gain a portion of their transform's momentum if it is moving.
- **Simulation Space**: This determines whether the particles will stay with the game object as it is moved (that is, local) or will remain where they are in the world.
- **Play On Awake**: This checkbox, if checked, will cause the emitter to start emitting as soon as it is spawned or the scene starts.
- **Max Particles**: This limits the total number of particles that this system supports at a single time. This value only comes into play if the rate particles are emitted or their life span is great enough to overbalance their rate of destruction.

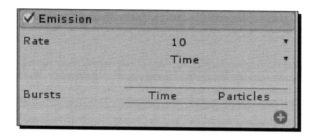

2. The **Emission** module controls how fast the particles are emitted.

- **Rate**: If set to **Time**, this is the number of particles per second that are created. If set to **Distance**, this is the number of particles per unit of distance the system travels as it moves.
- **Bursts**: This is only used when the **Rate** option is set to **Time**. It allows you to set points in the system's timeline when a specific number of particles will be emitted.

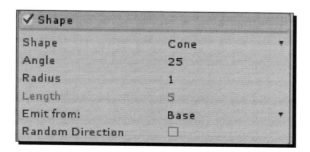

3. The **Shape** module controls how the system emits particles.

   ❏ **Shape**: This dictates what form the emission point will take. Each option comes with a few more value fields that determine its size.

   Sphere: This is the point from which particles are emitted in all directions. **Radius** determines the size of the sphere. **Emit from Shell** dictates whether the particles are emitted from the surface of the sphere or inside the volume.

   Hemisphere: This is, as the name suggests, half of a sphere. **Radius** and **Emit from Shell** work the same here as they do for **Sphere**.

   Cone: This emits particles in one direction. **Angle** determines whether the shape is closer to a cone or cylinder. **Radius** dictates the size of the emission point of the shape. **Emit From** will determine where the particles are emitted from. **Base** emits from the base disc of the shape. **Base Shell** emits from the base of the cone, but around the surface of the shape. **Volume** will emit from anywhere inside the shape and **Volume Shell** emits from the surface of the shape.

   ❏ **Box**: This emits particles from a cube-type shape. **Box X**, **Box Y**, and **Box Z** determine the size of the box.

   ❏ **Mesh**: This allows you to select a model to use as an emission point. All of the particles for the system will be emitted from the surface of the **Mesh**.

   ❏ **Random Direction**: This determines whether a particle's direction is determined by the surface normal of the shape chosen, or if it is chosen at random.

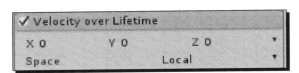

4. The **Velocity over Lifetime** module allows you to control the momentum of the particles after they have been spawned.

   ❏ **X**, **Y**, and **Z**: These define the number of units per second along each axis of the particle's momentum

❑ **Space**: This dictates whether the velocity is applied locally to the system's transform, or relative to the world

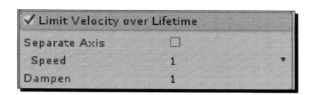

5. The **Limit Velocity over Lifetime** module dampens a particle's movement if it exceeds the specified value.

   ❑ **Separate Axis**: This allows you to define a value unique to each axis and whether that value is local or relative to the world

   ❑ **Speed**: This is how fast the particle has to be moving before the damp is applied

   ❑ **Dampen**: This is the percentage of speed to cut the particle by. It is a value between zero and one

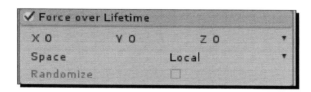

6. The **Force over Lifetime** module adds a constant amount of movement to each particle over the course of its life.

   ❑ **X, Y,** and **Z**: These define how much force to apply along each axis

   ❑ **Space**: This dictates whether the force is applied local to the system's transform or in the world space

   ❑ If **X, Y,** and **Z** are random values, **Randomize** will cause the amount of force to apply to be randomly picked each frame, resulting in a statistical averaging of the random values

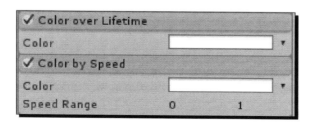

7. The **Color over Lifetime** module allows you to define a series of colors for the particle to transition through after it has been spawned.

8. The **Color by Speed** module causes the particle to transition through the defined range of colors as its speed changes.
   - **Color**: This is the set of colors to transition through
   - **Speed Range**: This defines how fast the particle must be going to be at the minimum and maximum ends of the **Color** range

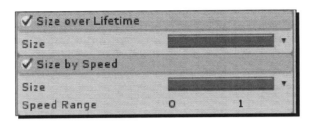

9. The **Size over Lifetime** module changes the size of the particle over the course of its life.

10. The **Size by Speed** module adjusts the size of each particle based on how fast it is going.
    - **Size**: This is the adjustment that the particles transition through
    - **Speed Range**: This defines the min and max values for each of the **Size**

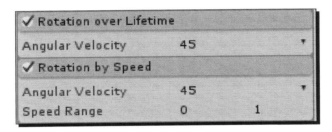

11. The **Rotation over Lifetime** module rotates particles over time after they have been spawned.

12. The **Rotation by Speed** module rotates particles more as they go faster.
    - **Angular Velocity**: This is the number of rotations to apply

  ❏ **Speed Range**: This is the min and max range for the **Angular Velocity** value if it is not set to **Constant**

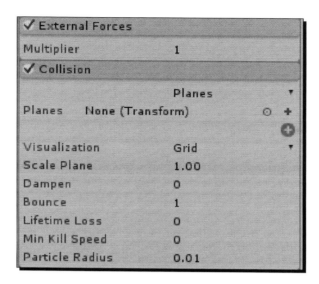

13. The **External Forces** module multiplies the effect of Wind Zone objects. Wind Zones simulate the effects of wind on particle systems and Unity's trees.

14. The **Collision** module allows particles to collide and interact with the physical game world.

  ❏ If set to **Planes**, you are able to define a number of flat surfaces for the particles to collide with. This is faster to process than World collisions.

  Planes: This is a list of transforms that define the surfaces to collide with. Particles will only collide with the local, positive y side of the transform. Any particles on the other side of the point will be destroyed.

  Visualization: This gives you the option to view the planes as a **Solid** surface or a **Grid** surface.

  Scale Plane: This adjusts the size of the **Visualization** option. It does not affect the actual size of the surface to collide with.

  Particle Radius: This is used to define the size of the sphere used to calculate the particle's collision with the planes.

  ❏ If set to **World**, the particles will collide with every collider in your scene. This can become a lot for the processor to handle.

Collides With: This defines a list of layers that will be collided with. Only colliders on layers that are checked in this list will be used for the collision calculation.

Collision Quality: This defines how precise the collision calculations are for this particle system. **High** will calculate precisely for every single particle. **Medium** will use an approximation and a limited number of new calculations each frame. **Low** just calculates less often than **Medium**.

If **Collision Quality** is set to **Medium** or **Low**, **Voxel Size** dictates how precise the system estimates the points of collision.

❏ **Dampen**: This removes the defined fraction amount of speed from the particle when it collides with a surface.

❏ **Bounce**: This allows the particle to maintain the defined fraction of its speed, specifically along the normal of the surface that was hit.

❏ **Lifetime Loss**: This is the percentage of life. When the particle collides, this percentage of life is removed from the particle. When the particle's life drops to zero over time, or through collision, it is removed.

❏ If, after collision, the particle's speed is below the **Min Kill Speed** value, it is destroyed.

❏ If the **Send Collision Messages** checkbox is checked, scripts attached to the particle system and the object that was collided with will be alerted every frame that the collision took place. Only one message is sent per frame, not per particle.

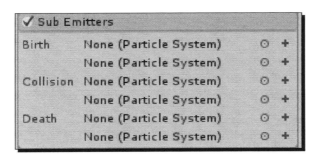

15. The **Sub Emitters** module allows additional particle systems to be spawned at points in the life of each particle of this system.

❏ Any particle systems in the **Birth** list will be spawned and follow the particle when it is first created. This could be used to create a fireball or smoke trail.

❏ The **Collision** list spawns particle systems when the particle hits something. This could be used for rain drop splashes.

□ The **Death** list spawns particles when the particle is destroyed. It could be used to spawn the firework explosion.

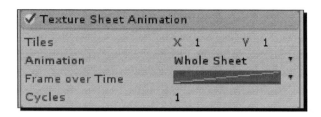

16. The **Texture Sheet Animation** module causes the particle to flip through a number of particles over the course of its life. The texture used is defined in the **Renderer** module.

 □ **Tiles**: This defines the number of rows and columns in the sheet. This will determine the total number of frames available.

 □ **Animation**: This gives you the options of **Whole Sheet** and **Single Row**. If set to **Single Row**, the row used can either be chosen at random or specified using the **Random Row** checkbox and **Row** value.

 □ **Frame over Time**: This defines how the particle transitions between frames. If set to **Constant**, the system will only use a single frame.

 □ **Cycles**: This is the number of times the particle will loop through the animation over the course of its life.

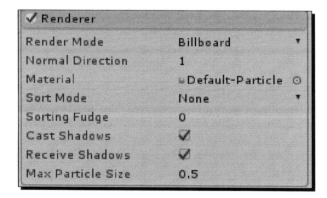

17. The **Renderer** module dictates how the particle is drawn on the screen.

 □ **Render Mode**: This defines which method a particle should use to orient itself in the game world.

    Billboard: This will always face directly at the camera.

Stretched Billboard: This will face particles at the camera, but stretch them based on the speed of the camera, the particle's speed, or by a specific value.

Horizontal Billboard: This is flat on the XZ plane of the game world.

Vertical Billboard: This will always face the player, but will always stay straight along the y axis.

If set to **Mesh**, you can define a model to be used as a particle rather than a flat plane.

❏ **Normal Direction**: This is used for the lighting and shading of the particles by adjusting the normal of each plane. A value of **1** points the normals directly at the camera while a value of **0** points them towards the center of the screen.

❏ **Material**: This defines the material used to render the particles.

❏ **Sort Mode**: This dictates what order the particles should be drawn in, by distance or age.

❏ **Sorting Fudge**: This causes particle systems to be drawn earlier than normal. The higher the value, the earlier it will be drawn on the screen. This affects whether the system appears in front of or behind other particle systems or partially transparent objects.

❏ **Cast Shadows**: This determines if the particles will block light.

❏ **Receive Shadows**: This determines if the particles are affected by the shadows cast by other objects.

❏ **Max Particle Size**: This is the total amount of screen space a single particle is allowed to fill. No matter what the real size of the particle is, it will never fill more than this space of the screen.

Creating engine trails

To enforce the player's impression that their ship is moving, we need to create some trails for the ship's engines. This exhaust will trail out as if the ship is moving even though it is not. By making the particle systems part of the group of objects that make up the ship, the engine trails will move and leave particles as one would expect them to.

Time for action – adding engine trails

Engine trails can easily be added and controlled with the use of only a particle system.

1. To begin with, we need to create a new particle system. Do this by going to the top of the Unity Editor and navigating to **GameObject | Create Other | Particle System**.

2. Rename the new particle system to `EngineTrail`.

3. First we look at the **Initial** module. We need the **Looping** and **Prewarm** checkboxes checked. This will keep the ship looking as if it is moving throughout the game and remove the build up the system would otherwise need to create the effect.

4. Next, we need to control the distance the particles travel. Do this by setting the **Start Lifetime** option to **3** and the **Start Speed** option to **1**.

5. To keep the particles sized and positioned properly in space, we need to set the **Start Size** option to **0.8** and choose **World** for **Simulation Space**.

6. Now we move on to the **Shape** module. We want the particles to fly straight out from the engines. So we use a value of **0** for the **Angle** option and **0.2** for the **Radius** option.

7. Exhaust tends to fade in color and dissipate in density over time. To achieve this effect, activate the **Color over Lifetime** and **Size over Lifetime** modules.

8. For the **Color** option, set the **Alpha** option to **0** at the beginning of the gradient and **255** a short way in. As to colors, select a vibrant blue at the beginning, transitioning to white, and then gray at the end.

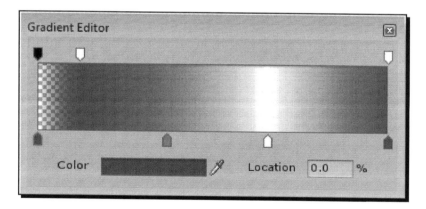

9. For the **Size** option, select a linear slope that is maximum at the beginning and minimum at the end. This is most easily done by clicking on the curve, to the right of the **Size** label, and selecting the third option from the bottom of the **Particle System Curves** window at the bottom of the **Inspector** window.

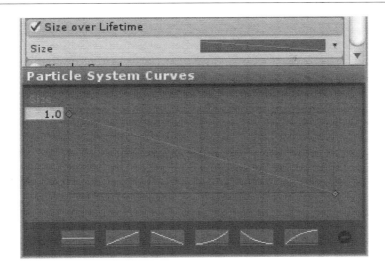

10. Now, in the **Scene** window, duplicate the `EngineTrail` object three times and position them behind the engines of the ship. Be sure to rotate them so the particles are emitted away from the ship.

11. Finally, make all of them children of the player's ship. If this step is skipped, they will not follow the ship as it moves.

What just happened?

We put into practice what we learned about particle systems to create trails for our space ship's engines. Because they are children of the ship and simulate in world space, they move with the ship and trail off as one would expect.

Have a go hero – more trails

The enemy ships have engines too. Try adding trails to the enemy ships. Be careful about picking the local or world space to simulate in. Because the ships move to make it look like the player is moving, simulating in world space could have some unusual side effects.

If you gave the player a turbo boost effect earlier, it is time to add some extra effects to it now. Try changing the length of the trails when the player is boosting. Perhaps the ship taps into a special type of fuel when it boosts. If it burns a different color, then the trails would have to be a different color, or series of colors, when the player is boosting.

Putting it together

So far, we learned about audio effects and particle systems on their own. They each can add a lot to the scene, setting the mood and giving that touch of polish that sets a game apart. But there are many effects that cannot stand on their own as one or the other. Explosions, for example, are simply not that impressive unless you have both the visual and auditory effects.

Explosions

It is so much more satisfying to destroy enemies when they explode. It takes both a particle effect and the sound effect to make a proper explosion. We will start by creating an explosion prefab. Then we will update the player's shooting to spawn the explosion when asteroids and enemy ships are destroyed.

Time for action – adding explosions

A single particle system and script will allow us to create some nice explosions that can be used everywhere.

1. We first need some new textures to make the explosion look like fire. Luckily, Unity provides a multitude of basic particle textures. To include them in your project, go to the top of the Unity Editor and navigate to **Assets | Import Package | Particles**.

2. In the resulting window, select **Import** and wait for Unity to finish importing them. This package is a great resource, including both textures and complete particle systems. However, all of the particle systems included use the old system that will be phased out of Unity over the next few versions. Despite this, we can still make full use of the included materials.

3. Create a new `particleSystem` object and name it `Explosion`.

4. First, in the **Initial** module, we need to make the effect last for a short time. Set the **Duration** to **0.5** and the **Start Lifetime** option to **1**.

5. To keep the particles close together, use a value of **0.5** for the **Start Speed** option.

 When we are done with this system, it will not loop. However, it is easier to see what we are working with if we let it loop for now.

6. Next, we need more particles, so go to the **Emission** module. Set the **Rate** option to **120** to generate the proper amount.

7. An explosion is generally round, so we need to adjust the **Shape** module next. Select **Sphere** for the **Shape** setting and set the **Radius** option to **0.5**.

8. Now for the **Color over Lifetime** module. An explosion is bright at the beginning and fades to brown, followed by black as it burns. For the **Color** option, start with an army green color, followed by faded yellow, then medium brown, and finally black at the end. Also, cause **Alpha** to fade in at the beginning and out at the end. This keeps the particles from popping in and out of existence.

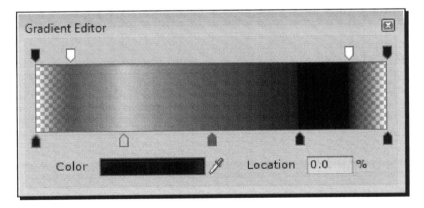

9. Next, we need a fire material for our particles. For the **Material** setting in the **Renderer** module, select the **Fire Smoke** material. It can also be found in your **Project** window by going to **Standard Assets | Particles | Sources | Materials**.

10. Once we are satisfied with the look of the system, make sure the **Play On Awake** checkbox is checked and the **Looping** checkbox is not checked in the **Initial** module.

11. As with the asteroids and enemy ships, the explosion needs to move around our player as they move. It also needs to destroy itself when it is done emitting. So, create a new script and name it `Explosion`.

12. This script is short and only includes two functions. The first function, `Update`, checks to see if the `particleSystem` object is missing or has finished playing. If either is true, the `gameObject` is destroyed.

```
public void Update() {
  if(particleSystem == null || !particleSystem.isPlaying)
    Destroy(gameObject);
}
```

13. The second function, `LateUpdate`, simply uses the `PlayerShip.Rotate` function, which we created in *Chapter 6, Specialities of the Mobile Device – Touch and Tilt*, to move the explosion for the player's movement. This is the same way we move the asteroids and enemy ships around as the player moves.

```
public void LateUpdate() {
  PlayerShip.Rotate(transform);
}
```

14. Return to Unity and add the script to the `Explosion` object.

15. Next, add an **Audio Source** component to the object.

16. For this component, we need the **Play On Awake** checkbox checked. Also select **Linear Rolloff** for the **Volume Rolloff** mode and **10** for the **Min Distance**, both found under **3D Sound Settings**.

17. And, of course, select the **Explosion** sound effect for the source's audio clip. These settings will cause the sound to play as soon as the explosion is spawned.

18. To complete the explosion's creation, turn the object into a prefab and delete the instance from the scene.

19. Next, we need to update the `TouchShoot` script to utilize the explosion. Open it now.

20. To the beginning, we add a variable to hold a reference to the explosion.

```
public GameObject explosion;
```

21. After the line where we make use of the `Physics.Raycast` function and before we destroy the shot object, add this line. If there is a reference to the explosion, it uses the `Instantiate` function to spawn a new instance of the explosion and sets its position and rotation to that of the object that was shot.

```
if(explosion != null) Instantiate(explosion, hit.transform.
position, hit.transform.rotation);
```

22. Back in Unity, find the instance of the `TouchShoot` script component on the player's ship. Add the reference to the `Explosion` prefab in the new **Explosion** slot.

What just happened?

We created an explosion. Unity provides us with a slew of particle textures with which we can create a multitude of effects. There are also a few particle systems already created, including an explosion. However, that explosion uses the old system and will not be included in Unity for much longer. We also updated our enemy ships and asteroids so they spawn the explosions when they are destroyed by the player.

Have a go hero – more types of explosions

One explosion is alright, but it is odd that the asteroids explode in the same manner as the ships. Different gases, fuels, and rock compositions all burn in different colors and with varying amounts of vigor. Create some more explosions for the different objects flying around your space. Change the colors and size to suit what is exploding. Also, explore other sound effects that provide differing auditory clues as to what is exploding. Finally, try to create a multi-explosion system. Perhaps the shots from the player cause the first explosion, and a chain reaction causes explosions in the weapon hold and engine compartment. To achieve this, take a look at using subemitters, or spawn a couple of different particle systems around the ship when it is destroyed.

Creating laser blasts

Being able to destroy objects and see them explode is great. It gives the player a reward for performing a simple action. However, when one fires a gun of any sort, you expect a reaction from it, whether or not anything is hit. To that end, we are going to create a muzzle-flash-type effect for the player's ship. Every time they tap the screen to fire, some particle systems will flash and a sound effect will play.

Time for action – adding laser blasts

A muzzle flash generally consists of two parts. The first is a straight blast, forward along the barrel. The second is a fan around the base of the first.

1. To begin, create a new `particleSystem` object and rename it as `LineBlast`; we will now proceed to make the first part.

2. The flash does not last for very long, so find the **Duration** option in the **Initial** module and set it to **0.1**.

3. Next, we need to set the **Start Lifetime** option to **0.1** so the particles do not stay on screen for very long.

4. The flash does not move away from the muzzle, so set the **Start Speed** option to **1**, keeping the particles close.

5. The particles need to be sized to correspond with the size of our ship's muzzle. Set the **Start Size** option to **0.2** to keep them small.

6. It is no fun if our laser blasts are just white, so change the **Start Color** value to an appropriate color for your lasers.

7. Last up for the **Initial** module is to uncheck the **Play On Awake** checkbox, keeping the system from triggering immediately when loaded.

8. Next we need to adjust the **Emission** module. The flash occurs in a burst, so set the **Rate** option to **0**.

9. To make the burst, click on the **+** sign to the right of the **Bursts** list. A value of **5** will work well.

10. Next we adjust the **Shape** module to emit the particles along a straight line. To this end, set the **Angle** option to **0** and the **Radius** option to **0.01**.

11. Finally, we need to adjust the **Renderer** module. To stretch out the particles, change the **Render Mode** option to **Stretched Billboard** and set the **Length Scale** option to **-4.5**.

12. Now that we are satisfied with the way this system looks, uncheck the **Looping** checkbox in the **Initial** module.

13. Now create the second `particleSystem` object and rename it as `SpreadBlast`.

14. These particles should last for as long as those of the first system. So, in the **Initial** module, set the **Duration** option to **0.1**, **Start Lifetime** to **0.1**, **Start Speed** to **1**, **Start Size** to **0.2**, and uncheck **Play On Awake**.

15. To make these particles distinct from the line, set the **Start Color** value to a slightly darker color.

16. Next, in the **Emission** module, set the **Rate** option to **0** and add the **Bursts** option with a **Particles** value of **30**.

17. For the **Shape** module, set the **Angle** option to **60** and the **Radius** option to **0.01**. This causes the particles to fan out when spawned.

18. For the **Renderer** module, set the **Render Mode** option to **Stretched Billboard** and the **Length Scale** option to **-3**.

19. Finally, once we are satisfied with the look of the system, again uncheck the **Looping** checkbox in the **Initial** module.

20. Before we put the particle systems in place, we need to create a script. Create a new one and name it `LaserBlast`. This script will trigger the particle systems and the audio clip to play.

21. This script starts with a single variable. This variable holds the list of systems to be triggered when the script is told to fire.

```
public ParticleSystem[] particles = new ParticleSystem[0];
```

22. Next we have the only function in the script, `Fire`. It starts by making sure there is an **Audio Source** component on the same `GameObject`. If it is present, `PlayOneShot` is called using the source's clip. This function plays the passed file once without blocking the playing of other clips.

```
public void Fire() {
  if(audio != null)
    audio.PlayOneShot(audio.clip);
```

23. The function continues by looping through the list of particle systems and using `Play` to trigger them if they exist.

```
    for(int i=0;i<particles.Length;i++) {
      if(particles[i] != null)
        particles[i].Play();
    }
}
```

24. Next, we need to update the `TouchShoot` script. It needs to call the `Fire` function on the `LaserBlast` script when the player touches the screen. To that end, we first add the `lasers` variable to hold the list of objects that need to be triggered.

```
public LaserBlast[] lasers = new LaserBlast[0];
```

25. To the beginning of the `Update` function, we add the `didFire` boolean value. It will keep the lasers from being triggered more than once per frame.

```
bool didFire = false;
```

26. We next set the Boolean to true after the `if` statement where we check to see if the touch's phase value is found to be equal to `TouchPhase.Began`.

```
didFire = true;
```

27. At the end of the `Update` function, if the `didFire boolean` is true, the `Fire` function that we will be writing shortly is called.

```
if(didFire) Fire();
```

28. Last up for the script, we add the `Fire` function. This function simply loops through the `lasers` array and calls their `Fire` function if they exist.

```
private void Fire() {
  for(int i=0;i<lasers.Length;i++) {
    if(lasers[i] != null)
      lasers[i].Fire();
  }
}
```

29. Now that we have all of the pieces, we need to put them together. Start by creating a new empty `GameObject` and naming it `LaserBlast`.

30. Next, make the `LineBlast` and `SpreadBlast` particle systems children of this new object. Be sure to set their positions and rotations to `0`.

31. Add our `LaserBlast` script to the object of the same name and add the two particle systems to the **Particles** list on the script component.

32. Next, add an **Audio Source** component to the object. Select the **Laser** sound effect for the **Audio Clip** value.

33. Finally for this object, expand the **3D Sound Settings** group and select **Linear Rolloff** for the **Volume Rolloff** value; otherwise, we will not be able to hear it.

34. Position the laser blast in front of the muzzles of the player's ship. Duplicate it as needed to cover all the points. Also, make sure their local z axis points forward along the muzzles.

35. Next, make all of your `LaserBlast` objects children of the player's ship so they keep moving with it.

36. Finally, add the objects to the **Lasers** list on the `TouchShoot` script component.

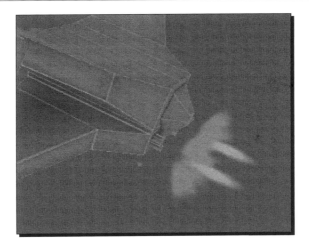

What just happened?

We created laser blasts for the player. Every time the player touches the screen, they are triggered. This way the player can tell that they are shooting even if they fail to hit anything. It is a quick and short effect, but adds a lot to the final experience.

Have a go hero – more types of lasers

The player can shoot lasers, now the enemy needs to too. Add some laser blasts to the enemy ships. Also, it is time to replace their sphere bullets with something better. Create a plasma ball to replace the sphere bullets. A smaller, looping version of the explosion could work for the ball. An appropriately colored version of the engine trails could work for the ball's trail as it flies towards the player. It might also be a good idea to add the alarms to the bullets. This way the player knows when they are about to be blasted out of the game.

Summary

In this chapter, we learned about special effects in Unity, specifically audio and particle systems. We started with understanding how Unity handles audio files. By adding background music and an alarm system, we put what was learned into practice. We moved on to understanding particle systems, and created engine trails for our player's ship. Finally, we put the two skill sets together and created explosions and laser blasts. Particle systems and audio effects add a lot to the final polish and look of a game.

In the next chapter, we complete our experience together by taking a look at optimization in Unity. We will take a look at the tools provided for tracking performance. We will also create our own tool to track specific parts of script performance. We will also create our own tool to track specific parts of script performance. We will explore asset compression and other points that we can change to minimize the application footprint. Finally, key points will be discussed for minimizing lag.

9
Optimization

In the previous chapter, we learned about special effects for our games. We added background music to our Space Fighter game. We also created engine trails for our ship. Combining both audio effects and particle systems, we created some explosions and gun blasts. Together, this rounds out the game experience and gives us a very complete-looking game.

In this chapter, we explore our options for optimization. We start by looking at the application footprint, and how to reduce it. We move on to look at the game's performance. We look at the tools that Unity provides and create another one ourselves. With the use of occlusion culling, we can improve the game's performance even further. Finally, we will explore some key areas that can cause lag and how to minimize their effects.

In this chapter, we will be covering the following topics:

- ◆ Minimizing the application footprint
- ◆ Tracking performance
- ◆ Minimizing lag
- ◆ Occlusion

We will be working on both our Space Fighter and Tank Battle games, for this chapter. Start by opening the Space Fighter project.

Minimizing the application footprint

One of the keys to a successful game is the size of the game itself. Many users will quickly uninstall any application that appears to be unnecessarily large. Also, all of the mobile app stores have limits to how your game will be supplied to users based on the size of the application itself. Becoming familiar with the options you have for minimizing the size of your game is the key to control how your game will be distributed.

The first thing to note when working to minimize the footprint is how Unity handles assets as it builds the game. Only assets that are used somewhere in one of the scenes for the build are actually included in the game. If it is not in the scene itself or referenced by an asset that is in the scene, it will not be included. This means you could have test versions of assets, or incomplete versions; as long as they are not referenced, they will not affect the final build size of your game.

Unity also allows you to keep your assets in the format you need for working on them. When the final build is made, all assets are converted to an appropriate version for their type. This means you can keep models in the format native to your modeling program. Or keep your images as Photoshop files, or any other format you work in, and they will be converted to JPG or PNG appropriately when the game is built.

Editor log

When you are finally ready to work with the footprint of your game, it is possible to find out exactly what is causing your game to be larger than desired. In the top-right corner of the **Console** window is a drop-down menu button. Inside this menu is **Open Editor Log**.

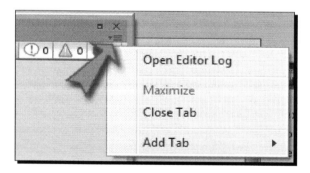

The editor log is the location where Unity outputs information while it is running. This includes information about the current version, license checks, and any asset importing. The log will also contain detailed information about the file size and assets included in the game, after it has been built.

```
Textures        2.0 mb      9.5%
Meshes          159.6 kb    0.7%
Animations      0.0 kb      0.0%
Sounds          15.4 mb     72.1%
Shaders         41.2 kb     0.2%
Other Assets    7.8 kb      0.0%
Levels          37.9 kb     0.2%
Scripts         14.0 kb     0.1%
Included DLLs   3.7 mb      17.2%
File headers    8.6 kb      0.0%
Complete size   21.4 mb     100.0%

Used Assets, sorted by uncompressed size:
 13.7 mb         64.1% Assets/Audio/Background.wav
 1.0 mb    4.7% Assets/Audio/Explosion.aif
 682.8 kb        3.1% Assets/Models/PlayerShip.png
 682.8 kb        3.1% Assets/Models/EnemyShip.png
 682.7 kb        3.1% Assets/Models/Asteroid.png
 516.9 kb        2.4% Assets/Audio/Alarm.wav
 189.7 kb        0.9% Assets/Audio/Laser.wav
 109.5 kb        0.5% Assets/Models/EnemyShip.blend
 41 1 kb         0 2% Assets/Models/PlayerShip blend
```

We can see a breakdown of the aspects of the final build. Every asset category has a size and percentage of the total build size. We are also supplied with a list of every asset that is actually included in the game, organized by their file size before being added to the build. This information becomes very useful when looking for assets that can stand to be made smaller.

Asset compression

Inside the **Import Settings** for models, textures, and audio there are options that affect the size and quality of imported assets. In general, the affected change is a reduction in quality. However, especially when working on mobile devices, asset quality can be reduced well below the levels required for a computer before the difference is noticeable on the device. Once you understand the options available for each type of asset, you will be able to make optimal decisions regarding the quality of your game. When working with any of these options, look for a setting that minimizes the size before introducing undesired artifacts.

Models

No matter what program or method you use to create your models, ultimately they are always a list of vertex positions and triangles, with a few references to textures. Most of the file size of a model comes from the list of vertex positions. To make sure the models in your game are of the highest quality, start in the modeling program of your choice. Delete any and all extra vertexes and faces. Not only will this result in a smaller file when building your final game, it will also reduce the import time when working in the editor.

The **Import Settings** for models consists of three pages, resulting in more options to adjust the quality. Each page tab corresponds to the relevant part of the model, allowing us to fine-tune each one of them.

Model tab

On the **Model** tab, we are able to affect how the mesh is imported. When it comes to optimizing our use of the models, there are many options here that are key to success. Once your game is looking and playing the way you want it to, we should have a good look at the settings shown in the following screenshot:

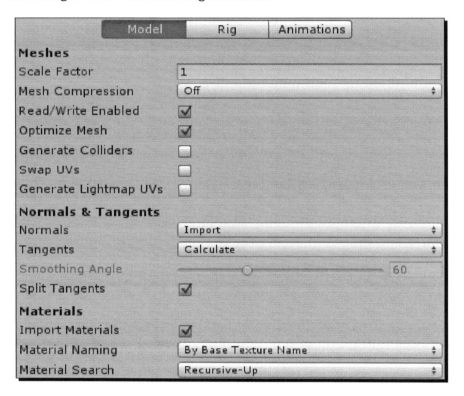

The settings available under the **Model** tab are explained as follows:

◆ **Mesh Compression**: This option lets us select how much compression should be applied to the model. The effect amounts to combining vertexes to reduce the overall amount of detail that has to be stored for the mesh. This setting is likely to introduce undesired oddities in the mesh. So, always pick the highest setting that does not introduce any artifacts.

- **Read/Write Enabled**: This option is only useful when you want to manipulate the mesh while the game is running, through the script. If you never touch the mesh with any of your scripts, uncheck this box. While not affecting the final build size, this will affect how much memory is required to run your game.

- **Optimize Mesh**: This option causes Unity to reorder the triangles list that describes the model. This is always a good one to leave checked. The only reason you might want to uncheck it is if you are manipulating the game or mesh based on the specific order of the triangles.

- **Generate Colliders**: This option is almost always a candidate to leave off. This option will add Mesh Collider components to every mesh in your model. These are relatively expensive to calculate when working with physics in your game. If possible, you should always use a group of the significantly simpler Box Colliders and Sphere Colliders.

- **Generate Lightmap UVs**: This option should only be used when working with objects that need static shadows. If the object does not, it will introduce excess vertex information and bloat the asset.

- **Normals**: This option is used by materials for determining which direction a vertex faces and how lighting should affect it. If the mesh never uses a material needing **Normals** information, be sure to set this to **None**.

- **Tangents**: This option is used by materials for faking detail with bump maps and similar special effects. Just as with the **Normals** setting, if you don't need them, don't import them. If **Normals** is set to **None**, this setting will automatically be grayed out and no longer imported.

Rig tab

The following is a screenshot that displays the **Rig** tab:

There are really only two things to keep in mind when working to optimize your animation rig. The first is, if the asset does not animate, then don't import it. By setting **Animation Type** to **None**, Unity will not try to import the rig or any useless animations. The second thing to keep in mind is to remove any unnecessary bones. Once imported to Unity, delete any and all objects from the rig that do not actually have an effect on the animation or character. Unity converts any inverse kinematics that you might use for animating into forward kinematics, so the guides used for it can be deleted once in Unity.

Animations tab

As with with the **Rig** tab, if the model does not animate, do not import animations. Unchecking the **Import Animation** box, when first importing the asset, will avoid any extra components being added to your GameObjects in Unity. Also, if any extra animations get added to your final build accidentally, they can quickly make your application over-sized.

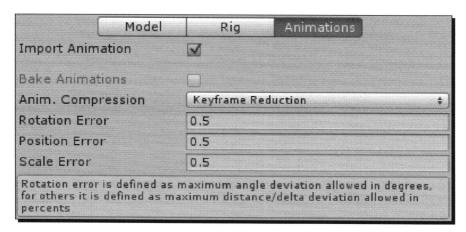

The settings available under the **Animations** tab are explained as follows:

- **Anim. Compression**: This option adjusts how Unity handles excess keyframes in your animations. For most situations, the default option works well.

    - **Off**: This option should only be used if you need a high-precision animation. This is the largest and most costly setting to choose.

    - **Keyframe Reduction**: This option will reduce the number of keyframes used by the animation based on the Error settings that follow. Essentially, if a keyframe does not have a noticeable effect upon the animation, it is ignored.

    - **Keyframe Reduction and Compression**: This option does the same as the previous option but additionally compresses the file size of the animations. At runtime, though, the animation will still require the same amount of processor resources to calculate as the previous option.

- **Rotation Error**: This option is the number of degrees different between keyframes that will be ignored when performing keyframe reduction.

- **Position Error**: This option is the movement distance that will be ignored between keyframes when performing the keyframe reduction.

- **Scale Error**: This option is the amount of size adjustment in the animation that will be ignored between keyframes when performing the keyframe reduction.

Textures

When working with textures in computer graphics, it is always better to work in **Powers of 2**. A Power of 2 is any value where it and its subsequent halves can be evenly divided by two until one is reached. This is important because they are faster for the computer to calculate and process. By default, Unity will convert any textures that do not meet this requirement by scaling them to the nearest Power of 2.

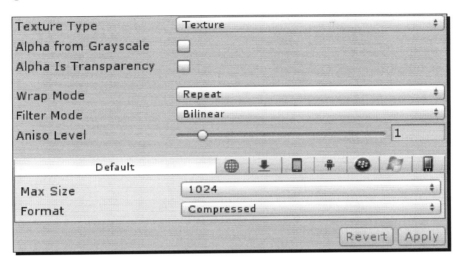

The various **Texture** settings available in Unity are explained as follows:

- ◆ **Texture Type**: This option affects what type of texture this image will be treated as. It is always best to select the type most appropriate for the intended use of the image.

  - ❑ **Texture**: This option is the most common and default setting. This should be used for your normal model textures.

  - ❑ **Normal Map**: This option is used for special effects such as bump maps. Materials using this type of texture will also need the normal and tangent information from the model import settings.

  - ❑ **GUI**: This option should be used if the image is going to appear in the GUI and not on any models.

  - ❑ **Reflection**: These textures are used for creating cube maps that imitate the reflective properties of real objects.

  - ❑ **Cookie**: These textures are used on lights, changing how the light is emitted from the light object.

- ❑ **Advanced**: This option gives full control over all of the settings concerned with importing images. You will only need this setting if you have special purposes for your textures.

  When the **Texture Type** option is set to **Advanced**, the **Read / Write Enabled** box becomes available. This should only be left checked if you plan on manipulating the texture from your scripts while the game is running. If unchecked, Unity does not maintain a copy of the data in the CPU, freeing memory for other parts of the game.

- ◆ **Generate Mip Maps**: This option is another **Advanced** setting that lets you control the creation of smaller versions of the texture. These are then used when the texture is small on the screen, reducing the amount of processing needed to draw the texture and the object using it on the screen.

- ◆ **Filter Mode**: This option is available for all of the texture types. It affects how the image will look when you are very close to it. **Point** will make the image look blocky, while **Bilinear** and **Trilinear** will blur the pixels. In general, **Point** is the fastest; **Trilinear** is the slowest but gives the best looking effect.

- ◆ **Max Size**: This option adjusts how large the image can be when it is used in the game. This allows you to work with images that are very large but import them to Unity in an appropriately small size. In general, values greater than **1024** are poor choices; not just because of the increased memory requirement, but also because the video cards on most mobile devices cannot handle textures that are any larger. Choosing the smallest size possible will have a great effect on the footprint size of the textures in your final build.

- ◆ **Format**: This option adjusts how the image should be imported and how much detail each pixel can hold. **Compressed** is the smallest, while **Truecolor** provides the most detail.

Audio

Giving a game quality sound always adds a lot to the final size of the game. It is one of those assets that a game cannot do without, but can be hard to include at a suitable level. When working on them in your audio program, keep them as short as possible to minimize their size. The audio import settings all have an effect on either their footprint in the build size, or the memory required to run the game.

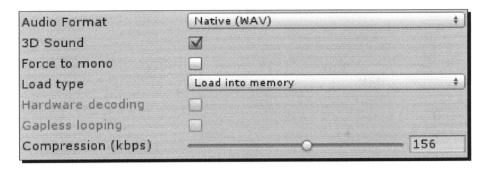

The various **Audio** settings available in Unity are explained as follows:

- ◆ **Audio Format**: This setting changes how the file will be stored in your game. **Native** offers higher quality while **Compressed** results in a smaller file size. As a special feature of mobile platforms, compressed audio can be retrieved relatively faster than on other platforms because of some special hardware in the mobile devices.

- ◆ **3D Sound**: This setting dictates whether or not the file will be affected by its position in the game relative to the **Audio Listener**. If this is unchecked, some calculations can be avoided, reducing the processing required in each frame of your game.

- ◆ **Force to mono**: This setting converts stereo audio into mono. While most devices are technically capable of playing stereo sounds, they do not always have the multiple speakers required for it to make a difference. Checking this box can significantly reduce the file size of the audio, by removing that extra audio channel.

- ◆ **Load type**: This setting affects how much of the system's memory is used, while the game is running, to handle loading audio files. **Decompress on load** uses the most memory, and is best for small, short sounds. **Compressed in memory** only decompresses the file while it is playing, using a medium amount of memory, and is best for medium-sized files. **Stream from disc** means that only the part of the file currently being played is stored in the runtime memory. This is like streaming video or music from the Internet. This option is best for large files but should only be used by a few at one time.

- ◆ **Compression (kbps)**: This setting adjusts the amount of detail in the audio file. A smaller value will reduce the file size, but also reduce quality. A larger value will result in a larger file size and greater quality. If the amount of compression already applied by your audio is smaller than the value here, the setting will have no effect on the sound. In general, it is best to pick the smallest size while maintaining the desired level of quality.

Player settings

Open your game's **Player Settings** by going to Unity's toolbar and navigating to **Edit | Project Settings | Player**. In the **Per-Platform Settings**, for Android, we have another few options under **Other Settings** that will affect the final size and speed of our game.

Rendering

The following is the screenshot that displays the **Rendering** settings:

The various **Rendering** settings available in Unity are explained as follows:

- When we worked with making lightmaps, we had to set some objects as static. This told Unity that the objects will never be moving and allows them to be lightmapped. It also allows Unity Pro users to utilize **Static Batching** that allows Unity to significantly speed up rendering times by grouping identical objects. For each group it then renders one object in multiple places, rather than each object individually. Potentially, this setting can add some extra girth to your final build size, because Unity will need to save extra information about your static objects to make it work.

- **Dynamic Batching** works the same as **Static Batching**, with two major differences. First, it is available to both Unity Pro and Basic users. Second, it groups objects that are not marked as static.

Optimization

The **Optimization** settings are shown in the following screenshot:

The various **Optimization** settings available in Unity are explained as follows:

- **Api Compatibility Level**: This setting determines which set of the .Net functions to include in the final build. **.Net 2.0** will include all of the available functions, making the largest footprint. **.Net 2.0 Subset** is a smaller portion of the functions, including only those that your programming is most likely to use. Unless you need some special functionality, **.Net 2.0 Subset** should always be the option you choose.

- **The Stripping Level**: This setting is a Unity Pro only feature. It allows you to reduce the size of your final build by removing all of the excess code before compiling it. System functions are grouped into what are called libraries for easy reference. **Strip Assemblies** removes the unused libraries from the final build. The **Use micro mscorlib** option performs the same function as the previous option, but utilizes a minimized form of the libraries. While significantly smaller, this library possesses fewer functions for your code to use. However, unless your game is complex, it should not make a difference.

- **Optimize Mesh Data**: This setting will remove extra information from all of your meshes that are not being used by any materials applied to them. This includes the **Normals**, **Tangents**, and a few other bits of information. Unless you have a very special case, this is a good box to always check.

Tracking performance

Unity provides us with many tools that allow us to determine how well our game is running. The first we will be covering is readily available for both Unity Pro and Basic users. However, the information is rather limited, though still useful. The second is only available to Unity Pro users. It provides significantly more detail and information on performance. Finally, we will create our own tool, allowing us to view the performance of our scripts in detail.

Editor statistics

In the top-right of the **Game** window, there is a button labeled **Stats**. Clicking on this button will open a window, giving us information about how the game is running. There is little bit of information about how fast the game is running. Most of the information in this window concerns how well the game is being rendered, largely amounting to how many objects are currently on the screen, how many are animating, and how much memory they take up.

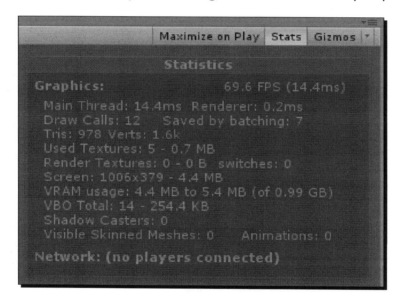

The various statistics in Unity Editor are explained as follows:

◆ At the top-right of the Unity Editor **Statistics** window is the current **FPS (Frames Per Second)** and the time in milliseconds that the last frame took to render. These values are unaffected by the rendering of the rest of the Unity Editor, though there is a slight performance hit by running the game in the Editor. In general, if you can keep your game running at more than 60 FPS, your game will run pretty well on your target platform.

- The **Main Thread** statistic provides us with the time in milliseconds that it took to run through the code for the frame and render everything to the screen. This is the total amount of time it takes to process a single frame of your game.

- To the right of **Main Thread**, we have **Renderer**. This statistic is the number of milliseconds the rendering of the frame alone took. This time is already included in the **Main Thread** statistic.

- The **Draw Calls** statistic is the number of unique objects that had to be drawn on screen. This is roughly equal to the number of objects that are currently visible to the camera. So, things behind the camera are not drawn and do not add to this value.

- The **Saved by batching** statistic is closely related to the number of **Draw Calls**. We will learn more about batching later. But, suffice it to say for now, batching is a special grouping process that reduces the number of **Draw Calls**, making the game render faster.

- Ultimately, every model in 3D graphics is made from a series of triangles. **Tris** is the total number of triangles seen and being rendered by the camera.

- Most of the information in a model file is concerned with the position of each vertex. **Verts** is the total number of vertexes seen and rendered by the camera. The lower the number of vertexes for each model, the faster it will be rendered to the screen.

- The first number for the **Used Textures** statistic is the total number of unique textures that are being used in this frame. The second is the total amount of memory they take up. By reducing texture quality or by combining textures, this statistic can be reduced, allowing the game to run faster.

- The **Render Textures** statistic is a special type of texture used for special effects such as security cameras and real-time reflections. This statistic displays the total number visible and the amount of memory needed for them.

- The **switches** statistic essentially amounts to how much work the **Render Textures** statistic is doing. Fewer **Render Textures** and simpler materials will reduce this number and the resulting cost to rendering time.

- **Screen** is the current width and height, in pixels, of the **Game** window. It also displays the amount of memory needed for rendering at that size. A smaller size results in less detail for your game, but also makes the game easier to render.

- The **VRAM usage** statistic gives the approximate minimum and maximum video memory currently being used. It also provides the current total amount of video memory available in parentheses. With this statistic and knowing the amount of video memory available in your target device, you can determine whether graphics of your game are simple enough to run on that device.

- The **VBO Total** statistic is the total number of unique meshes currently being rendered by your game. Every distinct model you might use will add to this statistic.

- The **Shadow Casters** statistic is used when making use of real-time shadows. Real-time shadows are expensive. If possible, they should not be used on mobile devices. But, if you have to have them, minimize the number of objects that cast those shadows. Limit it to moving objects that are large enough for the user to see the shadow. Small, static objects especially do not need to cast shadows.

- The **Visible Skinned Meshes** statistic is the total number of rigged objects currently in the view of the camera. **Skinned Meshes** are most often going to be your characters and just about anything else that animates.

- The **Animations** statistic provides the current total number of animations playing in the scene.

- The **Network** group of statistics only becomes visible when connected to other players in a multiplayer game. The information generally amounts to how many people the game is connected to and how fast those connections are.

The Profiler

The **Profiler** window, found in Unity's toolbar under **Window | Profiler**, is a great tool for analyzing how your game is running. It gives us a colorful breakdown of each part of our system and how much work it is doing. The only really unfortunate part of this tool is that it is only available for Unity Pro users.

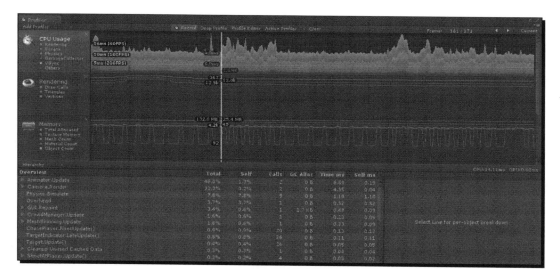

By first opening the **Profiler** window, we can then play our game in the window and watch the tool give us a fairly detailed breakdown of what is going on. We can click on any point and see detailed information about that frame in the bottom of the window. The information provided is specific to the lane that you clicked on, **CPU Usage**, **Rendering**, **Memory**, and so on.

The **CPU Usage** information is particularly useful when trying to find parts of our game that are taking too long to process. Spikes in processing cost stand out pretty easily. By clicking on a spike, we can see the breakdown of what each part of the game played in making that frame expensive. For most of these parts we can dig down to the exact object or function that is causing the issue. However, we can only get down to the function level. Just because we know where an issue in the code generally is, the Profiler will not tell us exactly which part of that function is causing the issue.

In order to actually work, the Profiler needs to hook into every part of your game. This introduces a little extra cost in the speed of your game. Therefore, when analyzing the information provided, it is best to consider the relative costs rather than hold each cost as an exact value.

Tracking script performance

All of these tools that Unity provides are great, but not always the right solution. The Unity Basic user does not have access to the Profiler. Also, both the Profiler and the Editor Statistics are fairly generalized. We can get a little more detail with the Profiler, but not always enough. In this next part, we will be creating a special script capable of tracking the performance of specific parts of any script. It should definitely become a regular piece of your developer kit.

Time for action – tracking scripts

We will be creating this script in the Space Fighter game:

1. First, we will need a special class that will keep track of our performance statistics. Create a new script and name it `TrackerStat`.

2. To begin this script, we first need to change the class definition line. We do not want or need to extend the `MonoBehaviour` class. So, find the following line of code:

```
public class TrackerStat : MonoBehaviour {
```

And, change it to the following:

```
public class TrackerStat {
```

3. This script starts with four variables. The first will be used as an ID, allowing us to track multiple scripts at once by supplying different key values. The second will keep track of the average amount of time that the tracked bits of code are taking. The third is just the total number of times the tracked code has been called. The fourth is the longest time the code has taken to execute.

```
public string key = "";
public float averageTime = 0;
public int totalCalls = 0;
public float longestCall = 0;
```

4. Next, we have two more variables. These will do the work of actually tracking how long the script takes to execute. The first is the time when the tracking starts. The second is a flag marking that tracking has started.

```
public float openTime = 0;
public bool isOpen = false;
```

5. The first function for this script is `Open`. This function is called when we want to start tracking a bit of code. It first checks to see if the code is already being tracked. It uses `Debug.LogWarning` to send a warning to the **Console** window, if it is. Next, it sets the flag marking that code is being tracked. Finally, the function tracks the time it was called by using `Time.realtimeSinceStartup`, which is the actual number of seconds since the game started.

```
public void Open() {
  if(isOpen) {
    Debug.LogWarning("Tracking is already open. Key: " + key);
  }

  isOpen = true;
  openTime = Time.realtimeSinceStartup;
}
```

6. The next function, `Close`, acts as the opposite of the previous one. It is called when we have reached the end of the code we want to track. The time when the tracking should stop is passed to it. This is done to minimize the amount of excess code being executed. As with the previous function, it checks to see if tracking is being done, sending out another warning and exiting early if it is not. Next, the `isOpen` flag is cleared by setting it to `false`. Finally, the amount of time since tracking was opened is calculated and the `AddValue` function is called.

```
public void Close(float closeTime) {
  if(!isOpen) {
    Debug.LogWarning("Tracking is already closed. Key: " + key);
    return;
  }
```

```
   isOpen = false;
   AddValue(closeTime - openTime);
}
```

7. This last function for this script is `AddValue`. This function is passed `callLength`, the length of time that the tracked bit of code took. It then uses some math to add the value to `averageTime`. Next, the function compares the current `longestCall` with the new value and selects the longest. Finally, the function increments `totalCalls`.

```
public void AddValue(float callLength) {
   float totalTime = averageTime * totalCalls;
   averageTime = (totalTime + callLength) / (totalCalls + 1);

   longestCall = longestCall < callLength ? callLength :
longestCall;

   totalCalls++;
}
```

8. Next, we need to create another new script and name it `ScriptTracker`. This script will allow us to do actual performance tracking.

9. This script starts off with a single variable. This variable maintains all of the stats that are currently being tracked. Note the use of `static` here; it allows us to easily update the list from anywhere in the game.

```
private static TrackerStat[] stats = new TrackerStat[0];
```

10. The first function for this script, `Open`, allows us to start tracking the code execution. It uses the `static` flag, so the function can be called easily by any script. A key value is passed to the function, allowing us to group track calls. The function starts by creating a variable to hold the `index` of the stat to start tracking. Next, it loops through the current set of `stats` to find a matching `key` value. If one is found, the `index` variable is updated with the value and the loop is exited.

```
public static void Open(string key) {
   int index = -1;

   for(int i=0;i<stats.Length;i++) {
      if(stats[i].key == key) {
         index = i;
         break;
      }
   }
}
```

[281]

11. The `Open` function continues by checking if a stat was found. The `index` variable will only be less than zero if we make it through the whole loop of current `stats` and are unable to find a matching `key`. If one is not found, we call `AddNewStat`, which will be created shortly, to create the new stat for tracking. The `index` is then set to that of the new stat. Finally, the stat is triggered to start tracking by using the stat's `Open` function.

```
if(index < 0) {
  AddNewStat(key);
  index = stats.Length - 1;
}

stats[index].Open();
}
```

12. The `AddNewStat` function is passed the `key` of the stat that is to be created. It starts by storing the list of `stats` in a temporary variable and increasing the size of the `stats` list by one. Each value is then transferred from the `temp` list to the larger `stats` list. Finally, a new stat is created, it is assigned to the last slot in the `stats` list, and the `key` is set.

```
private static void AddNewStat(string key) {
  TrackerStat[] temp = stats;
  stats = new TrackerStat[temp.Length + 1];

  for(int i=0;i<temp.Length;i++) {
    stats[i] = temp[i];
  }

  stats[stats.Length - 1] = new TrackerStat();
  stats[stats.Length - 1].key = key;
}
```

13. Next, we have the `Close` function. This function is passed the `key` value of the stat to be closed. It starts by finding the time that the function was called, minimizing the amount of excess code being tracked. It continues by looping through the list of `stats` to find a matching `key`. If one is found, the stat's `Close` function is called and the function is exited. If a match is not found, `Debug.LogError` is called to send an error message to the **Console** window.

```
public static void Close(string key) {
  float closeTime = Time.realtimeSinceStartup;

  for(int i=0;i<stats.Length;i++) {
    if(stats[i].key == key) {
```

```
            stats[i].Close(closeTime);
            return;
        }
    }

    Debug.LogError("Tracking stat not found. Key: " + key);
}
```

14. The last static function for this script is `Clear`. It only empties the stats list, making it ready for fresh tracking.

```
public static void Clear() {
    stats = new TrackerStat[0];
}
```

15. The last step for the script is the `OnGUI` function. This function will let us see our statistics while the game is playing. In it we make heavy use of the `GUILayout` class and its functions. `GUILayout` automatically arranges the various GUI elements, allowing us to spend less time arranging and more time analyzing. We first use `BeginVertical` to start a vertical list of elements. `BeginHorizontal` is used to start a horizontal list of elements. The `Label` function is then used to create titles for each row of our statistics. We are using the `GUILayout.Width` function to give each label a specific width, making the layout look much nicer. Next, `EndHorizontal` is called to close the horizontal list. Every call to `BeginHorizontal` must be paired with an `EndHorizontal` else Unity will make many complaints.

```
public void OnGUI() {
    GUILayout.BeginVertical();

    GUILayout.BeginHorizontal();
    GUILayout.Label("Key", GUILayout.Width(150));
    GUILayout.Label("Average", GUILayout.Width(100));
    GUILayout.Label("Total", GUILayout.Width(50));
    GUILayout.Label("Longest", GUILayout.Width(100));
    GUILayout.EndHorizontal();
```

16. Next, we loop through our list of stats. For each, we create a horizontal list and use `Label` to draw each stat on the screen. The `ToString` function is used to convert the numbers to strings, needed by the labels.

```
    for(int i=0;i<stats.Length;i++) {
        GUILayout.BeginHorizontal();

        GUILayout.Label(stats[i].key.ToString(), GUILayout.Width(150));
```

```
    GUILayout.Label(stats[i].averageTime.ToString(), GUILayout.
Width(100));
    GUILayout.Label(stats[i].totalCalls.ToString(), GUILayout.
Width(50));
    GUILayout.Label(stats[i].longestCall.ToString(), GUILayout.
Width(100));

    GUILayout.EndHorizontal();
  }
```

17. The OnGUI function finishes by creating a button, that calls upon the Clear function when clicked. And finally, the EndVertical function is called to end the vertical list of elements. Every call to BeginVertical must be paired with a call to EndVertical, just as the horizontal lists.

```
  if(GUILayout.Button("Clear"))
    Clear();

  GUILayout.EndVertical();
}
```

18. To test these scripts, open up your PlayerShip script. To the beginning of the Rotate function, add the following line to start tracking how long it takes to run.

```
ScriptTracker.Open("PlayerShip_Rotate");
```

19. Towards the end of the Rotate function, we need to call the Close function with the same key.

```
ScriptTracker.Close("PlayerShip_Rotate");
```

20. Finally, create an empty game object and add your ScriptTracker script to it. Start the game and take a look at the results.

Key	Average	Total	Longest
SpaceSpawn_Update	0.0004085933	43	0.001991361
PlayerShip_Rotate	0.0002421485	11910	0.0006141663
TouchShoot_Fire	7.281303E-05	35	0.0008485317
	Clear		

What just happened?

We created a tool for testing specific parts of code. By wrapping any bit of code in calls to the functions and sending a unique ID, we can determine how long it takes to execute the code. By averaging out the calls to the script, and wrapping different parts of code, we can determine exactly which parts of a script are taking the longest to complete. We can also find out if the parts of code have been called too many times. Both cases are ideal points to start looking at for minimizing processing and lag.

Be sure to remove any references to this tool before you deploy your game. If left in the final levels, it can add an unnecessary amount of load on the CPU. This adverse effect on the game could make the game unplayable. Always remember to clear out any uses of tools that are exclusively for Editor debugging.

Minimizing lag

Lag is one of those nebulous ideas used to describe an application performing slower than expected. As developers, we constantly fight against providing the highest quality experience we can, while maintaining the speeds and responsiveness that users expect. It essentially amounts to whether or not the processor on the user's device can handle the cost of providing the game experience. A few, simple objects in your game will result in fast processing. Several complex objects will cost the most processing.

Occlusion

Occlusion is great for games with a lot of objects. In its basic form, anything off to the sides or behind the camera is not seen and therefore not drawn. In Unity Pro, we are able to set up occlusion culling. This will calculate what can actually be seen by the camera, not drawing anything that is blocked from view. There is a balance that has to be achieved when using these tools. The cost of calculating what can not be seen needs to be less than the cost of just drawing those objects anyway. As a rule of thumb, if you have many smaller objects that are regularly blocked from view by larger objects, occlusion culling is the right choice.

Time for action – occluding tanks

We will add occlusion culling to the Tank Battle game, because it is the only one with anything large enough to block objects from view:

1. So, open up the Tank Battle game now. If you completed the challenges and added the extra debris and obstacles, this section will be particularly effective for you.

2. Open the Occlusion window by going to Unity's toolbar and navigate to **Window | Occlusion Culling**. This window is your primary point of access for modifying the various settings associated with occlusion in your game.

3. Switch to the **Bake** page and we can take a look at the options associated with occlusion culling.

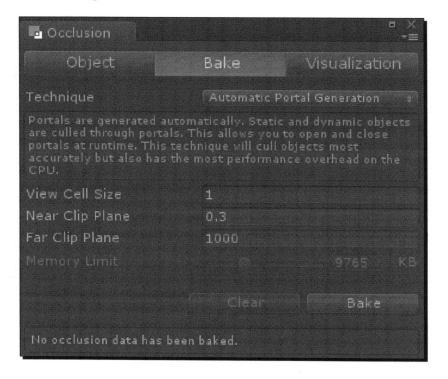

❑ **Technique**: This setting will determine what method to use when setting up occlusion culling.

> **PVS Only**: This setting will only calculate the static objects of your scene to have occlusion culling applied. This option is the least intensive for the processor but is only good if there are very few moving objects in the scene.
>
> **PVS and dynamic objects**: This setting will precompute what objects can be seen by the camera. For dynamic objects, the system will create portals. They are used to cull objects that are on opposite sides of the portals from the camera.
>
> **Automatic Portal Generation**: This setting will cull both static and dynamic objects based on portals. While giving the most accuracy, this option also has the highest cost for the processor.
>
> **View Cell Size**: This setting sets how detailed the occlusion calculations are. Smaller values will result in better culling but will cause the file size to increase to store the extra information.
>
> **Near Clip Plane** and **Far Clip Plane**: These settings are used by the system to estimate what a camera can see at any point in space. They should be set to the smallest **Near Clip Plane** and largest **Far Clip Plane** of all the cameras in your game.
>
> **Memory Limit**: This setting is used when either of the **PVS Techniques** have been chosen. It helps guide how much detail can be put into the calculation.

4. Select **PVS and dynamic objects** for **Technique** and 5 for **View Cell Size**.

5. In order to make the occlusion system work with dynamic objects, we need to set up a number of occlusion areas. To create them, create an empty **GameObject** and add an **Occlusion Area** component, found in Unity's toolbar under **Component | Rendering | Occlusion Area**.

6. They need to cover the area where any dynamic objects will be located. Create and position enough areas to cover the streets of our game. Their size can be edited just as when working with **Box Collider** components. Be sure to make them tall enough to cover all of your targets.

7. Hit **Bake** at the bottom of the **Occlusion** window. A progress bar will appear at the bottom-right of the Unity Editor, telling you how much longer the calculations will take. This process usually takes a good amount of time, especially as your game becomes more and more complex.

8. When the baking process has completed, the **Occlusion** window should have switched to the **Visualization** tab and the camera should be selected in your **Scene** window. If not, select them now. In the **Scene** view, Unity will give us a preview of how occlusion culling is working. Only those objects that can be seen will be visible while the rest are turned off.

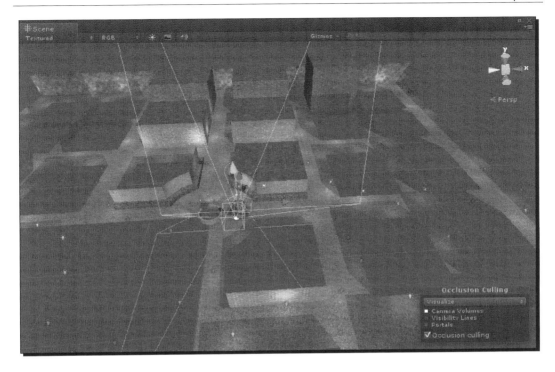

What just happened?

We went through the basic process for setting up occlusion culling. We took a look at the **Occlusion** window and learned about the settings available there. Occlusion culling is great for reducing the number of draw calls in a scene. However, that reduction needs to be balanced against the cost of storing and retrieving the occlusion calculations. This balance is achieved by selecting a proper **Technique** and an appropriate **View Cell Size**. Play around with the different values now, finding a cell size that gives the appropriate amount of detail without supplying too much information.

Points to remember

The following is a list of tips for dealing with and avoiding lag in your games. Not all of them will apply to every game you make, but they are good to keep in mind for every project:

◆ Avoid the transparent shaders, if possible, when creating your materials. They are a little more expensive to render. And, you can save yourself a world of headaches dealing with depth sorting, if you avoid them.

◆ Use one material per object. The greater the number of draw calls in your game, the longer each frame will take to render. Every mesh is drawn once per material on it, even if the material doesn't appear to do anything. By keeping to one material per object, especially on mobile platforms, you minimize the number of draw calls and maximize your rendering speed.

◆ Combine textures when possible. Not every texture you make will utilize the whole of the image. Whenever possible, combine the textures of objects that are in the same scene. This maximizes your efficient use of the images, while reducing the final build size and amount of memory needed to utilize those textures.

◆ Group objects in your **Hierarchy** using empty GameObjects. Though not specific to minimizing lag, it will make your project easier to work with. Especially with large and complex levels, you will be able to spend less time searching through the objects in your scene and more time making a great game.

◆ The **Console** window is your friend. Before worrying about your game not working, first take a look at the **Console** window or the bar at the bottom in Unity. Both will display any complaints that Unity might have about the way your game is currently set up. The messages here are great for pointing you in the right direction to fixing any problems. If you are ever unsure what the messages are trying to tell you, perform a Google search for the message and you should be able to easily find a solution from one of the many other Unity users. If your code ever appears to not be working and Unity isn't complaining about it, use the `Debug.Log` function to print messages to the **Console**. This will let you find places that your code might be exiting unexpectedly, or values that are not what they should be.

◆ Device testing is important. Working in the Editor is great, but there is nothing quite like testing on the target device. You can get a much better feel for how your game is performing when it is on the device. The Editor always introduces a small amount of additional processing overhead. Also, the computer you are working on will always be more powerful than the mobile devices you might intend on deploying to.

Summary

In this chapter, we learned about our options for optimization in Unity. We first took a look at the various settings, for the assets used in our games, used to keep their file size down while maintaining quality. Next, we learned about some settings that affect the overall game. After that, we explored options for tracking the performance of the game. We first looked at some tools provided by Unity for tracking that performance. Then, we created a tool of our own for tracking script performance in detail. We then took a look at some options for minimizing lag in our games, including utilizing occlusion culling. Now that we know about all of these tools and options, go through the games we created and optimize them. Make them the best they can be.

In this book we learned a whole lot. We started with learning about Unity, Android, and how to make them work together. Our journey continued with an exploration of Unity's GUI system and the creation of a Tic-tac-toe game. We then learned about the basic assets needed for any game, while starting the creation of a Tank Battle game. Our Tank Battle game then expanded with the addition of a few special camera effects and some lighting. We concluded the creation of the Tank Battle game by introducing some enemies and making them chase the player. The creation of our Space Fighter game taught us about the touch and tilt controls that we can utilize in our game. A short break from that game saw the creation of an Angry Birds clone while learning about physics and the possibilities of a 2D game in Unity. We then returned to the Space Fighter game to add some polish with the addition of sound and particle effects. Finally, our journey concluded by learning about optimizing our games. Thank you for reading this book. Enjoy your experiences with Unity and creating the awesome games you have always dreamed about.

Pop Quiz Answers

Chapter 5, Getting Around – Pathfinding and AI

Pop quiz – understanding enemies

Q1	3
Q2	2
Q3	1

Chapter 6, Specialties of the Mobile Device – Touch and Tilt

Pop quiz – understanding Android components

Q1	2
Q2	1
Q3	1
Q4	1
Q5	3

Index

E

Emission module
  Bursts 246
  Rate 246
EndGroup function 62
EndVertical function 284
enemy
  attacking 164, 165
  chasing 154, 155
  coloring 165
  creating 182, 204-208
  weakening 164
enemy ship
  adding 182-187
engine trails
  adding 254
explosions
  about 256
  adding 256-259
External Forces module 250

F

Field of View attribute 143
FireBird function 215
Fire function 161
Fixed Height 53
FixedUpdate function 156, 216
Fixed Width 53
flock variety
  black bird 230
  blue bird 228
  yellow bird 227
focused state 51
FollowBird function 222
Font attribute 49
Force over Lifetime module
  Space 248
  X, Y, and Z 248
FPS (Frames Per Second) 276
Full-Screen Post-Processing Effects feature 15

G

Game window tab 64, 65
General tab 36

GetCurrentAnimatorStateInfo function 111
GetRotation function 178
GetTouchPoint function 214
Google Play
  URL 26
Graphical User Interface (GUI) 35
GUI.Button function 44
GUI element states
  Border 52
  Margin 52
  Overflow 52
  Padding 52
GUI Skins
  creating 48
GUI Styles 49-51
gyroscope 173

H

Hierarchy window 56, 167
High Dynamic Range (HDR) 14
hover state 51

I

Image Position 53
Import settings
  3D Sound 237
  Audio Format 236
  compression 237
  Force to mono 237
  gapless looping 237
  hardware decoding 237
  Load Type 237
inheritance 227
Initial module
  Duration 245
  Gravity Multiplier 246
  Inherit Velocity 246
  Looping 245
  Max Particles 246
  Play On Awake 246
  Prewarm 245
  Simulation Space 246
  Start Color 246
  Start Delay 245
  Start Lifetime 245

N

navigation mesh. *See* NavMesh
NavMesh
  about 146
  creating 147-151
NavMeshAgent component
  about 152
  Acceleration 153
  Angular Speed 153
  Auto Repath 154
  Auto Traverse Off Mesh Link 153
  Avoidance Priority 154
  Base Offset 154
  enemy, creating 152-154
  Height 154
  Inspector window 153
  NavMesh Walkable 154
  Obstacle Avoidance Type 154
  Radius 153
  Speed 153
  Stopping Distance 153
New Game button 60
NewSlice function 125
normal state 51
Notepad++ 23

O

Occluder 148
occlusion
  about 148
  adding, to Tank Battle game 286-289
Occlusion Culling feature 15
OnCollisionEnter function 200
OnGUI function 42, 116, 130, 205, 233, 284
OnTriggerEnter function 182, 197
Open Editor Log 266
Open function 282
optimization
  application footprint, minimizing 266
  lag, minimizing 285
  occlusion 285
  performance, tracking 276
optimization settings
  Api Compatibility Level 275

Optimize Mesh Data 275
  Stripping Level 275
Optimize Mesh 76
OutOfBirds function 207

P

parallax background
  creating 224-226
particle systems
  about 244
  engine trails, adding 254-256
  settings 244-253
particle system settings
  about 244
  Collision module 250
  Color by Speed module 249
  Color over Lifetime module 249
  Emission module 246
  engine trails 253
  External Forces module 250
  Force over Lifetime module 248
  Initial module 245
  Limit Velocity over Lifetime module 248
  Renderer module 252
  Rotation by Speed module 249
  Rotation over Lifetime module 249
  Shape module 247
  Size by Speed module 249
  Size over Lifetime module 249
  Sub Emitters module 251
  Texture Sheet Animation module 252
  Velocity over Lifetime module 247
pathfinding 146
Pause button 29
performance tracking
  editor statistics 276-278
  Profiler window 278, 279
  script performance, tracking 279-284
physics materials
  about 203
  implementing 203
Physics.Raycast function 258
picture-in-picture (PIP) 61
pig. *See* enemy
platform-tools folder 33

turbo boost
  about 129
  creating 129-132

U

Unity
  drawback 8
  features 8, 9
  licensing options, Basic 11
  licensing options, Pro 11
  working, with Android 10
Unity Basic 11
Unity Pro 11
Unity Remote 26
Unreal Engine 9
Update function 68, 160, 213, 262

V

Velocity over Lifetime module
  Space 248
  X, Y, and Z 247
Video Playback and Streaming feature 12
Visit java.oracle.com button 18
Visualization tab 288

W

Word Wrap 53

Y

yellow bird
  creating 227, 228

Thank you for buying
Unity Android Game Development by
Example Beginner's Guide

About Packt Publishing

Packt, pronounced 'packed', published its first book "Mastering phpMyAdmin for Effective MySQL Management" in April 2004 and subsequently continued to specialize in publishing highly focused books on specific technologies and solutions.

Our books and publications share the experiences of your fellow IT professionals in adapting and customizing today's systems, applications, and frameworks. Our solution-based books give you the knowledge and power to customize the software and technologies you're using to get the job done. Packt books are more specific and less general than the IT books you have seen in the past. Our unique business model allows us to bring you more focused information, giving you more of what you need to know, and less of what you don't.

Packt is a modern, yet unique publishing company, which focuses on producing quality, cutting-edge books for communities of developers, administrators, and newbies alike. For more information, please visit our website: www.PacktPub.com.

Writing for Packt

We welcome all inquiries from people who are interested in authoring. Book proposals should be sent to author@packtpub.com. If your book idea is still at an early stage and you would like to discuss it first before writing a formal book proposal, contact us; one of our commissioning editors will get in touch with you.

We're not just looking for published authors; if you have strong technical skills but no writing experience, our experienced editors can help you develop a writing career, or simply get some additional reward for your expertise.

Unity iOS Game Development Beginners Guide

ISBN: 978-1-84969-040-9   Paperback:314 pages

Develop iOS games from concept to cash flow using Unity

1. Dive straight into game development with no previous Unity or iOS experience

2. Work through the entire lifecycle of developing games for iOS

3. Add multiplayer, input controls, debugging, in app and micro payments to your game

4. Implement the different business models that will enable you to make money on iOS games

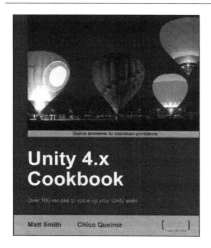

Unity 4.x Cookbook

ISBN: 978-1-84969-042-3   Paperback: 386 pages

Over 100 recipes to spice up you Unity skills

1. A wide range of topics are covered, ranging in complexity, offering something for every Unity 4 game developer

2. Every recipe provides step-by-step instructions, followed by an explanation of how it all works, and alternative approaches or refinements

3. Book developed with the latest version of Unity (4.x)

Please check **www.PacktPub.com** for information on our titles

Unity 4.x Game AI Programming

ISBN: 978-1-84969-340-0   Paperback:232 pages

Learn and implement game AI in Unity3D with a lot of
sample projects and next-generaion techniques to use
in your Unity3D projects

1. A practical guide with step-by-step instructions
   and example projects to learn Unity3D scripting

2. Learn pathfinding using A* algorithms as well as
   Unity3D pro features and navigation graphs

3. Implement finite state machines (FSMs), path
   following, and steering algorithms

Unity 4 Character Animation with Mecanim

ISBN: 978-1-84969-636-4   Paperback: 260 pages

A detailed guide to the complex new animation tools in
Unity packed with clear instructions and illustrated with
original content in the context of a next generation zombie
apocalypse adventure game

1. Create and export models and animation sequences
   to Unity from 3ds Max, Maya and Blender

2. Prepare character models and animation for games
   using Mecanim's rigging tools

3. Retarget, adjust, and mix and match motion capture
   and other animation data

Please check **www.PacktPub.com** for information on our titles

8859430R00177

Printed in Great Britain
by Amazon.co.uk, Ltd.,
Marston Gate.